WESTERN FILMS 2

GARLAND REFERENCE LIBRARY
OF THE HUMANITIES
(Vol. 638)

WESTERN FILMS 2
An Annotated Critical Bibliography from 1974 to 1987

Jack Nachbar,
Jackie R. Donath
and
Chris Foran

GARLAND PUBLISHING, INC. • NEW YORK & LONDON
1988

Library of Congress Cataloging-in-Publication Data

Nachbar, John G.
Western films 2.

(Garland reference library of the humanities;
v. 638)
Includes indexes.
1. Western films—Bibliography. I. Donath,
Jackie R., 1952– . II. Foran, Chris, 1961– .
III. Title. IV. Title: Western films two. V. Series:
Garland reference library of the humanities; vol. 638.

Z5784.M9N332 1988 016.79143'09'093278 87-38487
ISBN 0-8240-8640-6 [PN1995.9.W4]

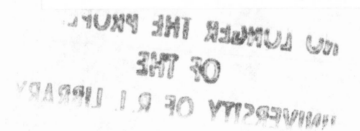

Printed on acid-free, 250-year-life paper
Manufactured in the United States of America

CONTENTS

ACKNOWLEDGMENTS

This sequel to *Western Films: An Annotated Critical Bibliography* would have been impossible without the willing aid of countless friends and associates. Special thanks go: to Ray Merlock, for his help in providing sources on the relationship between country-western music and the B Western; and to Grady Franklin, editor of *Western Film*, for providing material for this volume's periodical index. We are particularly grateful to the staff of the interlibrary loan office of Jerome Library at Bowling Green State University for their willingness to supply us with much of the material in this bibliography, as well as for their endurance of our slapdash methods.

The faculty, staff and graduate assistants of the Popular Culture Department at B.G.S.U. also added considerable support, and also channeled a lot of possible material our way.

The result of this work is dedicated to Lynn Nachbar, Bruce Springborn and Susan Bushouse Foran, who between them have shown more patience and love than we could have hoped for.

INTRODUCTION

This second volume of *Western Films: An Annotated Critical Bibliography* attempts to identify, describe and evaluate books and articles about Western movies written in English from 1974 through the spring of 1987. Our intention was to include everything published with the exception of materials appearing in Western-movie fan magazines. Appendix B lists the fan periodicals. A hint of how far we have probably missed the mark of complete coverage is that the second section of this volume lists 71 items missed in the first volume. Our apologies to authors and researchers who know of important publications which were unintentionally omitted.

When the first volume of this ongoing bibliography was completed in mid-1974, Western movies were riding tall in the saddle. Veteran directors such as Robert Aldrich (*Ulzana's Raid*, 1972) and John Huston (*The Life and Times of Judge Roy Bean*, 1972) had recently each produced his best Western. And younger directors including Phillip Kaufman (*The Great Northfield Minnesota Raid*, 1971), Robert Altman (*McCabe and Mrs. Miller*, 1971), and James Frawley (*Kid Blue*, 1973) had recently created new types of Westerns, self-reflexive and stylistically experimental. Perhaps even more important to the promising future of Westerns at that time was the simple economic fact that a number of Westerns were rounding-up cash at the box-office. In 1974 for example, *Blazing Saddles*, a reissue of *Butch Cassidy and the Sundance Kid* (1969), a reissue of *Billy Jack* (1970), and a reissue of *Jeremiah Johnson* (1972) all were among the top twenty grossing films of the year.

By the time of this writing (in late 1987) however, it is all too obvious that by 1974 the Western film was riding into the sunset. Since the mid-1970s, the production of Westerns has been punctuated by critical and popular failure. Notable directors such

as Arthur Penn (*The Missouri Breaks*, 1976) and
Michael Cimino (*Heaven's Gate*, 1980) made hugely ex-
pensive films which were pummeled by the critics and
ignored by moviegoers. Since 1974, only two Westerns
have made it into their particular year's top twenty
box-office films--*The Outlaw Josey Wales* (1976) and
Pale Rider (1985), both directed by and starring
Clint Eastwood, a star who would have a large following no matter what genre he played in. In 1980, only
six Westerns were released and in 1986 and 1987
Hollywood did not release a single major-budget Western. Although Westerns are still commonly shown on
some cable television networks and an occasional made
for-television Western manages to win its time period
on a major television network, it is now obvious that
the past dozen years have witnessed the death of the
Western film as a significant factor in American cultural life.

Given the dying public interest in new Western
movies, it seems somewhat surprising that during the
last few years articles and books about Westerns have
thrived. The first volume of this bibliography contained just under 400 entries that covered almost 75
years of Western film scholarship. This second volume
covers just over twelve years of scholarship but includes more than 700 entries, almost double the amount
in the first volume. One reason for this is a better
selection of bibliographic tools available now. Com-
puters and useful printed resources such as *Film Literature Index* have made it possible to be more thorough than in the earlier volume in searching for
materials. Another reason is the deaths of notable
Western movie legends such as directors John Ford and
Howard Hawks and stars such as John Wayne and Randolph
Scott. Biographies and critical reappraisals seem
nearly as inevitable as death itself. An even more
important reason, we suspect, is the very fact of the
Western's demise. There is about the genre at this
time a sense of completeness, the feeling that the
story has been told and that the time has come to
gather together its many strands and to figure out
its patterns, directions and meanings. A final
reason for the active interest in Western scholarship
may be quite simply a sense of loss for the genre,
with the writing serving as a sort of meager compen-
sation. A few of the authors listed here have re-
examined Western film history, found it weighted down
with sexism, racism and violence, and have consequently
written with disillusionment and bitterness. Recent
books by Jon Tusca (7.15) and J. Fred MacDonald (9.8)

are notable examples. A vast majority of the works cited here, however, speak of Westerns with respect and affection.

The books and articles in this bibliography, outside of the reference works, fall into four general categories which together suggest the dimensions of Western film scholarship since 1974:

1. HISTORIES. These may be divided into two categories: Western film history and comparisons between Westerns and the history of the American West. Histories of Westerns, such as Jon Tuska's *The Filming of the West* (6.28), survey one development of the entire genre or, like Kevin Brownlow's *The War, the West, and the Wilderness* (6.5), examine more specialized periods. A favorite tactic of fans of the historical West in both volumes of this bibliography has been to compare historical incidents such as Custer's last stand with the movie versions of the incident. Invariably the movies are condemned for being historically inaccurate. An obvious example of this means of finding fault with Westerns is Michael Sarf's *God Bless You, Buffalo Bill* (6.22).

2. DESCRIPTIONS AND ANALYSES OF FILMMAKERS AND PERFORMERS. Clear evidence of the continuing academic fascination with movie stardom and the influence of the *auteur* theory of film analysis may be seen in sections four and five of this bibliography, "Performers" and "Makers," which are the two largest of the ten sections. Eighteen books and articles are devoted to the career of John Wayne, for example, while 70 detail the career and films of Wayne's mentor, director John Ford.

3. STUDIES OF INDIVIDUAL FILMS. These works show a surprising variety, ranging from books about the production of certain Westerns, to how specific films represent the vision of certain auteurs, to sophisticated interpretations of the films themselves. Since 1974 the most written about films have been John Ford's *Stagecoach* (1939), and *The Searchers* (1956), Howard Hawks' *Red River* (1948), and Sam Peckinpah's *The Wild Bunch* (1969), all auteurist favorites. No Western outside the films of a major auteur, with the exception of *High Noon* (1952), is discussed more than a few times.

4. CULTURAL ANALYSES. This category includes many books and articles which also should appear in one of the other three categories. It also includes a great deal of the theory section of the bibliography.

It is distinguished by an assumption that Western
films are not essentially historical recreations of
the West but rather are metaphors of the twentieth
century culture which produces them and consumes them
Under this assumption, Western movies are analyzed as
cultural artifacts. Whatever the validity of this
assumption, cultural analyses have dominated in-
depth research and speculation about Westerns since
1974. Examples of provocative cultural analyses include Laura Mulvey's feminist analysis of *Dual in the
Sun* (7.33), John Lenihan's study of Westerns from 195(
through the mid-1970s (7.7) and Stephen Tatum's exami
nation of the evolving popular image of Billy the Kid
(9.17).

One surprise we experienced in gathering these
materials was the lack of contemporary, "post-struc-
turalist" methods in the analysis of the films.
Besides auteurism, a number of theoretical approaches
already common by 1974 continued to be utilized, including psychoanalytical, Marxist, structuralism and
semiotics. Post-structuralism, on the other hand, is
currently all the rage in a number of graduate film
studies programs in Great Britain and the United
States. Yet, except for some of the feminist analyse:
of Westerns, books and articles about Westerns writter
since 1974 have not utilized the concepts of major
European post-structuralists such as Jacques Lacan an(
Michel Foucault.

Hopefully, research interest in Westerns will
remain at a high enough level to justify a third
volume of this bibliography at the beginning of the
twenty-first century. Much remains to be written
about Western movies. New theories and methods
necessitate new analyses. And a comprehensive, cultural study of Westerns has never been published.
For those of us who grew up watching Westerns as a
loved weekly ritual, it is sad to think that writing
about them will not renew Western production. But
continuing research will lead to imaginative new perspectives and ideas about this most prolific and
resonant of genres. And, when it comes right down to
it, the movie West has always been an area of the min(
and the imagination anyway.

Western Films 2

BIBLIOGRAPHY

This bibliography continues the annotated list of books and articles in English devoted to Western films which was originally published in 1975. It begins with materials published in 1974 that were not included in the initial volume, and ends with materials published in the early part of 1987. In addition, older books and articles missed in the initial volume are included here. A complete list of published materials on Western movies would be virtually impossible to compile. Too many articles are published in obscure journals or limited circulation fan magazines to make hope of absolute coverage realistic. All of the books and articles included in this volume were available through the resources of a large university library and were read by the authors. No attempt was made, however, to include film reviews or the many worthwhile articles published in magazines and newsletters aimed at Western fans and collectors. Those who wish information from these magazines and newsletters can consult the Appendix of this volume for titles currently being published.

Articles and books appear under one of the following ten categories:

1. Selected Reference Sources
2. Western Film Criticism, Pre-1974
3. Specific Western Films
4. Western Film Performers
5. Makers of Western Films
6. Western Film History
7. Theories of Western Films
8. Theses and Dissertations on Western Films
9. Comparative Studies
10. Westerns in the Classroom

In general, these categories are the same as those

used in the first volume. There are two exceptions. The second category in the first volume
covers books and articles published before 1950.
Since the category in this volume is intended to
cover those materials missed in the initial
bibliography, the date was put forward to the end
of the first volume. The other category that is
different is the eighth, which originally was
entitled "The Western Audience" and included
mainly sociological studies of those who attend
Westerns. Since 1975, however, no such studies
have apparently been published. Consequently,
the subject matter has been changed to allow for
the inclusion of other potentially important
information--theses and dissertations wholly or
in part about Western films.

As in the first volume, each entry in this
bibliography is subdivided into "Books" and
"Articles." Entries are arranged under these
subdivisions in alphabetical order according to
author or according to the first word of the
entry.

A number of books and articles include
detailed information or ideas that fit more than
one category. And sometimes, materials about
specific topics such as Native Americans are mixed
among different categories. Two methods of cross-
referencing are therefore included to simplify the
finding of specific kinds of materials. At the
end of the general descriptions of each category,
references to materials in other categories that
could have been included within that category are
listed under "Related Materials." John Lenihan's
book *Showdown* (7.7), for example, is listed under
the category "Theories of Western Film." But
since the book examines the Westerns made from
about 1950 through the 1970s, a reference to the
book is included at the end of the description of
"Western Film History." The second method is an
index of specific references and an index of
authors.

Each entry in the bibliography is preceded by
a number. The digits before the decimal point
signify in which category the item appears--1.0 is
references, 6.0 is Western film history, etc.
These numbers are used in the "Related Materials"
listing at the end of the general description of
each category and in both of the indexes.

1. Selected Reference Sources

Following the precedent set in the first volume, this section surveys sources of information about Westerns published after 1974 beyond the scope of this bibliography. Much of this material falls into several major categories:

a. Information about films. These sources generally offer filmographic information on production and cast credits, release dates, plot synopses, and so on: 1.1; 1.3; 1.4; 1.5; 1.6; 1.7; 1.15; 1.17; 1.18; 1.19; 1.20; 1.21; 1.22; 1.23; 1.24; 1.25; 1.26; 1.27; 1.28; 1.30; 1.31; 1.32; 1.39; 1.44; 1.46; 1.48; 1.49. Among the best are *The Western* (1.21), an encyclopedic volume devoted to the genre, and *American Film Index* (1.28), an alphabetical listing of over 2,300 silent films. *American Indians in Film* (1.22) provides an annotated filmography of movies from 1903 to 1984 in which Native Americans appear.

b. Compilations of film reviews: 1.2; 1.12; 1.33; 1.34; 1.35; 1.36; 1.40; 1.42; 1.50; 1.52; 1.56. *Film Review Annual* (1.42) is a particularly valuable source as it includes production information and extensive indexes in addition to reviews of films produced since 1981. *The New York Times Encyclopedia of Film 1898-1979* (1.12) is an excellent source for commentary and profiles, reproduced from the newspaper's pages, and *The New York Times Film Reviews 1913-1978* (1.40) continues to be a useful source.

c. Bibliographies and collections of critical articles: 1.9; 1.13; 1.47; 1.48; 1.58; 1.59; 1.60; 1.61; 1.67. Many of the sources mentioned in this category in the first volume (see page 2 and pages 10-18) continue to be of value. A new, important bibliographic source is *The Macmillan Film Bibliography* (1.47) published in 1982, which annotates entries for almost 7,000 books. Native Americans in film are well represented by bibliographies compiled by Gretchen Bataille and Charles L.P. Silet (1.9; 1.58; 1.59; 1.60).

d. Non-film materials: 1.11; 1.16; 1.37; 1.38; 1.41; 1.53; 1.54; 1.62; 1.63; 1.64; 1.65; 1.66. A number of works on Westerns in other media provide useful perspectives and insights to students of Western films. Two volumes by Jon Tuska and Vicki Piekarski chronicle Western fiction and historical

writing (1.53; 1.54). *Max Brand: Western Giant*
(1.41) also offers critical and bibliographic
information about Frederick ("Max Brand") Faust's
books and the films made from them. Several
sources (1.7; 1.11; 1.37; 1.38; 1.62; 1.63; 1.64;
1.65; 1.66) provide production and cast list
information, as well as plot synopses, for television Westerns. Radio Westerns are treated in
Tune In Yesterday (1.16), which discusses various
kinds of radio programming from 1926 to 1962.
     For additional reference sources, see section
one of Volume I.
     Other reference sources and related material:
3.9; 3.11; 4.26; 6.1; 6.17; 6.27; 6.72; 9.5; 9.9.

2. Western Film Criticism, Pre-1974

     The books and articles in this section were
discovered in the process of collecting materials
for this edition of the bibliography and were, for
various reasons, omitted from the first volume.
Much of this material centers on actors and
directors identified with the genre. For example,
John Ford (2.8; 2.17; 2.22; 2.27; 2.36; 2.46; 2.57;
2.60; 2.62) and Sam Peckinpah (2.7; 2.25; 2.37;
2.39; 2.61) are both heavily represented.

3. Specific Western Films

     Writings about individual Westerns reflect the
diverging streams of criticism. Fans, historians,
auteur enthusiasts and structural analysis buffs
all approach specific films from their distinctive
perspectives. As a result, the books and articles
in this category are a mixed collection of remembrances, production histories, microcosm director
studies and systems analyses. Interestingly,
these often opposing strategies are frequently
focused on the same movies.
     The continuing pre-eminence of the *auteur*
theory in film scholarship is reflected in the
films discussed in these writings. The Westerns
of John Ford, particularly *Stagecoach* (1939) (3.2;
3.3; 3.11; 3.28; 3.30; 3.81; 3.111), *Wagonmaster*
(1950) (3.10; 3.35; 3.119), *The Searchers* (1956)
(3.16; 3.25; 3.27; 3.28; 3.59; 3.68; 3.69; 3.70;
3.83; 3.90; 3.95; 3.99; 3.100) and *The Man Who
Shot Liberty Valance* (1962) (3.33; 3.34; 3.94;
3.105), dominate the category. Those made by

distinctive stylists like Sam Peckinpah (3.47;
3.50; 3.71; 3.86; 3.89; 3.106; 3.110) and Howard
Hawks (3.22; 3.42; 3.98; 3.102; 3.109; 3.112) are
also strongly represented. Though the director-as-
author approach to film should translate into the
movie-as-text, relatively few Western screenplays
have been reprinted. Hopefully, as studios like
Warner Bros. and RKO open their archive collections to publishing houses (to University of Wisconsin Press and Frederick Ungar Publishing Co.
Inc., respectively), more original source material
will be given popular circulation.
    The writings included in this category are
those which focus on specific Western films.
    Related materials: 2.1; 2.5; 2.9; 2.17; 2.21;
2.25; 2.39; 2.62; 2.71; 5.5; 5.16; 5.53; 5.57;
5.58; 5.83; 5.94; 5.129; 5.130; 5.132; 5.133;
5.135; 5.145; 5.148; 6.72; 7.33; 7.37; 7.43; 8.1;
8.13; 8.14; 9.19; 9.21; 9.22; 9.26; 9.40; 10.7.

4. Western Film Performers

    The importance of the Western hero to the
genre is underscored by the proliferation of books
and articles written about specific performers.
Thus, the importance of the performer as an
onscreen persona reinforces the fan-related focus
of most of the writings in this category. Book-
length profiles, usually tracing the career of a
major box-office star, are often rich in filmographic detail, but are lacking in information about
the cultural relevance of the profiled performer.
Exceptions to the rule are some of the studies of
the two most iconographic Western stars, John
Wayne (4.8; 4.11; 4.32; 4.33; 4.38; 4.39; 4.49;
4.50; 4.55; 4.59; 4.62; 4.72; 4.76; 4.86) and
Clint Eastwood (4.8; 4.16; 4.17; 4.46; 4.47; 4.57;
4.73; 4.74; 4.77). The introductory chapters of
some of the *Films of...* series published by
Citadel Press (4.6; 4.10; 4.12; 4.32; 4.37; 4.41;
4.42; 4.47) also go further in their examinations
of the impact of major performers.
    Because of the fan appeal of much of this
material, some of the books noted in this section
feature self-serving or apologetic perspectives.
    The books and articles in this section focus
on performers whose work in Westerns has either
had important impact on the genre or is represen-

tative of its history.
Related materials: 1.5; 1.43; 1.45; 1.52;
1.55; 2.3; 2.4; 2.10; 2.12; 2.14; 2.18; 2.19;
2.20; 2.50; 2.63; 2.64; 2.65; 2.66; 3.40; 5.60;
5.62; 5.81; 5.82; 5.134; 5.138; 6.6; 6.14; 6.18;
6.23; 6.30; 6.40; 6.41; 6.69; 8.5.

5. Makers of Western Films

The strengths and weaknesses of the *auteur*
theory, in which the director is the "author" of a
film, are well documented and do not need reitera-
ting here. In terms of the Western genre, the
approach's contributions and limitations can be
spelled out in two words: John Ford. Though other
directors' works receive some attention, it is
Ford's which critics dwell on and use as para-
meters for the genre (5.1; 5.13; 5.14; 5.15; 5.36;
5.41; 5.56; 5.60; 5.62; 5.63; 5.66; 5.68; 5.73;
5.77; 5.81; 5.86; 5.90; 5.92; 5.97; 5.100; 5.102;
5.111; 5.118; 5.120; 5.121; 5.122; 5.127; 5.131;
5.134; 5.145; 5.147).

Fortunately for those interested in Westerns,
Ford's popularity among film scholars has forced
writers to look to other directors with which to
make their mark. Howard Hawks (5.4; 5.15; 5.25;
5.26; 5.33; 5.37; 5.46; 5.52; 5.54; 5.71; 5.72;
5.93; 5.95; 5.101; 5.110; 5.112; 5.141) and Sam
Peckinpah (5.6; 5.28; 5.38; 5.40; 5.48; 5.87;
5.97; 5.104; 5.113; 5.114; 5.115; 5.128; 5.131;
5.133; 5.142), both responsible for some of the
most important films in the genre, have been early
and frequent subjects for discussion, and other
filmmakers have also received attention, though
generally of a more idiosyncratic sort.

Jon Tuska and Vicki Piekarski's *Close-Up*
series (5.46; 5.47; 5.48), featuring in-depth
interviews with major and minor filmmakers, shows--
to its credit--little discretion, mixing B-movie
directors with feature-making individualists like
Alfred Hitchcock and studio directors like Henry
King. Such an indiscriminate focus not only
brings little-mentioned directors into focus, but
also opens the way to a broader examination of
other films in the genre that have received less
attention.

The filmmakers discussed in the books and
articles in this category are those whose work

includes a sizeable share of Westerns, or those
whose work in the genre constitutes an important
contribution to it.

Related materials: 1.13; 1.14; 1.27; 1.48;
1.52; 2.1; 2.2; 2.7; 2.13; 2.15; 2.22; 2.24; 2.25;
2.26; 2.27; 2.28; 2.29; 2.31; 2.34; 2.36; 2.37;
2.39; 2.41; 2.42; 2.43; 2.46; 2.49; 2.51; 2.54;
2.55; 2.56; 2.57; 2.58; 2.59; 2.60; 2.61; 3.1;
3.4; 3.5; 3.33; 3.34; 3.35; 3.36; 3.86; 3.87;
3.88; 4.4; 4.16; 4.19; 4.20; 4.57; 4.68; 8.4; 8.9;
8.10; 8.11; 8.12; 8.16; 8.18; 8.21; 8.25; 8.26;
8.27; 8.28; 8.29; 8.32; 8.34; 8.36; 8.37; 9.26;
9.27; 10.8.

6. Western Film History

It might be argued that all books and articles
about Western movies contribute to Western film
history just as studies of specific authors of
literary genres contribute to the history of
literature. The large number of items included
in the "Related Materials" section listed below
suggests how potentially inclusive this category
is. For purposes of maintaining a genuine
relationship between the materials included under
this heading, however, only items which examine
Westerns within an actual historical context have
been included. The bibliography includes four
types of historical studies: studies of the
popular culture of historical events, such as
Custer's Last Stand, or of historical figures such
as Billy the Kid, which include some emphasis on
Western films; studies in the historical development of the Western film genre itself; studies of
Westerns as they exist within the development of
various types of Hollywood products such as B
movies or movie serials; and studies of different
types of Westerns, such as the "singing cowboy"
films.

Several of the books included in this category
restate or expand on historical data and conclusions published earlier (see section 6 of Volume
I). Worth mentioning, however, are three books
which add crucial new information or suggest
important new directions in the study of Western
film history. Kevin Brownlow's *The War, The West
and The Wilderness* (6.5) provides invaluable
information about the pre-feature Western and

should serve as a model of how to intelligently
integrate photos with text. Jon Tuska's *The
Filming of the West* (6.28) adds to our knowledge
of B Westerns, detailing information lacking in
other historical overviews. Gretchen Bataille
and Charles L.P. Silet's anthology *The Pretend
Indians* (6.1), which traces the mostly negative
or condescending images of Native Americans in
American films, especially Westerns, suggests the
continuing need to examine the cultural implications of all elements of Westerns, including those
which may suggest the negative implications of a
genre usually described as a celebration of the
American historical past.

Even though the number of items in this
category is nearly one-third longer than the
listed items under the same heading in Volume I,
a thorough, overall critical-cultural history of
the Western has yet to appear. Books and articles
on the cultural history of Westerns are so far
limited to specific topics or historical periods.
General histories of Westerns have emphasized
factual information. Still to be written is a
definitive history of Western movies which will
combine accurate facts and brilliant analysis.

Related materials: 1.1; 1.20; 1.46; 1.54;
2.12; 2.16; 2.23; 2.30; 2.35; 2.44; 2.45; 2.47;
2.48; 2.53; 3.5; 3.9; 3.52; 3.104; 4.15; 4.35;
4.44; 4.48; 4.69; 4.81; 5.16; 5.30; 5.82; 5.85;
7.1; 7.4; 7.7; 7.10; 7.11; 7.12; 7.17; 7.23; 7.39;
8.2; 8.3; 8.15; 8.17; 8.30; 8.33; 8.35; 9.3; 9.5;
9.7; 9.8; 9.9; 9.10; 9.13; 9.16; 9.17; 9.20; 9.23;
10.1; 10.2.

7. Theories of Western Films

Although a quick scanning of the books and
articles in this section of the bibliography will
reveal a number of materials likely to stimulate
almost anyone interested in Western movies, those
interested in bold, new approaches to Westerns may
well be disappointed. During the late 1960s and
early 1970s so many exciting theoretical works on
Westerns were published that the introduction to
this section in Volume I suggested a glorious
future for theories of Western films. But such a
future has not been realized during the last
decade. Some theorists like John G. Cawelti in

Adventure, Mystery and Romance (7.4), have
re-presented in new forms the theoretical concepts
about the Western they had developed earlier.
Others, such as Will Wright in *Sixguns and Society*
(7.17), have employed new strategies for the study
of Westerns but, like Wright, have used flawed
methods or have arrived at already established
conclusions. Old theoretical debates such as
whether Westerns primarily present cultural
mythology or inaccurate American history still
rage on while no book-length study of Westerns
employing some of the more recent academic methods
of studying American films--Marxism, feminism,
Freudianism, semiotics--has yet been published.
In fact, those desiring intelligent and contemporary theoretical approaches to Westerns may be
better off consulting section 3 of this bibliography, where a number of exciting theoretical
concepts are applied to the analysis of specific
films.
    Two books and one article do provide important
new concepts for the study of Westerns. Robert B.
Ray's *A Certain Tendency of the Hollywood Cinema,
1930-1980* (7.10) is about narrative strategies in
American movies in general and how these strategies are related to Hollywood ideologies. Several
Westerns serve as extended examples of Ray's
arguments and thus, indirectly, Ray provides
valuable perspectives on how Westerns fall within
broader Hollywood storytelling traditions. Jon
Tuska's *The Filming of the West* (7.15) once again
centers on the rather tiresome argument that
Westerns distort the American frontier past.
Tuska, however, provides two important new perspectives to this argument. First, he insists
that by distorting frontier history Westerns help
perpetuate harmful stereotypes, especially of
Native Americans and women. Second, he savagely
attacks a vast majority of recent academic analyses of Westerns which for the most part have
argued that historical inaccuracy in Westerns is
irrelevant. Tuska's strongly stated perspectives
will offend most Western fans and a large number
of Western scholars, but his arguments will hopefully force a re-examination of much of what has
been written about Western movies. Finally, Laura
Mulvey's essay on the problems of Pearl Chavez in
Duel in the Sun (7.33) applies feminist and

Freudian tools of analysis to the study of a single
Western in order to arrive at some fascinating
insights that may apply to a large number of
Westerns. The article should serve as a model of
what may be accomplished when an active mind
creatively uses the tools of contemporary film
theory.
     Related materials: 1.54; 2.23; 2.40; 2.48;
2.70; 3.8; 3.22; 3.36; 3.43; 3.52; 3.54; 3.75;
3.81; 3.83; 3.86; 3.94; 3.99; 5.19; 5.38; 5.62;
5.90; 5.115; 5.123; 5.126; 8.7; 8.8; 8.13; 8.26;
8.31; 9.12; 9.17; 9.38; 10.4; 10.5.

8. Theses and Dissertations on Western Films

     This section is an alphabetical listing of
M.A. theses and Ph.D. dissertations on a variety of
Western film topics. It is drawn from two sources:
Raymond Fielding's *A Bibliography of Theses and
Dissertations on the Subject of Film* (Houston:
University Film Association, 1979) and his later
articles in the *Journal of Film and Video* (34:1 and
37:4).
     Although frequently using specific films as
the foundation for a selective theoretical
approach, the theses and dissertations noted here
also analyze the work of prominent directors (8.4;
8.9; 8.10; 8.11; 8.12; 8.16; 8.18; 8.21; 8.25;
8.26; 8.27; 8.28; 8.29; 8.32; 8.34; 8.36, 8.37) and
aspects of the genre's economic and stylistic
history (8.3; 8.7; 8.8; 8.15; 8.17; 8.20). Annotations have been added to a number of entries,
directing the reader to later books by some of the
authors.
     Related materials: 5.38; 6.21; 7.7; 9.2; 9.12.

9. Comparative Studies

     This section of the bibliography describes
books and articles which compare or supply the
means for comparison between American Western films
and Westerns in other forms, including Westerns on
radio and television, foreign Westerns and Westerns
in literature. It also includes materials about
related genres such as the Japanese samurai films.
Overall, the differences between this section in
Volume I and in this volume suggest that a striking
increase in interest in these materials developed
after 1975. The present section includes more than

twice the number of entries than the corresponding
section in Volume I. And, whereas this bibliography lists seventeen published books that
emphasize comparative studies, the first volume
lists only two. The first volume includes four
articles on Italian Westerns; this volume includes
three book-length studies of the subject as well
as three articles.

Two books in this section provide useful new
models for future publications in comparative film
studies. Christopher Frayling in *Spaghetti
Westerns* (9.3), though his style is unnecessarily
dense in places, provides not only an excellent
examination of the Italian Westerns so popular in
the United States between 1967 and 1975, but also
does an exemplary job of showing how the films
relate to Italian culture. In addition, Frayling
examines cross-cultural patterns of the genre and
shows how Italian Westerns influenced American
productions. Stephen Tatum, in *Inventing Billy the
Kid* (9.17), breaks new scholarly ground by examining
the evolving cultural meanings of one historical
character through analysis of Billy's image in all
types of popular media including fiction, films and
dance.

Also noteworthy in this section are the
several books and articles devoted to the Lone
Ranger. Such attention is long overdue. The
"Masked Rider of the Plains" has been popular for
more than fifty years in thousands of different
stories in at least half a dozen different media.
All of the published material discussed in this
bibliography about the "Masked Man" has so far been
primarily factual, however. A detailed analysis of
why the Lone Ranger has been so popular for so long
still has not been published.

Related materials: 1.7; 1.9; 1.11; 1.16; 1.35;
1.37; 1.38; 1.62; 1.63; 1.64; 1.65; 1.66; 2.32;
2.68; 2.69; 3.12; 3.24; 3.25; 3.29; 3.30; 3.55;
3.84; 3.97; 3.101; 3.115; 3.118; 3.121; 4.26; 4.45;
5.40; 5.90; 5.121; 5.128; 5.145; 6.1; 6.3; 6.10;
6.14; 6.18; 6.21; 6.23; 6.26; 6.30; 6.32; 6.37;
6.38; 6.46; 6.71; 7.3; 7.4; 7.8; 7.11; 7.14; 7.19;
7.20; 7.21; 7.41; 7.44; 7.45; 7.46; 8.6; 8.19;
8.20; 8.23; 8.24; 8.31; 10.3.

10. Westerns in the Classroom

        During the last decade film studies courses
have become a regular part of the curriculum at
thousands of colleges and universities all over the
world. At the same time, however, books and
articles on the teaching of Western movies at the
college or high school levels has actually
declined. Since the publication in 1971 of Frank
Manchel's *Cameras West* (I, 6.42), for example, no
book or article intended as a text for high school
students has been published. In this section,
easily the shortest in this bibliography and the
only section shorter than its corresponding section
in Volume I, there are only three articles whose
subject matter is strategies for teaching Westerns.
The other listed publications are from college
textbooks on the general study of film in which
materials about Westerns is only one small part.
        It is certainly no secret that Westerns have
played a key role in the development of American
film history and that they provide important clues
as to how twentieth century Americans have perceived their past. Westerns, therefore, despite
their recent dramatic decline in popularity, are
potentially rich source materials in both film
studies and studies in American social history.
Clearly more source materials for students on
Western films and more articles on using Westerns
in the classroom need to be published. The
teaching models included in this volume are all
about using specific Westerns for specialized
purposes. The articles by John Frayne (10.7) and
Richard Maynard (10.8), as well as the articles on
The Searchers (1956) published in an Autumn 1975
special issue of *Screen Education* (3.100) are on
John Ford's Westerns. The course outline by
Michael Marsden and Jack Nachbar (10.9) isolates
films depicting images of Native Americans. In
addition to these specialized materials, what is
also needed are descriptions of how to teach
Westerns on a broader level, a level that will incorporate several thematic elements and will
include the historical evolution of the genre.
        Related materials: 1.57; 3.27; 3.28; 3.70;
3.83; 3.95; 3.99; 3.100; 6.65; 7.24; 7.30; 7.42.

SELECTED REFERENCE SOURCES

Books

1.1   Adams, Les and Buck Rainey. *Shoot-Em-Ups*.
            New Rochelle, N.Y.: Arlington House,
            1978.

            This filmographic listing of the
        credits of over 3,300 Westerns shown
        between 1929 and 1977 calls itself "a
        complete reference guide to Westerns of
        the sound era." It is not. Some films
        are missing (*Fort Apache*, 1948, is the
        most notorious omission), and there is
        no description of plots. Nevertheless,
        as the most complete reference work on
        Western films available to this time, it
        is an important and valuable resource.
        Also includes rather forgettable intro-
        ductions to the films of each decade and
        a title index.

1.2   Alvarex, Max Joseph. *Index to Motion
            Pictures Reviewed by Variety, 1907-
            1980*. Metuchen, N.J.: The Scarecrow
            Press, Inc., 1982.

            A useful, one-volume title index of
        reviews of motion picture features and
        short subjects reviewed by *Variety* from
        1907 to 1980.

1.3   *The American Film Institute Catalog of
            Motion Pictures 1961-1970*. 2 volumes.
            New York: R.R. Bowker, 1976.

            Most complete source of basic infor-

mation about films released during the
period. Includes credits, sources,
subjects, production indexes and brief
plot summaries. Indexed.

1.4   *Annual Index of Motion Picture Credits.*
         5 volumes. Westport, Conn.: Greenwood
         Press, 1978-1982.

         Each volume is a cross-referenced
listing of credits for the films of a
year gathered by the Academy of Motion
Picture Arts and Sciences. Credits are
listed under four sections: film titles,
credits (actors, producers, technicians,
etc.), releasing companies and alphabetical index of individual credits.

1.5   Aros, Andrew. *An Actor Guide to the
         Talkies 1965-1974.* Metuchen, N.J.:
         The Scarecrow Press, Inc., 1977.

         This volume continues Richard
Dimmitt's earlier *An Actor's Guide to the
Talkies* volumes (see I, 1.12). Arranged
alphabetically by film title, with a
performer index volume.

1.6   ———. *A Title Guide to the Talkies
         1964-1974.* Metuchen, N.J.: The
         Scarecrow Press, Inc., 1977.

         A continuation of Richard Dimmitt's
A Title Guide to the Talkies volumes (see
I, 1.15). Includes year of release,
production company, producer and story
source. Features index.

1.7   *ATAS/UCLA Television Archives Catalog.*
         Pleasantville, N.Y.: Redgrave
         Publishing Co., 1981.

         An alphabetical listing of the
holdings of the study collection of the
Academy of Television Arts and Sciences-
University of California at Los Angeles
television archives. Entries follow the
format of the archive's card catalog, and

include episode number, network, air
date, production credits, cast members,
running time and format (videotape, 16mm,
etc.). Also includes lists of materials
acquired but uncatalogued at the time of
publication, and programs for which the
archive holds only the audio portion. Of
some value to researchers who could visit
the archives, but without episode synopses
and updated lists of current holdings, not
as useful a volume as it might be.

1.8   Baer, Richard D., ed. *The Film Buff's
         Checklist of Motion Pictures (1912-
         1979)*. Hollywood, Calif.: Hollywood
         Film Archive, 1979.

Nineteen thousand titles are alphabetically indexed and rated on a scale of
one to ten, the criteria of which is left
unstated. Of marginal use only.

1.9   Bataille, Gretchen M. and Charles L.P.
         Silet. *Images of American Indians on
         Film: An Annotated Bibliography*. New
         York: Garland Publishing Inc., 1985.

An invaluable source for those
researching the relationship between
images of Native Americans and the mass
media. The book is divided into four
sections: general background books and
articles, books and articles on American
Indians in films, reviews of individual
films and a filmography of sound films
dealing with American Indians. Annotations are brief but clear. Includes an
index.

1.10   Bawden, Liz-Anne, ed. *The Oxford
         Companion to Film*. New York: Oxford
         University Press, 1976.

This competent reference work features
biographical, subject, theme and
individual film entries. Includes
separate entries for "Westerns" and for
some individual Western films.

1.11   Brooks, Tim and Earle Marsh. *The*
            Complete Directory to Prime-Time
            Network TV Shows 1946-Present.
            New York: Ballantine Books, revised
            edition, 1981.

            An alphabetical listing of nighttime
            network series is at the center of this
            reference work. Entries include first
            and last telecast dates, network and
            broadcast information, cast lists, and
            synopses of the series' premises, which
            often includes information which places
            the series within broader network and
            cultural contexts.

1.12   Brown, Gene, ed. *The New York Times*
            Encyclopedia of Film 1898-1979.   13
            volumes. New York: New York Times
            Books, 1984.

            An exceptional compilation of
            articles, interviews, profiles and com-
            mentary reproduced from the pages of the
            New York Times. Includes a separate
            index volume. Look under "Westerns," as
            well as individual title, performer and
            creator entries.

1.13   Coursodon, Jean-Pierre with Pierre
            Sauvage. *American Directors.*   2
            volumes. New York: McGraw-Hill Book
            Co., 1983.

            In addition to the authors, a number
            of contributors wrote literate essays to
            accompany better-than-average filmogra-
            phies. Although there is no particular
            organization to the work, "older"
            directors seem to be gathered in the
            first volume, while "newer" ones are in
            the second.

1.14   Dixon, Wheeler W. *The "B" Directors: A*
            Biographical Directory. Metuchen,
            N.J.: The Scarecrow Press, Inc., 1985.

            Information about more than 350

directors of low-budget movies, arranged
in alphabetical order by the last name of
the director. Information about each
filmmaker includes a chronologically
arranged list of films and a brief
description including some biographical
details about the director and a short
assessment of the director's style.
Dixon never defines what a B film is,
and he says in his introduction that he
excluded directors whose films do not
reflect a personal signature. As a
result, the selection of directors he
includes is somewhat arbitrary. Nevertheless, the book focuses on a large
number of directors not often documented
elsewhere and is therefore a valuable
resource. Includes a film title index.

1.15   ————, ed. *Producers Releasing Corporation: A Comprehensive Filmography
and History*. Jefferson, N.C.:
McFarland and Company, Inc., 1986.

Most of this book is a compilation of
earlier writings that contain references
to the 1940s B movie studio, PRC (see I,
6.18; 6.39). Information between
sources is occasionally contradictory.
Information about PRC-made Westerns is
limited to three pages (pp. 35-37), and
PRC's three best-remembered Western
performers, Al St. John, Buster Crabbe
and Lash La Rue, are not included in a
section of brief biographies of key PRC
personnel. Of most value is a checklist
of PRC films which includes credits and
is the most complete PRC filmography to
date. Other reference materials include
a chapter of statistics about the
American film industry in 1944, a filmography of the films of principal PRC
directors, a miniscule bibliography and
an index.

1.16   Dunning, John. *Tune in Yesterday: The
Ultimate Encyclopedia of Old-Time
Radio*. Englewood Cliffs, N.J.:

Prentice-Hall, Inc., 1976.

A description of individual comedy,
variety and dramatic series programming
on radio from 1926 to 1962, including
Westerns. Programs are arranged in
alphabetical order by full title. Information on each program, incorporated into
the text, includes key members of the
production staff, principal players,
sponsors, networks, time slots, a
description of the overall plot format
and a discussion of noteworthy details.
Descriptions range from a single, long
paragraph to, as in the cases of *The Lone
Ranger* and *Gunsmoke*, several pages.
Dunning collected his information both
from listening and from thousands of
magazine articles. The most comprehensive source on series radio available.
Includes index.

1.17   Eames, John Douglas. *The M.G.M. Story*.
            New York: Crown Publishers, Inc.,
            1975.

Brief descriptions of M.G.M. films
released between 1924 and 1974. Films
are arranged by year. Partial credits
are included. Features index. Lavishly
illustrated.

1.18   ————. *The Paramount Story*. New York:
            Crown Publishers, Inc., 1985.

Brief descriptions of Paramount
feature films released between 1916 and
1984. Partial credits are included.
Films are arranged by year. Also
includes miscellaneous appendixes and
film and personnel indexes. Extensively
illustrated.

1.19   Fitzgerald, Michael G. *Universal
            Pictures*. New Rochelle, N.J.:
            Arlington House, 1977.

An adequate studio history, long on

lists and short on exposition. Includes
useful star filmographies and a complete
filmography for Universal from 1930 to
1976.

1.20   Garfield, Brian. *Western Films: A
            Complete Guide.* New York: Rawson
            Associates, 1982.

         In his preface to this filmography
of over 2,000 Westerns, Garfield states,
"This is a book of personal opinions ...
you may find this book a bit iconoclastic." Forewarned, the reader may
experience the book enjoyably.
Garfield's comments about individual
films tend to praise technically well-
made classic Westerns and to lambast
movies with pretensions of seriousness.
His polemical style is lively and an
entertaining contrast to more academic,
analytical approaches to Westerns. A
rather detailed introduction to the
filmography is just as opinionated.
Unfortunately, the filmography itself is
less useful as an information resource
than it is as entertainment. Despite
the title of the book, it is considera-
bly less than complete. Silent Westerns
are skipped entirely. Most B Westerns
are missing too, except for a few that
Garfield includes apparently at his own
whim. Entries are arranged alphabetically. Each includes only a partial
list of credits and about a one-sentence
plot description. The remaining one or
two paragraphs are Garfield's opinions.
Some of the credit information is wrong.
Also included are 100 stills and selective indexes on documentary films about
the West, children's Westerns and made-
for-TV and spaghetti Westerns. Also
included is a two-page, briefly
annotated bibliography.

1.21   Hardy, Phil. *The Western.* New York:
            William Morrow and Co., 1983.
            Reprinted as *The Encyclopedia of*

Western Movies. Minneapolis:
Woodbury Press, 1984.

A filmography of about 1,800 A and
B Westerns from 1929 through 1983.
Entries are arranged alphabetically
under the year of their release. Information on each film includes producing
studio, running time, primary screen
credits and one or more paragraphs in
which Hardy describes the story and
points out other information of interest.
There also are a series of appendixes
with information about the most finan-
cially successful Westerns, Westerns
which won or were nominated for Academy
Awards, favorite Westerns of selected
critics and a list of Westerns with
partial credits not included in the
regular text. A title index is also
included. Adding an attractive dimen-
sion to all of this are some 450 still
photos from the collection of John Kobal.
Overall, this is an excellent resource.
Hardy's opinions about specific films
are informed by a genuine affection for
the genre tempered by an informed sense
of film history.

1.22   Hilger, Michael. *The American Indian in
           Film.* Metuchen, N.J.: The Scarecrow
           Press, Inc., 1986.

An annotated filmography of 830
films from 1903 through 1984 that
include Native Americans as important
characters. Entries are arranged
alphabetically under their year of
release. Information about each film
includes title, distributor, director,
the performers playing the prominent
Native American characters and a brief
summary of that part of the plot that
features Native Americans. Perhaps
because Hilger acquired his plot information from magazine reviews as well as
personal viewings, a number of his plot
descriptions are misleading. Indian

actions are described without an explanation of what motivated them. And what
are only minor elements of some films
are described as if they are the central
features in the stories. Also included
is a brief bibliography, and name and
subject indexes. Unfortunately, there
is no title index, which makes finding a
film very difficult if one does not know
the year of its release.

1.23   Hirshhorn, Clive. *The Universal Story*.
New York: Crown Publishers, Inc.,
1983.

Brief descriptions of Universal
feature films released between 1913 and
1982. Partial credits are included.
Films are arranged by year. Miscellaneous appendixes and film and personnel
indexes are also included. Extensively
illustrated.

1.24   ————. *The Warner Bros. Story*. New
York: Crown Publishers, Inc., 1979.

Brief descriptions of Warner Bros.
features released between 1929 and 1978.
Includes partial credits. Films
arranged by year. Also includes index.
Lavishly illustrated.

1.25   Jewell, Richard B. with Vernan Harbin.
The RKO Story. New York: Arlington
House, 1982.

Brief description of RKO features
released between 1929 and 1960. Partial
credits are included. Films are listed
by year. Title and personnel indexes
are also included. Features photos.

1.26   Katz, Ephraim. *The Film Encyclopedia*.
New York: Thomas Y. Crowell Publi-
shers, 1979.

Entries are primarily on film
performers and directors. Listing of

films under each person is included.
Film genres, including Westerns, do not
receive separate listings.

1.27   Langman, Larry. *A Guide to American
          Film Directors: The Sound Era 1929-
          1979.* 2 volumes. Metuchen, N.J.:
          The Scarecrow Press, Inc., 1981.

          Volume I lists directors of American
films. Volume II is a title index.

1.28   Lauritzen, Einar and Gunnar Lundquist.
          American Film Index 1908-1915.
          Stockholm: Film Index, 1976.

          An alphabetical listing of over
2,300 American films produced between
July 1908 and December 1915, most drawn
from *Moving Picture World* magazine.
Entries include, when possible, production company, release date, director,
author, scenario writer, cinematographer,
art director and actors.

1.29   Leff, Leonard J. *Film Plots: Scene-by-
          Scene Narrative Outlines for Feature
          Film Study.* Ann Arbor: Pierian
          Press, 1983.

          Volume I includes scene-by-scene
summaries and details of *High Noon*
(1952), *Red River* (1948), *Viva Zapata!*
(1952), *Stagecoach* (1939) and *The Wild
Bunch* (1969).

1.30   Lyon, Christopher, ed. *The International
          Dictionary of Films and Filmmakers.*
          2 volumes. Chicago: St. James
          Press, 1984.

          Volume I treats films. Entries
include information about publications
about the movie, short essays and
production information. Volume II
provides similar information on directors and filmmakers.

1.31   Magill, Frank N., ed. *Magill's American Film Guide.* 5 volumes. Englewood Cliffs, N.J.: Salem Press, 1983.

A description of 3,691 American films arranged in alphabetical order. Each entry includes production and cast credits and about three pages of plot summary, analysis and evaluative comments. Volume V includes indexes of titles, directors, screenwriters, cinematographers, editors, performers, sources, subjects and a chronological list of titles. Unfortunately, Westerns do not receive a separate listing in the subject index. Most of this material appeared earlier in *Magill's Survey of Cinema* (1.33, 1.34, 1.36).

1.32   ———. *Magill's Cinema Annual.* Englewood Cliffs, N.J.: Salem Press, 1982 to date.

Each volume details selected world films of the previous year. Entries include credits, plot synopsis, critical commentary and a selected list of film reviews. Also includes indexes of titles, directors, cinematographers, art directors, music, performers and subjects. Check each subject index under "Westerns."

1.33   ———. *Magill's Survey of Cinema: English Language Films, First Series.* 4 volumes. Englewood Cliffs, N.J.: Salem Press, 1980.

Reviews, analyses and summaries of 515 English-language films, including some notable Westerns. A cross-referenced index is included in the Second Series (see 1.34).

1.34   ———. *Magill's Survey of Cinema: English Language Films, Second Series.* 6 volumes. Englewood

Cliffs, N.J.: Salem Press, 1981.

Reviews, analyses and summaries of 751 English-language films, including several notable Westerns. The set features an index of both the First (see 1.33) and Second Series, with cross-referenced indexes by creator, actor, title and year of release.

1.35　　　　　———. *Magill's Survey of Cinema: Foreign Language Films*. 8 volumes. Englewood Cliffs, N.J.: Salem Press, 1985.

Reviews, analyses and summaries of a selection of foreign-language films, including some Westerns. Includes a separate index volume. Look under "Westerns" in the subject section.

1.36　　　　　———. *Magill's Survey of Cinema: Silent Films*. 3 volumes. Englewood Cliffs, N.J.: Salem Press, 1982.

Prefaced by a series of short topical essays, this survey of silent films includes production credits and summaries of 308 movies. The third volume includes indexes by director, screenwriter, cinematographer, editor and performers, as well as a chronological listing. Topical essay subjects include acting style in silent films, stars and a focusing essay on Thomas H. Ince.

1.37　　　　　Marill, Alvin H. *Movies Made for Television: The Telefeature and the Mini-Series, 1964-1984*. New York: New York Zoetrope, 1984.

A chronological list of 1,693 films. Each item includes production and cast credits and a brief annotation summarizing the plot. Title, cast, producer and writer indexes are also included.

1.38   McNeil, Alex. *Total Television: A
          Comprehensive Guide to Programming
          from 1948 to the Present.* New York:
          Penguin Books, second edition,
          1984.

          This updated version of the first
          edition (1980) provides comprehensive
          listings of series, specials, network
          schedules and award-winning productions.
          Alphabetized index of genres includes
          listing of network prime-time Western
          series, and will lead researcher to
          entries in which author includes
          synopses of story lines, air dates and
          names of main characters and actors
          who played recurring roles. This is an
          important basic resource for those
          interested in television Westerns.

1.39   Meyer, William R. *The Film Buff's
          Catalog.* New Rochelle, N.Y.:
          Arlington House, 1978.

          Dated, unsophisticated introductory
          reference to film books, magazines,
          directors, archives, distributors, film
          schools, fan clubs, soundtracks and
          nostalgia outlets. Includes an
          eccentric five pages on Westerns giving
          synopses, production information and
          rental information for ten "classics."

1.40   *The New York Times Film Reviews, 1913-
          1978.* 10 volumes. New York: Arno
          Press, 1979.

          Continuation of *The New York Times
          Film Reviews* series (see I, 1.45).

1.41   Nolan, William F. *Max Brand: Western
          Giant.* Bowling Green, Ohio: Bowling
          Green State University Popular Press,
          1985.

          About evenly divided between essays
          about Frederick Faust (Max Brand) and
          lists of information about Faust's

writings. Included in the lists is a
filmography of movies based on Faust's
fiction and of films Faust helped
script.

1.42   Ozer, Jerome S., ed. *Film Review
              Annual*, 1981 to date. Englewood
              Cliffs, N.J.: Jerome S. Ozer, 1982
              to date.

              Annual volumes of reprinted and
        unedited reviews of feature films
        released in major markets in the United
        States. Reviews include production
        information, cast and crew listings,
        running time and MPAA rating. Each
        volume features separate indexes for
        film critics, publications, actors,
        producers, directors, screenwriters,
        cinematographers, editors, music
        composers and production crews.

1.43   Parish, James Robert. *Hollywood
              Character Actors*. New Rochelle,
              N.Y.: Arlington House, 1978.

              Illustrated guide to character
        actors which includes filmographies.
        Also adds a fun touch--a memorable quote
        from one of the actors' better-known
        roles.

1.44   Parish, James Robert and Michael R.
              Pitts. *The Great Western Pictures*.
              Metuchen, N.J.: The Scarecrow Press,
              Inc., 1976.

              Information about some 200 Westerns,
        arranged chronologically by title. Each
        entry includes production and cast
        credits and about one page of discussion
        which includes miniscule plot summaries,
        references to reviews, comparisons and
        evaluative comments. Included at the
        end of the volume are alphabetical lists
        of radio and TV Westerns and a selected
        bibliography of Western novels. The
        Westerns chosen for detailing seem to

have been selected based on the personal
choices of the authors rather than on
any rational system. This, coupled with
the lack of any indexes, sadly limits
the book's use as a reliable source.

1.45   Pickard, Roy. *Who Played Who in the
            Movies: An A-Z.* New York: Schoken
            Books, 1979.

        Organized around film characters,
entries in this book include a brief
biographical introduction to each
character and lists of portrayals which
include actor, film director and year of
release.

1.46   Pitts, Michael R. *Hollywood and Ameri-
            can History.* Jefferson, N.C.:
            McFarland and Company, Inc., 1984.

        This alphabetical filmography of
about 250 movies depicting American
history and historic personalities
includes as its best features a useful
subject index and competent cast information for many of the films listed.
Inconsistent selection process results
in some startling omissions (*Red River*,
1948, for one, because its characters
are fictional--although *Gone With the
Wind* is included), and the questionable
criteria--whether historical figures are
included in the story line--prevents
Pitts' work from being more useful than
as a general reference tool.

1.47   Rehrauer, George. *The Macmillan Film
            Bibliography.* 2 volumes. New York:
            Macmillan Publishing Co., 1982.

        An invaluable critical, annotated
bibliography of almost 7,000 books about
film and film scripts. Volume II is a
subject, author and script index. Books
with information about Westerns may be
searched in the subject index under the
names of specific performers, makers or

films and under the general heading of
"Western films."

1.48   Sarris, Andrew. *The American Cinema:*
               Directors and Directions, 1929-1968.
               Chicago: University of Chicago
               Press, 1985.

               Originally published in 1968,
          Sarris' pantheon of American film
          directors is still compelling, if you
          can get past the *auteur* critic's
          idiosyncracies. His directorial
          profiles, nearly 200 in all, include
          several of directors whose reputations
          were made (or broken) in the Western
          genre. Includes chronological and film-
          by-film indexes. The 1985 edition
          features Sarris' 1977 essay, "The *Auteur*
          Theory Revisited."

1.49   Sigoloff, Marc. *The Films of the*
               Seventies. Jefferson, N.C.:
               McFarland and Company, Inc., 1984.

               A filmography of American, British
          and Canadian feature films, including
          Westerns, from 1970 to 1979. Includes
          production and cast credits, running
          times, quality ratings and one-paragraph
          evaluations. The annotations and
          ratings seem somewhat arbitrary.

1.50   Slide, Anthony, ed. *Selected Film*
               Criticism, 1896-1960. 7 volumes.
               Metuchen, N.J.: The Scarecrow Press,
               Inc., 1982-1985.

               A collection of popular criticism
          of 1,146 feature films released in the
          United States between 1896 and 1960,
          arranged alphabetically and by period.
          Includes title and reviewer indexes.

1.51   Smith, John M. and Tim Cawkwell, eds.
               The World Encyclopedia of the Film.
               New York: World Publishing/Times

Mirror, 1972.

Sketchy biographical encyclopedia of film performers and filmmakers. Volume is incomplete and severely dated. Includes confusing title index.

1.52   Thomsen, David. *A Biographical Dictionary of Film*. New York: William Morrow and Co., revised second edition, 1981.

A highly opinionated compilation of biographies and film reviews. Flavored by author's dislike of Westerns, including a scurrilous attack on John Ford.

1.53   Truitt, Evelyn Mack. *Who Was Who on Screen*. New York: R.R. Bowker, third edition, 1983.

Alphabetically lists performers who died between 1905 and 1982, giving brief biographies and as full as possible lists of screen credits.

1.54   Tuska, Jon and Vicki Piekarski, ed. *Encyclopedia of Frontier and Western Fiction*. New York: McGraw-Hill Book Co., 1983.

This is, as the title suggests, a reference book about Western writers. It is of some use for those interested in Western films, however. Each entry includes a list of films based on the writings of the author.

1.55   ————. *The Frontier Experience: A Reader's Guide to the Life and Literature of the American West*. Jefferson, N.C.: McFarland and Co., Inc., 1984.

Although this reference book is mostly an annotated bibliography of historical studies and novels about the

West, it also contains information of
possible use for those interested in
Western films. A list of related films
is included at the end of each chapter on
historical resources. In addition, there
is an entire section devoted to Western
films. This includes a detailed annotated filmography of sixty Western films
and a brief but detailed annotated
bibliography of books about Western
movies. The annotations in both the
filmography and the bibliography deal
mainly with the filmic treatment of
Native Americans and with the relationship of the films with actual Western
history.

1.56   *Variety Film Reviews, 1907-1984.* 18
                volumes. New York: Garland
                Publishing Inc., 1982-1986.

        Complete and comprehensive reproduc-
tions of original reviews printed in
Variety from its first film reviews in
January 1907 to 1984. Series includes a
separate title index volume for volumes
1 through 15.

1.57   *Your Movie Guide to Western Video Tapes
                and Discs.* New York: Signet Books,
                1985.

        A quick guide to over 500 Westerns
for sale on disc or tape compiled by the
editors of *Video Times Magazine.* Each
entry includes brief credits, a one- or
two-sentence plot summary and a concise
critical evaluation. Included are the
retail purchase prices in disc, VHS and
Beta formats. Also included is a list of
video suppliers. Films are rated on a
four-star scale. This is a possibly
useful resource, but fluctuating prices
and ever-increasing titles will quickly
make such usefulness dated.

Articles

1.58   Bataille, Gretchen M. and Charles L.P.
        Silet. "The American Indian on Film:
        An Annotated Critical Bibliography."
        In *The Native American Image on Film*,
        ed. Annette Traversie Bagley.
        Washington: The American Film
        Institute, 1980, pp. 59-90.

        A checklist of articles, books or
        portions of books and selected reviews on
        the topic from 1909 through the 1970s.
        Annotations mainly summarize the content
        of the items. A slightly revised version
        of this checklist was used as the biblio-
        graphy in the authors' anthology, *The
        Pretend Indians* (6.1).

1.59   ———. "A Checklist of Published
        Materials on Popular Images of the
        Indian in the American Film."
        Journal of Popular Film, 5:2 (1976),
        170-182.

        A compilation of books, articles and
        reviews with brief, descriptive anno-
        tations. Materials included with much
        additional information became a part of
        the authors' *Images of American Indians
        on Film* (1.9).

1.60   ———. "Bibliography: Additions to 'The
        Indian in American Film.'" *Journal
        of Popular Film and Television*, 8:1
        (Spring 1980), 50-53.

        Includes additions to the authors'
        earlier checklist (see 1.59).

1.61   Etulain, Richard W. "Recent Interpreta-
        tions of the Western Film: A Biblio-
        graphical Essay." *Journal of the
        West*, 22:4 (October 1983), 72-81.

        A descriptive and evaluative essay
        about major writings on Western films
        published in Europe and America from 1950

to the present. The discussion of each
work considered includes a description of
the work's thesis and a discussion of the
work's critical strengths and weaknesses.
Comparisons between certain works are
also included. Etulain concludes his
essay with a discussion of notable gaps
in Western film scholarship and calls for
articles and books featuring cross-
disciplinary commentary and an extended
analytical work on Western films with an
emphasis on the Western's cultural
implications. Overall, this is an
informed and balanced essay on published
materials about Western movies. For
those desiring a reliable, brief introduction to important Western scholarship,
it is the best source available.

1.62   Frederiksson, Kristine. *"Gunsmoke*:
Twenty-Year Videography--Part I."
*Journal of Popular Film and Tele-
vision*, 12:1 (Spring 1984), 16-33.

The author was a production assistant
on the CBS series from 1967 to 1974, and
her personal involvement adds immediacy
to the introductory essay which accom-
panies the videography of the 1955-1958
seasons. Organized chronologically,
entries include production numbers, air
dates, episode titles, directors, story
and script credits, guest stars and brief
plot synopses.

1.63   ———. *"Gunsmoke*: Twenty-Year Video-
graphy--Part I Continued." *Journal
of Popular Film and Television*, 12:2
(Summer 1984), 73-86.

This continuation of the Frederiksson
videography treats the 1958-1961 seasons.

1.64   ———. *"Gunsmoke*: A Videography--Part
II." *Journal of Popular Film and
Television*, 12:3 (Fall 1984), 127-143.

This installment of the videography

provides information on episodes
broadcast between 1961 and 1965.

1.65   ————. "*Gunsmoke*: Twenty-Year Video-
graphy, Part III." *Journal of
Popular Film and Television*, 12:4
(Winter 1984-85), 171-186.

This installment of the videography
provides information on episodes
broadcast between 1965 and 1970.

1.66   ————. "*Gunsmoke*: Twenty-Year Videography, Part IV." *Journal of Popular
Film and Television*, 13:1 (Spring
1985), 31-45.

This final installment of the videography provides information on episodes
broadcast between 1970 and the last
season of the show, 1974-1975.

1.67 Landrum, Larry M. and Jack Nachbar. "The
Serials: A Selected Checklist of
Published Materials." *Journal of
Popular Film*, 3:3 (Summer 1974),
272-276.

This brief bibliography includes
articles and books about movie serials,
including Westerns, published through
1974. Some items are briefly annotated.

WESTERN FILM CRITICISM,
PRE-1974

<u>Books</u>

2.1   Behlmer, Rudy, ed. *Memo from David O.
            Selznick.* New York: Viking Press,
            1972.

            This collection of memoranda issued
by producer Selznick from 1926 to 1962
includes an extensive section on *Duel in
the Sun* (1946). The material stresses
production problems and postproduction
publicity campaigns.

2.2   Bogdanovich, Peter. *Allan Dwan: The Last
            Pioneer.* New York: Praeger Publi-
            shers, Inc., 1971.

            Dwan directed some 400 films in his
fifty-year career, many of them Westerns.
Bogdanovich's monograph includes a brief
introductory overview of Dwan's career, a
long interview arranged chronologically
around Dwan's films and a thorough
filmography. References to Westerns are
scattered throughout the book.

2.3   Carpozi, George Jr. *The John Wayne
            Story.* New Rochelle, N.Y.: Arlington
            House, 1972.

            A gossipy biography by a journalist
who promises to "shoot from the hip and
hit 'em between the eyes." Only a small
step up from a *National Enquirer* profile,
this fawning, folksy bit of fluff is

unredeemed by the addition of a filmography at its conclusion.

2.4   Carroll, David. *The Matinee Idols*. New
York: Galahad Books, 1972.

This collective biography of male
stars stresses the silent era, and
includes mentions of Tom Mix and William
S. Hart.

2.5   Christina, Frank and Teresa Frank. *Billy
Jack*. New York: Avon Books, 1973.

The screenplay of the 1971 film
written by Tom Laughlin and Delores
Taylor under assumed names. Includes
seven photos from the film and an introduction by Laughlin and Taylor describing
their distribution problems with the film.

2.6   Cowie, Peter, ed. *International Film
Guide, 1966*. New York: A.S. Barnes
and Co., 1966.

Cowie's annual overview includes one
chapter on the Western: "The Growth of
the Western" (pp. 39-43). The chapter
includes a brief description of the
history and main conventions of the
genre, a list of main directors and a
list of fifty "important examples."
Cowie criticizes the genre for being
unrealistic but admits that the lack of
realism is also the genre's greatest
glory because it adds to its emotional
punch.

2.7   Evans, Max. *Sam Peckinpah, Master of
Violence*. Vermillion, S.D.: Dakota
Press, 1972.

A description of the activities surrounding the make of one of Peckinpah's
best films, *The Ballad of Cable Hogue*
(1970). Evans, a novelist and personal
friend of Peckinpah's, was hired to play
a small role in the film. His

descriptions of the troubles with getting
the film finished and the pranks and high
living off the set by the cast and crew
read much like literary tall tales. The
title of the book is misleading, since
only a few incidental comments are made
to violence in other Peckinpah films.

2.8   Gassner, John and Dudley Nichols. *Best
       Film Plays of 1943-1944.* New York:
       Crown Publishers, 1945.

Includes a version of Lamar Trotti's
screenplay for *The Ox-Bow Incident* (1943)
(pp. 511-560). Though it differs in many
ways from the filmed version, it does
offer an interesting and useful glimpse
of the film at an earlier stage in its
production. The printed script also
features an alternate, more upbeat ending
for the film, which was excised in the
final release.

2.9   Jodorowsky, Alexandro. *El Topo.* Ross
       Firestone, ed. New York: Douglas
       Book Corp., 1971.

Part one is the screenplay of Jodorowsky's surreal 1970 Western, *El Topo*,
including footnotes by Jodorowsky nearly
as enigmatic as the film itself. Part
two is a long interview with Jodorowsky
discussing what the film means.

2.10   Lahue, Kalton Co. *Riders of the Range:
       The Sagebrush Heroes of the Sound
       Screen.* New York: Castle Books,
       1973.

Thumbnail sketches of two to four
pages each of 28 B Western stars whose
careers in Westerns began after the
coming of sound. Each sketch is, as the
author admits, "subjective" and includes
minimal specific information. About half
the book is stills. Will provide some
pleasure to fans, perhaps, but of little
or no value for research. Meant as a

companion volume to Lahue's earlier book
about silent Western stars, *Winners of
the West* (I, 4.21).

2.11   Miller, Don. *"B" Movies: An Informal
            Survey of the American Low-Budget
            Film, 1933-1945*. New York: Curtis
            Books, 1973.

            A survey of low-budget films of the
1930s and 1940s arranged mainly according
to the producing studios. There is no
separate chapter on B Westerns;
references to Westerns are sprinkled
throughout the text. The book is best
used as a means of establishing a general
context for understanding the production
of all types of B films, including
Westerns. Miller tends to write in short
spurts, rarely giving more than one paragraph to a single film. Overall,
however, this is the best survey of B
movies available. Includes index.

2.12   Quirk, Lawrence. *The Films of Paul
            Newman*. New York: Citadel Press,
            1971.

            A film-by-film study of actor
Newman's career, which at the time of the
book's publication had important Western
roles ahead of it. Dated.

2.13   Richie, Donald. *George Stevens: An
            American Romantic*. New York: The
            Museum of Modern Art, 1970.

            Placing director Stevens within a
tradition of American romanticism, Richie
argues that Stevens' films resolve their
basically romantic themes by insisting on
the complexities of the individual within
society. In the director's films, the
author asserts, to be a true individual
is to insist on one's own individuality,
and to be responsible for oneself and
for one's beliefs. Richie's provocative
monograph surveys the tensions resulting

from these themes in Stevens' work, using
Shane (1953) as a principal example.
Unlike the director's other important
heroes, Shane does not let his status as
an outsider prevent him from acting on
his inner values, but allows those values
to force him to be a man of action.
Includes detailed filmography through
1970.

2.14   Schickel, Richard. *His Picture in the
        Papers.* New York: Charterhouse,
        1973.

This biographical essay on Douglas
Fairbanks Sr., and his rise and fall as a
celebrity, includes incidental mention of
the actor's work in Westerns. Schickel's
emphasis is on the interrelationship
between Fairbanks' personal values,
including his love for the American West,
and his onscreen persona.

2.15   Sherman, Eric and Martin Rubin. *The
        Director's Event: Interviews with
        Five American Film-Makers.* New York:
        Atheneum, 1970.

In-depth interviews with five idiosyncratic directors, including three with
distinctive work in Westerns: Budd Boet-
ticher, Samuel Fuller and Arthur Penn.
Each section includes plot summaries and
filmographies, now dated.

2.16   Slide, Anthony. *Early American Cinema.*
        New York: A.S. Barnes and Co., 1970.

This monograph on the pre-feature
film era of American movies is arranged
according to the important film production companies before 1914. References
to early Westerns appear occasionally
throughout the text, but of special
importance is a chapter on Essanay, which
made the Broncho Billy films, and a
chapter on the American Biograph studio
which details a number of early Westerns

made by D.W. Griffith.

2.17   *Stagecoach. A Film by John Ford and
            Dudley Nichols.* New York: Simon and
            Schuster, 1971.

     This screenplay of Ford's 1939
Western, *Stagecoach*, is accompanied by
84 stills from the film. Also includes
the Ernest Haycox short story, "Stage to
Lordsburg," upon which the film was based,
and notes explaining the differences
between the original screenplay and the
final version of the film.

2.18   Thomas, Tony. *The Films of Kirk Douglas.*
            Secaucus, N.J.: Citadel Press, 1972.

     A film-by-film description of the
movie career of Kirk Douglas, including
the 12 Westerns in which Douglas starred
between 1951 and 1971. Each chapter
includes credits, about eight stills and
about two pages of commentary which
summarizes the story, comments on the
quality of the film and points out the
importance of the movie in Douglas'
career. Thomas' comments are knowledge-
able and insightful, making this book one
of the best star studies in the Citadel
series.

2.19   Tomkies, Mike. *The Robert Mitchum Story:
            'It Sure Beats Working.'* Chicago:
            Henry Regnery Company, 1972.

     A personal anecdote story of actor
Mitchum's life, Tomkies' book is light on
specifics about individual films,
emphasizing instead Mitchum's cynical
worldview. Includes filmography.

2.20   Twomey, Alfred E. and Arthur F. McClure.
            The Versatiles. New York: A.S.
            Barnes and Co., 1969.

     A biographical dictionary of charac-
ter actors and actresses, including a

number who appeared in Westerns, between
1930 and 1955. Each entry is about one
paragraph in length and includes birth
and death years, a brief description of
the performer's movie career with
selected films being mentioned. A photo
of each performer is also included. The
lack of an index limits the use of the
book as a research tool.

2.21   Wald, Malvin and Michael Werner, eds.
              Three Major Screenplays. New York:
              Globe Book Company, Inc., 1972.

              Includes Lamar Trotti's screenplay
         for *The Ox-Bow Incident* (1943) and Carl
         Foreman's script for *High Noon* (1952).
         Each is introduced with curt biographies
         of the screenwriters, histories of each
         production and a survey of critical
         responses to each movie.

Articles

2.22   "About John Ford." *Action*, 8 (November-
              December 1973), 9-11.

              Directors Guild of America members
         remember the director of several classic
         Westerns on the occasion of his death.

2.23   Alloway, Lawrence. "Lawrence Alloway on
              the Iconography of the Movies."
              Movie, no. 7 (February 1963), 4-6.

              Alloway's discussion of the changing
         iconography of postwar American films
         includes some recommendations for
         examining changes in the Western genre.
         Arguing Robert Warshow's image of "a
         figure in repose" was fixed too early in
         the movie genre's development, Alloway
         claims that by the 1950s heroes had
         become more desperate and violence more
         brutal or ironic. He also claims that
         certain cycles, particularly within
         established genres like the Western, need

to be more carefully explored.

2.24   Apra, Adrian, Barry Boys, Ian Cameron, et
           al. "Interview with Nicholas Ray."
           Movie, no. 9 (April 1963), 14-25.

           Interview with director Ray includes
           a limited discussion of *The True Story of
           Jesse James* (1954), stressing the use of
           folk balladry in the film and Ray's
           battles over the structure of the
           project.

2.25   Armes, Roy. "Peckinpah and the Changing
           West." *London Magazine*, 9 (March
           1970), 101-106.

           In a spirited defense of *The Wild
           Bunch* (1969), Armes argues that Sam
           Peckinpah's approach to the Western is
           charmingly innovative. What the director
           does, Armes asserts, is take the
           established characteristics of the genre
           and look at them with a new awareness.

2.26   Austen, David. "Out for the Kill."
           Films and Filming, 14:8 (May 1968),
           4-9; 14:9 (June 1968), 10-15.

           A two-part study of Don Siegel's
           major films, emphasizing their reliance
           on violence and action. Austen's
           selected analyses include a look at *Duel
           at Silver Creek* (1952), Siegel's first
           Western which Austen describes (in part
           one) as an "extraordinary mixture of pure
           comic strip and, seemingly, a parody of
           that very style." In part two, Austen
           claims that *Flaming Star* (1960) is an
           unusual work for Siegel because it
           presents its narrative within the context
           of a family background.

2.27   Barkun, Michael. "Notes on the Art of
           John Ford." *Film Culture*, no. 25
           (Summer 1962), 9-13.

           The second half of this descriptive

and evaluative essay on Ford's films concentrates on Ford's Westerns, with a special emphasis on *Fort Apache* (1948). Barkun concludes that Ford is an American folk artist with an exceptional control of the film medium. This is best realized in his Westerns, which "represent a fusion of conventional, popular material and the shaping hand of the artist." Other elements of Ford's Westerns such as his use of Irish characters and the presence of sentimentality are also briefly discussed.

2.28   Bogdanovich, Peter. "Interview (with Howard Hawks)." *Movie*, no. 5 (December 1962), 8-18.

Brief film-by-film discussion with director Hawks includes limited information on his involvement in several Westerns, including *The Outlaw* (1943), *Red River* (1948), *The Big Sky* (1952) and *Rio Bravo* (1959). Interview featured in an issue of *Movie* devoted to Hawks' work.

2.29   ———. "Working Within the System: Interview with Don Siegel." *Movie*, no. 15 (Spring 1968), 1-17.

Interview features extensive discussion of Siegel's pre-director career, and a wealth of details covering most of his films through 1968, including two Westerns: *Duel at Silver Creek* (1952) and *Flaming Star* (1960). Also includes a detailed but dated filmography.

2.30   Bradshow, Bob. "They Still Go Thisaway and Thataway in the Redrock Country." *Arizona Highways*, 35:5 (May 1959), 6-9.

A listing of the Westerns made in the Sedora-Oak Creek country of Arizona after 1940 and a brief description of filmmaking in the area by an extra in most of those films. Includes sixteen stills.

2.31   Brownlow, Kevin. "The Early Days of
          William Wyler." *Film*, no. 37 (Autumn
          1963), 11-13.

          An interview with Wyler during which
          the director discusses the making of his
          silent two-reel Westerns at Universal.

2.32   Bryan, J., III. "Hi-Yo Silver!"
          Saturday Evening Post, 212 (Oct. 14,
          1939), 20-21, 131, 134, 136, 138.

          An invaluable resource for anyone
          doing research on the popularity of
          Westerns during the late 1930s or on the
          history of *The Lone Ranger*. The article
          includes data on the number of radio
          stations carrying the radio show (140),
          the number of newspapers carrying the
          comic strip (123), radio sponsors, etc.
          It also includes a short profile of Earl
          W. Graser, the radio voice of the Ranger
          during the 1930s, and brief biographical
          sketches of writer Fran Striker and
          producer George Trendle. There are some
          factual errors about the origins of the
          show, but overall this is the most
          usefully detailed record available about
          the most famous of all radio Westerns,
          written when *The Lone Ranger* was in the
          middle of its radio popularity.

2.33   Buscombe, Edward. "The Idea of Genre in
          the American Cinema." *Screen*, 11:2
          (March/April 1970), 33-45. Reprinted
          in *Film Genre*, ed. Barry K. Grant.
          Metuchen, N.J.: The Scarecrow Press,
          Inc., 1977.

          Argues that genre study is a better
          approach for the analysis of movies as a
          popular art form than the *auteur* theory.
          In trying to arrive at the elements that
          constitute a film genre, Buscombe argues
          that the "outer form" of movies, their
          visual qualities, is the central element
          for defining a genre and that these outer
          forms determine the "inner forms" of

themes, plot structures, etc. When
visual elements such as setting, costume,
tools and other objects are perceived by
the movie-going audience as conventions,
a popular genre exists. Buscombe's
central example is the Western, and his
only detailed example is Sam Peckinpah's
Ride the High Country (1962). Buscombe's
thesis that iconology and semiology are
the sole determinants of a genre is
controversial and contradicts most other
genre theory. A critique of Buscombe's
article, generally critical of the entire
concept of movie genres by Richard
Collins, appeared in *Screen* just a few
months later (see I, 7.33).

2.34   Cameron, Ian and Mark Shivas. "Interview
         with Robert Aldrich." *Movie*, no. 8
         (March 1963), 8-11.

         Interview with director Aldrich
features discussion of improvisational
qualities of *Vera Cruz* and *Apache* (both
1954) as well as the conflicts in production for both films. Includes a dated
filmography.

2.35   Carroll, Sidney. "Lo, the Poor Cowboy."
         Esquire, 18:5 (November 1942), 47,
         140-142.

         A brief overview of the history of
the Western prepared with the help of
veteran Western director George Marshall.
The tone of the article emphasizes the
humor of the topic rather than detailed
information. Includes no information not
covered in more detail in later histories
of Western movies.

2.36   Cherniak, Samuel. "Toward *Liberty
         Valance*." *Moviegoer*, no. 2 (Summer-
         Fall 1964), 34-37.

         Argues that Ford's questioning of his
earlier idealization of the West, as seen
in *The Man Who Shot Liberty Valance*

(1962), may be traced back to an earlier
Ford Western, *The Horse Soldiers* (1959).
Liberty Valance represents a fully
realized critique on Ford's part, but *The
Horse Soldiers* should not be overlooked
as a signpost of Ford's changing
perspectives.

2.37   Crist, Judith, Bruce Kane, Philip K.
            Scheuer and Joel Reisner. "Special
            Report: The Western." *Action*, 5:3
            (May/June 1970), 11-29.

        Includes an attempt to establish the
top 12 Westerns of all time and articles
about the Westerns of Sam Peckinpah and
Henry Hathaway.

2.38   Denton, James F. "The Red Man Plays
            Indian." *Colliers*, 113 (March 18,
            1944), 18-19.

        Describes the Navaho training to play
Cheyenne warriors for the film *Buffalo
Bill* (1944). The overall tone is one of
amusement and slight condescension. For
the most part, the Navaho are described
as childlike. Such an attitude in an
article in a popular magazine offers a
useful hint about general public
attitudes toward Native Americans in
1944. Includes five photos of the film
in production.

2.39   Farber, Stephen. "Peckinpah's Return."
            Film Quarterly, 23:1 (Fall 1969),
            2-11.

        Farber's in-depth analysis of *The
Wild Bunch* (1969) stresses its relationship to traditional Western motifs and
conventions. Director Peckinpah's mix of
realism and romanticism "illuminates the
Western myths so that they seem relevant,
not remote." Includes an interview with
Peckinpah in which the director discusses
his relationship with movie studios and
his intentions for *The Wild Bunch* and *The

Ballad of Cable Hogue (1970), then in
production.

2.40   "The Great American Horse Opera." *Life*,
        26:2 (Jan. 10, 1949), 42-46.

        In this photo essay, photographer
John Florea attempts to reduce Westerns
to their formulaic essence by creating
photos of the key moments of *Yellow Sky*
(1949) with the costumed cast but without
the backgrounds. Twelve of 13 photos are
in color even though the film itself was
in black and white.

2.41   Hanson, Curtis Lee. "William Wyler."
        Cinema (California), 3 (Summer 1967),
        22-35.

        Interview with Wyler includes some
discussion of the director's early
apprenticeship making silent Westerns for
Universal and problems shooting *Hell's
Heroes* (1929), Wyler's first sound
picture. Includes a lengthy filmography
with commentary.

2.42   Hillier, Jim. "Arthur Penn." *Screen*,
        10:1 (January-February 1969), 5-12.

        Tracing Penn's biography to put his
work in context, Hillier argues that the
director's films deal in popular American
legends (like Billy the Kid and Bonnie
and Clyde) in order to remove their
mythic props. Hillier's essay includes
analysis of *The Left-Handed Gun* (1958).

2.43   "Howard Hawks Filmography." *Movie*, no. 5
        (December 1962), 31-34.

        Detailed but dated filmography of
Hawks' movie career. Featured in an
issue of *Movie* devoted to Hawks' work.

2.44   Hughes, Albert. "Jesse James: Outlaw
        with a Halo." *Montana*, 17:4 (October

1967), 60-75.

A survey of movies featuring the James gang, with an emphasis on how the films have distorted history and glorified Frank and Jesse James as heroes.

2.45   Kahn, Gordon. "Lay That Pistol Down." *Atlantic*, 173 (April 1944), 105-108.

An attempt to relate Westerns of the period to the preoccupations of the world movie audience. Kahn argues that fears of violence and the war have turned the formerly tough, aggressive Western hero into the safer and gentler singing cowboy.

2.46   Libby, Bill. "The Old Wrangler Rides Again." *Cosmopolitan* (March 1964), 13-21.

An informal interview with John Ford in which Ford dismisses those who do not discuss Westerns as seriously as other films and in which he expresses his own deep affection for the genre. Reprinted in part in *My Darling Clementine. John Ford, Director* (pp. 136-140) (see 3.6).

2.47   Mantell, Harold. "Counteracting the Stereotype." *American Indian*, 5 (Fall 1950), 16-20.

A report about the formation and initial activities of the National Film Committee of the Association on American Indian Affairs, a group charged with recommending to the film industry ways of eliminating negative stereotypes of Native Americans in the movies. *Broken Arrow* (1950) is praised as an initial success in this effort. The article is of historical interest for those researching a history of activism in Hollywood against Native American stereotyping.

2.48   Markfield, Wallace. "The Inauthentic
                Western." *American Mercury*, 75:345
                (September 1952), 82-86.

            A critique of the more serious,
        reflective Westerns that were appearing
        in the early 1950s. Markfield praises
        older Westerns, including the Bs, for
        their moral clarity and uninhibited sense
        of movement. Recent Westerns, he
        concludes, violate these earlier models
        by bogging themselves down with social
        problems, moral ambiguities and an
        inflated sense of their own significance.
        A more famous article with a similar
        perspective by Andre Bazin was published
        in France about the same time (I, 7.3).

2.49   Mayersberg, Paul. "*The Miracle Worker*
                and *The Left-Handed Gun*." *Movie*,
                no. 3 (October 1962), 26-28.

            Mayersberg argues that Arthur Penn's
        first two films share important elements,
        particularly in their concern with the
        problems of physical communication
        between people and their treatment of
        situations in which the spoken word is
        virtually useless. In *The Left-Handed
        Gun* (1958), Mayersberg asserts, Billy's
        emphasis on gesture and his skill with a
        gun are reflections of his difficulties
        in more verbal forms of communication.

2.50   Maynard, Ken. "The Modern Westerner."
                Breaking into the Movies, ed. Charles
                Reed Jones. New York: Unicorn Press,
                1927, pp. 52-58.

            Written by perhaps the greatest
        stuntman of all the Western stars just as
        he was reaching the height of his popula-
        rity. Offered as advice to those who
        want to appear in Western movies, Maynard
        says the four most important ingredients
        for such a career are good riding skills,
        a personality that "screens well," acting
        skills and having the right producer. In

the last few paragraphs, Maynard insists
that all of his pictures are "historically accurate."

2.51   McVay, Douglas. "Greatest--Stevens."
            Films and Filming, 11 (April 1965),
            10-14; 11 (May 1965), 16-19.

McVay devotes more than half of the
first part of his two-part examination of
Stevens' major films to an in-depth
analysis of *Shane* (1953). Unlike some of
Stevens' other important works, McVay
argues, *Shane* keeps its passages of
realism unprosaic and its passages of
stylization "powerful and disciplined."
As a result, *Shane* is more than just a
Western; according to McVay, it is a
universal morality play in an abstract
Western setting.

2.52   Millstead, Thomas. "The Movie the
            Indians Almost Won." *Westways*, 62
            (December 1970), 24-26, 55.

Relates the story of Buffalo Bill
Cody's filming of a re-enactment of the
Battle of Wounded Knee in 1913. Millstead tells the tale as a yarn rather
than as serious historical research. He
emphasizes the fact that at one point in
the filming the Sioux participating in
the film secretly planned to use live
ammunition instead of blanks in the
climactic battle scene. Although the
facts seem generally correct here, those
who wise a more serious perspective with
accompanying photos of the same film
should examine Kevin Brownlow's *The War,
The West and the Wilderness* (6.5).

2.53   Moser, Don. "The Western Hero." *Life*,
            55:25 (Dec. 20, 1963), 104-111.

Brief, disconnected comments about
Western movies with an emphasis on their
long and international popularity.
Includes 18 photos, one of them a

sculpture of John Wayne as Western hero
by Marisol. Part of a special issue of
Life devoted to American movies.

2.54   Mundy, Robert. "Don Siegel: Time and
        Motion, Attitudes and Genre." *Cinema*
        (Cambridge), no. 5 (February 1970),
        10-13.

        Examining principal themes in
Siegel's work, Mundy briefly looks at the
director's approach to two genres with
conflicting settings: the gangster story
and the Western. According to Mundy, the
urban-rural conflict plays an important
role in Siegel's approach to both genres,
but the author is unable to explain in
any detail its impact on the director's
work in Westerns, though Mundy does make
a claim that Siegel had an uncredited
hand in shaping *Death of a Gunfighter*
(1969).

2.55   Perkins, V.F. and Mark Shivas. "Inter-
        view with King Vidor." *Movie*, no. 10
        (July/August 1963), 7-10.

        Interview with director Vidor
features a brief mention of *Man Without a
Star* (1955) and a lengthy discussion of
Duel in the Sun (1946), stressing Vidor's
technical contributions to the film and
his early conflicts with producer David
O. Selznick.

2.56   Perkins, V.F. "The Cinema of Nicholas
        Ray." *Movie*, no. 9 (April 1963),
        4-10.

        Perkins discusses the major themes of
director Ray's work, including *Johnny
Guitar* (1954) and *The True Story of Jesse
James* (1957). In these Westerns in
particular, Perkins argues, decor is used
in highly symbolic ways to show isolation
and distance. The discussion is part of
an issue of *Movie* devoted to Ray's films.

2.57   Reed, Allen C.   "John Ford Makes Another
         Movie Classic in Monument Valley."
         Arizona Highways, 32:4 (April 1956),
         4-11.

         A brief description of the making of
         five John Ford Westerns in Monument
         Valley, including the making of the then
         recent *The Searchers* (1956). Includes
         details about Ford's initial choice to
         use the location in *Stagecoach* (1939) and
         his relationship with the Navahos who own
         Monument Valley. Includes 27 photos of
         Ford's Monument Valley Westerns,
         including a number that show the films
         in production. The article is part of a
         special issue of *Arizona Highways* devoted
         to Monument Valley.

2.58   Reid, John Howard. "A Comparison of
              Size." *Films and Filming*, 6:6 (March
              1960), 12, 31-32, 35.

         The second part of Reid's two-part
         study of William Wyler (see 2.59)
         emphasizes the director's major works
         from 1939 to 1959, including some
         discussion of *The Westerner* (1940), which
         Reid ranks among Wyler's best because of
         the director's use of natural sound,
         composition and expert photography.
         Inexplicably, *The Big Country* (1958) is
         not even mentioned.

2.59   ————.   "A Little Larger Than Life."
              Films and Filming, 6:5 (February
              1960), 9-10, 32.

         Compact history of William Wyler's
         career from his first job with his
         second cousin's studio (Carl Laemmle's
         Universal) in 1920 through his work on
         Dead End (1937). Scant mention is made
         of the director's early films, most of
         which were one- and two-reel Westerns.
         The article is the first of a two-part
         study on Wyler (see 2.58).

2.60   Russell, Lee. "John Ford." *New Left*
                 Review, no. 29 (January/February
                 1965), 69-73.

              A brief summing up of the major
         themes in John Ford's films, especially
         his Westerns. Russell argues that Ford
         is a Jacksonian populist and as such the
         political implications of his films are
         both liberal and conservative. He also
         sees Ford's films evolving from an early
         celebration of American history to a
         viewing of the past as a pleasant memory
         set against the failures of the present.

2.61   Schrader, Paul. "Sam Peckinpah Going to
                 Mexico." *Cinema* (California), 5:3
                 (1969), 19-25.

              Examining *The Wild Bunch* (1969),
         Schrader asserts that the film is not,
         like Peckinpah's previous work, about an
         outmoded Western code, but "about
         Westerners bereft of the code," thus
         giving a perspective on an age that could
         believe the Western code was valuable.
         Includes a handful of stills from *The
         Wild Bunch*, and is accompanied by a brief
         history of Peckinpah's troubled career.

2.62   Shivas, Mark. "*How the West Was Won*."
                 Movie, no. 6 (January 1963), 28-29.

              Shivas sorts out the directorial
         efforts shared in making *How the West Was
         Won* (1963), arguing that John Ford's
         misty-eyed nostalgia is outgunned by
         Henry Hathaway's unassuming sense of
         spectacle.

2.63   Smith, H. Allen. "King of the Cowboys."
                 Life, 15:2 (July 12, 1943), 47-48,
                 50, 52, 54.

              This *Life* cover story is a brief
         biographical profile of Roy Rogers by the
         noted American humorist. Smith portrays
         Rogers as a rather simple-minded hick and

the overall tone of the article is condescending and insulting to both Rogers
and his fans. Includes some data about
the cost of Rogers' gaudy Western clothes
and the quantity of his fan mail. Also
includes six photos.

2.64   Stein, Jeanne. "Gregory Peck." *Films in*
                   Review, 18:3 (March 1967), 129-145.

Biography of Peck, based on lengthy
letter from the actor, features Peck's
reflections on his major films. Includes
brief anecdotal material on Peck's work
in *Duel in the Sun* (1946) and *The Gun-*
fighter (1950). Also features useful
filmography, though dated.

2.65   Stewart, James. "One Hat's Enough For
                   Me." *Films and Filming*, 12 (April
                   1966), 19-22.

Stewart details his philosophy of
acting, and discusses his work with
various directors and in different
genres. The Western, he argues, is
ageless because of its reliance on visual
communication.

2.66   Sweigart, William R. "James Stewart."
                   Films in Review, 15 (December 1964),
                   585-605.

Sketchy account of Stewart's career,
with little more than incidental background information about any of Stewart's
films, particularly his Westerns.
Includes a useful but dated filmography.

2.67   Vestal, Stanley. "The Hollywood Indian."
                   Southwest Review, 21:4 (July 1936),
                   418-423.

Argues that inaccuracy in the
portrayal of Native Americans on screen
is present in the casting of whites as
Indians, fake costuming and a false
detailing of day-to-day tribal life. As

a result, of all the Indians on the
screen, "there is not a human being in a
carload." Vestal's arguments are long
familiar but the article is interesting
in being one of the first to appear in an
academic journal condemning Hollywood
stereotyping of Native Americans.

2.68   Walker, Stanley. "Let the Indian be the
            Hero." *The New York Times Magazine*
            (April 24, 1960), 50, 52, 55.

A criticism of television Westerns
for portraying Native Americans according
to formula conventions instead of
according to history. Walker calls for
truer stories in which sometimes "the
Indian (may) be the hero." Since no TV
shows are detailed, Walker's argument
seems well-intentioned but superficial.
It may, however, be of some historical
value as an early discussion of stereotyping in television written at the
height of the fad for TV Westerns.

2.69   Wallington, Mike and Chris Frayling.
            "The Italian Western." *Cinema*
            (Cambridge), nos. 6-7 (August 1970),
            31-38.

An attempt to establish the forms and
themes of "spaghetti" Westerns when they
were at the height of their American
popularity. Special attention is given
to the films of Sergio Leone. For a more
detailed presentation of these materials,
see Frayling's book *Spaghetti Westerns*
(9.3).

2.70   Williams, John. "The Western: Definition
            of the Myth." *The Nation*, 193:17
            (Nov. 18, 1961), 401-406.

Although this article is about
Western fiction, many of Williams'
generalizations might also be applied to
Western films. Formula Westerns,
Williams argues, reflect a New England

Calvinistic sense of the predestined
triumph of good over evil. More serious
Western fiction tends to mistakenly be
epic whereas they more properly should be
mythic. The Western hero is not epical
because his quest is not national; he is
mythic because "(h)e is an adventurer in
chaos, searching for meaning there."
Williams' perceptions tend to ignore the
social implications of Westerns and need
to be balanced by other theorists, such
as John Cawelti (see 7.4 and 7.5), who
discuss Westerns as a perception of
social history. However, Williams' ideas
about the sense of inevitability in
formula Westerns and his ideas about the
inner quest of the Western hero make his
essay provocative and useful reading.

2.71   Wood, Robin. "Rio Bravo." *Movie*, no. 5
          (December 1962), 25-27.

Wood stresses the importance of
Hawksian themes such as self-respect in
Rio Bravo (1959), and claims that the
director's acceptance of underlying
generic conventions gives the film the
timeless, universal quality of myth. The
essay is featured in an issue of *Movie*
devoted to Hawks' work.

SPECIFIC WESTERN FILMS

Books

3.1   Bach, Steven. *Final Cut: Dreams and Disasters in the Making of Heaven's Cut*. New York: William Morrow and Company, Inc., 1985.

An articulate first-person narrative of Bach's rise and fall as an executive at United Artists, centering on the making of *Heaven's Gate* (1980). While not an expose, *Final Cut* reveals exactly what it is like to be in the *business* of making movies. Bach gives an almost excruciating amount of detail on *Heaven's Gate* as well as insights into other films being made by United Artists at that time.

3.2   Behlmer, Rudy. *America's Favorite Movies: Behind the Scenes*. New York: Frederick Ungar Publishing Co., 1982.

This description of the making of 15 famous films includes one chapter each on the making of *Stagecoach* (1939) and *High Noon* (1952). Behlmer discusses location choices, casting, filming and editing decisions as well as special circumstances and incidents occurring in the making of each film. Of special interest in the discussion of *High Noon* is how and why Carl Foreman changed his original concept of the film from an allegory about the United Nations to one which condemned the investigations of the House

Committee on Un-American Activities. A
short bibliography for each chapter is
included.

3.3   Ford, John and Dudley Nichols. *Stage-*
           coach. London: Lorrimer Publishing
           Inc., revised edition, 1984.

           A reproduction of the screenplay to
Ford's 1939 movie, matched with the final
version of the film currently in distribution. The book includes Ernest
Haycox's "Stage to Lordsburg," the short
story on which the film is nominally
based, and more than 75 production
photos. Also included is an afterword by
Andrew Sinclair, in which he combines
production history with analysis to argue
that *Stagecoach* was Ford's presentation
of the Old West in mythic terms as a way
of mourning the death of Tom Mix.

3.4   Haver, Ronald. *David O. Selznick's*
           Hollywood. New York: Alfred A.
           Knopf, 1980.

           This sinfully opulent book traces the
career and productions of Hollywood's
legendary producer. Of special interest
for those dealing with Westerns are pages
352-369, which detail the making of
Selznick's erotic Western, *Duel in the*
Sun (1946). Dozens of stills accompany
the text, 55 of them in color.

3.5   Koszarski, Richard, ed. *The Rivals of*
           D.W. Griffith: Alternate Auteurs
           1913-1918. New York: New York
           Zoetrope, 1976.

           A catalog of the films shown in a
series at Walker Art Center in Minneapolis in 1976. Brief description of
several Westerns are included: John
Emerson's *Wild and Wooly* (1917),
described by Eileen Bowser; Charles
Swickard and William S. Hart's *Hell's*
Hinges (1916), described by William K.

Everson; John Ford's *Straight Shooting*
(1917), described by Tag Gallagher; and
Frank Borzage's *The Gun Woman* (1918),
described by Richard Koszarski.

3.6   Lyons, Robert, ed. *My Darling Clementine.*
          John Ford, Director. New Brunswick,
          N.J.: Rutgers University Press, 1984.

Includes the continuity script and
shooting script of Ford's classic 1946
Western. Also featured are interviews
with Ford on Westerns in general and an
interview with Winston Miller, who wrote
the script for *Clementine*. Final
sections of the volume include a selection of reviews of the film, critical
commentaries on the film and Westerns in
general and a brief filmography of Ford's
work after 1930 and a short bibliography.
It is a handy collection, weakened
slightly by the inclusion of only 16
stills, hardly enough to give the rich
visual nature of *My Darling Clementine*.
In the book's well-argued introduction,
Lyons concludes that "*My Darling Clementine* is ultimately a film of reconcilia-
tion in which Ford uses the historical
legend of Wyatt Earp to create an
affirmation, perhaps his most confident
affirmation, of American moral values and
social purpose."

3.7   McClelland, Doug. *The Golden Age of "B"*
          Movies. Nashville: Charter House
          Publishers, Inc., 1978.

Summaries and stills of a handful of
"favorite" B movies from the late 1940s.
An interesting work which, though it
features detailed discussions of the
films in their contexts, includes mention
of only one Western (the 1948 *Thunder-
hoof*), making it marginally useful here.

3.8   McConnell, Frank D. *The Spoken Seen:*
          Film and the Romantic Imagination.
          Baltimore: The Johns Hopkins

University Press, 1975.

Argues that films reflect a parallel
vision to that presented in great romantic literature. In a provocative analysis of the 1959 film *Warlock* (pp. 146-
161), McConnell sees the film using as a
theme a topic usually unstated but
inherent in the genre itself: the
founding and establishment of a city.
The shamanistic Western hero founds the
city; the priestly Western hero establishes and maintains laws within the
city, something the shamanistic hero is
not concerned with. *Warlock* presents
both types of heroes and shows how they
are antithetical to one another. Further-
more, it presents this conflict within an
ambiguous environment that may not be
worth the struggle between the two
heroes. The film is therefore about some
of the complexities within the Western
genre itself. It anticipates self-
reflexive Westerns, which would come a
decade later. Some of these ideas about
Westerns are developed in more detail in
McConnell's later book, *Storytelling and
Mythmaking* (7.8).

3.9   Meyer, William R. *The Making of the
           Great Westerns*. New Rochelle, N.Y.:
           Arlington House, 1979.

Largely anecdotal production histories of 30 Western films. Relying
heavily on publicity information and
selected autobiographical accounts, the
histories are sketchy and often incomplete. Each includes brief excerpts from
a handful of important movie review
sources. A flimsy bibliography and a
strong postwar bias (only 11 of the
productions discussed were released
before 1950, and only two of those before
1939) hamper the work's pretense of
eclectic coverage. Useful for its
general background information.

3.10   Nugent, Frank and Patrick Ford. *Wagon-*
            master. New York: Frederick Ungar
            Publishing Co., Inc., 1986.

            The complete final screenplay of John
            Ford's 1950 film which he often listed as
            the favorite of his Westerns. Also
            includes 23 full-page stills from the
            film.

3.11   Pilkington, William and Don Graham, eds.
            Western Movies. Albuquerque:
            University of New Mexico Press, 1979.

            This collection of essays begins with
            a short and sweet introduction of a
            variety of approaches which may be
            applied to Westerns, before turning to
            treatments of a number of films,
            including: *The Virginian* (1929); *Stage-*
            coach (1939); *Fort Apache* (1948); *High*
            Noon (1952); *Shane* (1953); *Rio Bravo*
            (1959); *The Wild Bunch* (1969); *Little Big*
            Man (1970); *A Man Called Horse* (1970);
            The Great Northfield, Minnesota Raid
            (1972); *Ulzana's Raid* (1972); and *The*
            Missouri Breaks (1976).

3.12   Schaefer, Jack. *Shane: The Critical*
            Edition. James C. Work, ed.
            Lincoln, Neb.: University of
            Nebraska Press, 1984.

            Although this book is mainly devoted
            to reprinting Schaefer's novel and to a
            series of critical essays about it, one
            section of the book deals with critical
            studies of the film and reprints three
            reviews and three articles. In addition,
            many of the critical analyses of the
            novel are applicable to the film as well.
            Overall, the book is a convenient and
            essential starting place for anyone
            beginning a close study of this most
            famous of Western stories.

3.13   Thomas, Tony. *Hollywood and the American*
            Image. Westport, Conn.: Arlington

House, 1981.

This coffee table book is attractively packaged with movie photos, but
its commentary is too lightweight to have
more than fan appeal. One chapter, "The
West that Never Was" (pp. 130-149),
claims, "Of all the kinds of American
life depicted on the screen, it (the
Western) is the most exciting and least
accurate." Thomas illustrates the
comment with brief discussions of three
films: *Santa Fe Trail* (1940), *Abilene
Town* (1946) and *Angel and the Badman*
(1946).

Articles

3.14   Abbott, L.B. "*Butch Cassidy and the Sun-
          dance Kid*." *Special Effects*. Holly-
          wood, Calif.: The ASC Press, pp.
          161-168.

A technical description of three
special effects devised by Abbott for
Butch Cassidy and the Sundance Kid
(1969). Includes seven color stills from
the film.

3.15   Albert, Steven. "*The Shootist*: Redemp-
          tion of Discredited Authority." *Jump
          Cut*, no. 26 (December 1981), 9-12.

An analysis of *The Shootist* (1976)
within the cultural context of its
original release. Albert argues that the
film was an attempt to reinstate the
dignity and value of the figure of authority during the muddled days of the post-
Watergate years. The film is analyzed as
a redemption of the John Wayne persona,
and as a myth narrative from the perspective of the political right in which
those with power and authority are
re-established to the elevated positions
which are their natural due. Although
Albert sometimes forces the meaning of
specific scenes to fit his arguments,

especially in interpreting the final
sequence of the film, his overall perspectives are original and thought-
provoking. Of special interest is a
comparison of *The Shootist* with *High Noon*
(1952). While *The Shootist* shows a world
of finalized hierarchies, Albert
concludes, *High Noon* presents a world
where people can make choices and change.

3.16   Anderson, Lindsay. *"The Searchers."*
        Sight and Sound, 26 (Autumn 1956),
        94-95. Reprinted in *Theories of*
        Authorship: A Reader, ed. John
        Caughie. London: Routledge & Kegan
        Paul, 1981, pp. 75-77.

This brief study of John Ford's 1956
film starring John Wayne argues that *The*
Searchers is, despite its promise,
without feeling. The movie's focus on a
bitter and obsessed hero, as in the
director's earlier *Fort Apache* (1948),
results in uneven portrayals and reflects
the director's "unease" with his subject.

3.17   Appelbaum, Ralph. *"The Long Riders*: The
        Rebirth of the American Western?"
        Filmmaker's Monthly, 13 (June 1980),
        16-19.

A brief discussion of the Walter Hill
film *The Long Riders* (1980). Most of the
information is provided by comments made
by those involved with the production of
the film. At the end, Appelbaum speculates that *The Long Riders* might create a
renewed public interest in Westerns, a
speculation which proved to be incorrect.

3.18   Bach, Steven. "Once Upon a Time in the
        West." *American Film*, 10:9 (July-
        August 1985), 46-49.

Bach, an executive at United Artists
at the time of the production of Michael
Cimino's *Heaven's Gate* (1980), details
how the legendary cost overruns of that

film began to accumulate. The article is
a selection from Bach's book on *Heaven's Gate, Final Cut* (3.1).

3.19   Bazin, Andre. "Beauty of a Western."
            Cahiers du Cinema, no. 55 (January
            1956), trans. Liz Heron. Reprinted
            in *Cahiers du Cinema, the 1950s:
            Neo-Realism, Hollywood, New Wave*,
            ed. Jim Hillier. Cambridge: Harvard
            University Press, 1985, pp. 165-168.

            Review of Anthony Mann's *The Man From
            Laramie* (1955) focuses on director's use
            of landscape as atmosphere in his films.
            Bazin claims contemplation is the ulti-
            mate goal of Mann's use of *mise en scene*.

3.20   ────. "An Exemplary Western." *Cahiers
            du Cinema*, no. 74 (August-September
            1957), trans. Phillip Drummond.
            Reprinted in *Cahiers du Cinema, the
            1950s: Neo-Realism, Hollywood, New
            Wave*, ed. Jim Hillier. Cambridge:
            Harvard University Press, 1985, pp.
            169-172.

            Review of *Seven Men From Now*
            describes Budd Boetticher's 1956 film as
            the best Western made after World War II.
            Bazin credits the film's use of landscape
            and highly conventional characterizations
            in inventive situations with its success.

3.21   Belton, John. "The Bionic Eye: Zoom
            Esthetics." *Cineaste*, 11 (Winter
            1980-81), 20-27.

            Belton discusses the evolution of
            zoom-lens techniques used in Hollywood
            moviemaking, with some emphasis on Robert
            Altman's use of zoom shooting in *McCabe
            and Mrs. Miller* (1971). The author
            argues that the use of zoom techniques
            reflects a shift in cinematic codes, that
            space is now defined in terms of changing
            image size and time.

3.22   Benequist, Lawrence. "The Semiotic Mode:
            Anchor and Relay as Sign Function in
            Red River." *Cine-Tracts*, 3 (Spring
            1980), 72-82.

            When Howard Hawks made *Red River*
            (1948), he made it in two versions: in
            one, a cowhand played by Walter Brennan
            narrated the story; in the other, the
            oral commentary was replaced with hand-
            written text presented as legend. Using
            Roland Barthes' definition of the
            relation between the linguistic and the
            iconic in communication, Benequist
            analyzes the different comments made by
            Hawks in each version. Benequist con-
            cludes that the narrated version
            humanized the protagonists' actions,
            while the text left central characters in
            historically determined poses. The
            article includes a chart comparing the
            two versions, applying both to the same
            photographed sequences. The study is
            part of a special section of *Cine-Tracts*
            on *Red River*, resulting from a 1978
            seminar on semiotics and film.

3.23   Bernstein, Gene W. "Robert Altman's
            *Buffalo Bill and the Indians, or
            Sitting Bull's History Lesson*: A
            Self-Portrait in Celluloid." *Journal
            of Popular Culture*, 13:1 (Summer
            1979), 17-25.

            Argues that Altman's 1976 film is
            reflexive about three subjects concur-
            rently: the film medium itself, the
            Western and the creation of a superstar.
            This is accomplished by Altman through a
            constant comparison of illusion, repre-
            sented by Buffalo Bill, with history,
            represented by Sitting Bull. Ironically,
            Bernstein concludes, to debunk the false
            version of history created by the Wild
            West show, Altman creates his own dis-
            torted version of history in his movie,
            yet another kind of show. This suggests
            "what other recorders of history can

loath to admit, that the record can never
be set straight, it can only be added to
by new portraits of ourselves." Bernstein does not argue his thesis by
comparing historical details with the
Wild West show. Rather, he shows how the
theme of illusion versus history is
developed within the film itself. He is
thus able to explore the structure of the
film itself in more detail than most
other critics who have written about the
film.

3.24   Billman, Carol W. "Illusions of
            Grandeur: Altman, Kopit and the
            Legends of the Wild West."
            Literature/Film Quarterly, 6:3
            (Summer 1978), 253-261.

            A comparison of themes and charac-
terizations between Arthur Kopit's play
Indians and Robert Altman's film adaptation, *Buffalo Bill and the Indians, or
Sitting Bull's History Lesson* (1976).
The theme of *Indians* is the distortion of
American history and Kopit's Buffalo Bill
is a man with a conscience beginning to
realize that his glorification of the
white taking of the West has contributed
to the demise of the Indians. Altman's
film, on the other hand, is thematically
concerned with the broader question of
illusion and reality and the relation of
this question to the world of show business. Altman's Buffalo Bill is unable to
determine the differences in his own
person between the real Bill and Buffalo
Bill the show business creation. In both
versions "we are indeed at others' mercy
for a perception of both America's past
and its heroes."

3.25   Boyd, David. "Prisoner of the Night."
            Film Herald, 12:2 (Winter 1976-77),
            24-30.

            Argues that the "most prevalent
influence" on Martin Scorsese's *Taxi*

Driver (1976) was a film that on the
surface seems to be its direct opposite,
John Ford's *The Searchers* (1956). Boyd
attempts to demonstrate this thesis by
describing parallels between the two
films in locale, characters, theme and
social critique. He concludes that,
ultimately, *Taxi Driver* is a much darker
film than *The Searchers*. Boyd never
tries to directly prove his argument, but
through his process of finding numerous
parallels, he is able to intelligently
analyze both films. See also (9.22).

3.26   Browne, Nick. "The Spectator-in-the-
            Text: The Rhetoric of *Stagecoach*."
            Film Quarterly, 29 (Winter 1975-76),
            26-38.

            Browne argues that the requirements
of a rhetorical presentation are articulated as a set of integrated structures
and strategies that give form to the work
and, at the same time, determine the
viewpoint of the spectator in his reading
of the film. The author uses *Stagecoach*
(1939) as a model for semiological study
of filmic texts which incorporate the
place and role of the spectator. Browne
argues that the viewer's vantage point
determines how the action in John Ford's
film is interpreted. This article is an
expanded version of a piece that originally appeared in *Communications*, no. 23
(1975); first printed in French, the
original article can be found in English
translation as "The Rhetoric of Specular
Text With Reference to *Stagecoach*," in
Theories of Authorship: A Reader, edited
by John Caughie (London: Routledge &
Kegan Paul, 1981, pp. 251-260).

3.27   Buscombe, Edward. "Critics on *The
            Searchers*." *Screen Education*, 17
            (Autumn 1975), 49-52.

            As evidenced by the reviews of *The
Searchers*, Buscombe argues that critics

are relatively unconcerned with matters
of form and style in film. His rather
odd point seems to be that, because
critics offer distorted "readings" of
films, teachers should be wary of both
their methods and their conclusions.
Included in an issue of *Screen Education*
devoted to *The Searchers*.

3.28   Caughie, John. "Teaching Through Author-
              ship." *Screen Education*, 17 (Autumn
              1975), 3-13.

With mixed success, this essay
attempts to "locate the uses and limitations" of an *auteur* approach in the
classroom. Within the context of John
Ford's freedom, or lack thereof, to
control "meaning," Caughie deals with *The
Searchers* (1956) in terms of themes,
ideologies and style. The essay also
provides a concise description of the
development of the *auteur* theory as
Caughie argues that interest in the
director should be a point of departure
rather than a final destination.
Included in an issue of *Screen Education*
devoted to *The Searchers*.

3.29   Cawelti, John. "The Frontier and The
              Native American." *America as Art*,
              ed. Joshua C. Taylor. Washington,
              D.C.: Smithsonian Institution Press,
              1976, pp. 133-184.

Within the context of Turner's
frontier thesis as an expression of Anglo
domination, Cawelti traces the myths of
the frontier and images of Native
Americans in a variety of cultural expressions. The essay centers on painting
but includes examples drawn from advertising, fiction and film to reinforce his
points. Provides interesting information
about images in paintings which found
their way into films.

3.30   Clandfield, David. "The Onamastic Code

of *Stagecoach*." *Literature/Film Quarterly*, 5 (Spring 1977), 174-179.

Using a basically linguistic approach, Clandfield compares the original story by Ernest Haycox to the script of the 1939 film by Dudley Nichols. He believes changes in place and personal names reveal the film's "deep structure," and illuminate dramatic and ideological matters.

3.31   Comolli, Jean-Louis. "Signposts on the Trail." *Cahiers du Cinema*, no. 164 (March 1965), 75-76. Reprinted in *Theories of Authorship: A Reader*, ed. John Caughie. London: Routledge & Kegan Paul, 1981, pp. 109-116.

Comolli's defense of *Cheyenne Autumn* (1964) centers on the interference of the producing studio (Warner Bros.) which crippled the movie director John Ford wanted to make. The author claims that the film--Ford's last Western--still manages to emphasize important Fordian themes, such as the Quest, the conflicts between white "civilization" and Indian culture and the compressed use of generic symbols. *Cheyenne Autumn*, Comolli argues, seems to "condense the whole stock of Fordian material into the compass of a single film."

3.32   Cook, David A. "*The Wild Bunch*, Fifteen Years After." *North Dakota Quarterly*, 51:3 (1983), 123-130.

Cook argues that *The Wild Bunch* was often misunderstood when it was first released in 1969. Hindsight reveals that it is an American masterpiece. Most of the article is an interpretive discussion of the plot. The arguments are solidly presented but add little to what had been published earlier. A number of other sources are mentioned but not footnoted.

3.33   Coombs, Richard. "At Play in the Fields
            of John Ford." *Sight and Sound*, 51:2
            (Spring 1982), 124-129.

                In a complicated argument, Coombs
            suggests that *Seven Women* (1966) is John
            Ford's last "Western," albeit a "back-
            wards" one. Within his schema, *The Man
            Who Shot Liberty Valance* (1962) signals
            the death of the genre for Ford, and
            Seven Women becomes a "real" revision--
            treating myths and issues found in other,
            clearer examples of Fordian Westerns--by
            focusing its attention on women missio-
            naries as agents of civilization. While
            Coombs' argument for *Seven Women* as a
            Western seems, ultimately, misguided, he
            nevertheless raises some interesting
            questions about the centrality of the
            genre to Ford's work as a whole.

3.34   Coursen, David F. "John Ford's Wilder-
            ness: *The Man Who Shot Liberty
            Valance*." *Sight and Sound*, 47:4
            (1978), 237-241.

                For Coursen, *The Man Who Shot Liberty
            Valance* (1962) is unlike other Ford
            Westerns because it extends the tradi-
            tional "historic moment" of the frontier
            to deal in a rich and complex fashion
            with the after-effects of civilization.

3.35   D'Arc, James V. "'I Want Stone-Age
            Faces!': A Behind-the-Scenes Look
            with Harry Carey, Jr., Patrick Ford
            and Wes Jefferies at the Making of
            John Ford's Favorite Film." *American
            Classic Screen*, 4:2 (Winter 1980),
            31-33.

                A collection of brief interview-
            reminiscences of actors (Carey), screen-
            writer (Patrick Ford) and costume
            supervisor (Jefferies) about John Ford's
            Wagonmaster (1950). Focusing primarily
            on pre-production details, the article
            centers on the director's perfectionist

approach to the film and on the evolution
of the film from idea to script. Also
features several candid photos taken by
Jefferies on the production's location.
Part of an *American Classic Screen*
"Special Western Issue."

3.36   Degenfelder, E. Pauline. "McMurtry and
            the Movies: *Hud* and *The Last Picture
            Show*." *Western Humanities Review*, 29
            (Winter 1975), 81-91.

        The first part of the essay illus-
trates a point made earlier by Larry
McMurtry (see I, 7.85) that modern
Westerns reflect Northrup Frye's
fictional modes of low mimetic and ironic
whereas earlier Westerns are usually high
mimetic or romantic. The modern Western
examples are *Hud* (1963) and *The Last
Picture Show* (1971), two films adapted
from McMurtry novels. The second half of
the essay argues that *The Last Picture
Show* is more successful than *Hud* in
dramatizing declining heroism in modern
Westerns. For parallel arguments, see
I, 3.48; and I, 7.52.

3.37   Dervin, Daniel A. "Creativity and Colla-
            boration in Three American Movies."
            American Imago, 34:2 (Summer 1977),
            179-204.

        A psychoanalytic look at the use of
the "Primal Scene" ("a child's witnessing
of, or his fantasies or theories about,
parental intercourse") in three 1970s
films, including one Western, *Little Big
Man* (1970). Dervin praises the film for
its complex use of the Primal Scene in
its circular narrative structure. The
protagonist, Jack Crabbe, learns that
"the meaning of the Primal Scene is not
death but *birth* ... sexuality is a
private human act which generates a
modicum of peace in order for the human
family to survive." This interpretation
of the film is useful in that it provides

a fresh perspective on a Western usually
discussed in comparison with Thomas
Berger's novel or as a study of Native
American-white conflict.

3.38   Ellis, Kirk. *"The Shootist*: Going in
                Style." *Literature/Film Quarterly*,
                14:1 (1986), 44-52.

A comparison and contrast between
Glendon Swarthout's 1975 novel, *The
Shootist*, and the 1976 film of the same
name directed by Don Siegel. Ellis
concludes that the film is a more significant artistic accomplishment than the
novel and that thematically, "Swarthout's
distasteful depiction of the gunman's
decline and fall has been transformed in
the film into a gentle paean to a way of
life on the wane." This change is
accomplished in the film through an
infusion of warm humor and mainly because
of the legendary presence of John Wayne
as the dying gunfighter, J.B. Books.
Ellis' thematic comparison is convincingly detailed but his insistence on the
superiority of the film over the novel
seems justified by his enthusiasm for the
film rather than from substantive arguments.

3.39   Evans, J. Greg. *"The Ballad of Gregorio
                Cortez."* *American Cinematographer*,
                64 (October 1983), 60-64.

A production history of *The Ballad of
Gregorio Cortez* (1983). Emphasis is on
shooting details and financing.

3.40   Everson, William K. "A Film History
                Mystery." *Films in Review*, 35:10
                (December 1984), 591-594.

Subtitled "An Early Ken Maynard
Talkie Begs For a Solution--Or At Least
An Explanation," this article is a call
for information about a Ken Maynard film
called *Song of the Caballero* (1929). It

is also a good, albeit short, introduction to this popular star of silent
Westerns.

3.41   Falkenberg, Pamela. "The Third Term is
          not Always the Father: Women and/as
          the 'Paternal Function' in *Destry
          Rides Again*." *Enclitic*, 5/6:1/2
          (1981-82), 55-65.

A Freudian analysis of the 1939
version of *Destry Rides Again*. According
to Falkenberg, the film deals with symbolic questions of fatherhood, husband-
hood and fantasies of true love.
Ironically, the siren Frenchy, by assu-
ming control over males through verbal
irony assumes the male function in the
film. When she gives up this irony for
true love, she dies; the mantle of irony
passes to Tom Destry. This argument is
presented in considerable detail by
Falkenberg with much of the complicated
diction of European-influenced film
analysis. Within itself, the article is
convincing. Little or no consideration
is given to the fact that the film is at
least partially a comedy, however, and
Falkenberg makes no attempt to consider
the implications of her thesis beyond the
boundaries of the film itself.

3.42   Fete, Margaret. "Women as an Element of
          Narrative in *Red River*." *Cine-Tracts*,
          3 (Spring 1980), 68-71.

Fete examines the role women play in
Howard Hawks' 1948 film, claiming that
women function at best as extensions or
possessions of the male protagonists.
The movie includes women, the author
argues, solely because of audience expectations, not for essential reasons of
narrative, thus presaging the 1950s male-
defined action/adventure films. The
piece appears in a special section of
Cine-Tracts on *Red River*, resulting from
a 1978 seminar on semiotics and film.

3.43   Fetherling, Doug. "Recent Westerns."
                Canadian Forum, 56:665 (October 1976),
                40-42.

                Brief discussions of three 1976
            Westerns, *Buffalo Bill and the Indians,
            or Sitting Bull's History Lesson, The
            Missouri Breaks* and *The Shootist*.
            Concludes that Westerns have always been
            about "the eternal verities" and not
            history. This is true in 1976 even
            though the three Westerns discussed give
            a good deal of attention to looking like
            the historical eras in which they take
            place.

3.44   Foreman, Carl. "*High Noon*." In *Film
                Scripts Two*, ed. George P. Garrett,
                O.B. Hardison Jr. and Jane R.
                Gelfman. New York: Meredith Corp.,
                1971, pp. 37-155.

                Reprint of Foreman's screenplay for
            Fred Zinneman's 1952 film. Includes an
            introduction with some weak attempts at
            analysis.

3.45   Galperin, William. "History into
                Allegory: *The Wild Bunch* as Vietnam
                Movie." *Western Humanities Review*,
                35 (Summer 1981), 165-172.

                Galperin compares *The Wild Bunch*
            (1969) with *The Deer Hunter* (1978) and
            concludes that the former, released
            during the Vietnam War, has more to say
            about our involvement in Vietnam than the
            film actually set there. This is so, he
            says, because Sam Peckinpah is
            "unflagging in his support for Thornton,"
            a man who has eschewed all ideals in
            order to survive, whereas Michael Cimino
            in *The Deer Hunter* allows idealism to
            persist as a value when nationalistic
            idealism was the actual cause of the
            Vietnam War. This interpretation of *The
            Wild Bunch* contradicts the more generally
            accepted conclusion that Thornton regains

his own sense of ideals at the end of the
film. Insufficient evidence is presented
to support Galperin's unusual reading of
the ending.

3.46   Gans, Herbert J. "*Billy Jack*: A Pacifist
          Western." *Social Policy*, 4:5 (March-
          April 1974), 57-59.

          After discussing the plot and
characters in *Billy Jack* (1971), Gans
concludes that the film is a vaguely conceived fantasy of a "middle American
utopia." As a reflection of its
audience, the film suggests that "many
middle Americans are antiwar and liberal."
Since very few Westerns reflect such an
ideology, *Billy Jack* deserves a place in
the history of American films for advo-
cating a pacifist-liberal position.

3.47   Garfield, Brian. "*The Wild Bunch*
          Revisited." *Armchair Detective*, 13:2
          (1980), 141-144.

          Argues that "*The Wild Bunch* ...
clearly represents the total union of the
Western and crime genres." The body of
the article, however, does not develop
this thesis. Instead, Garfield drifts
rather aimlessly from short comment to
short comment considering Sam Peckinpah's
films in comparison to John Ford's, the
long history of the outlaw hero and other
topics. The final conclusion that *The
Wild Bunch* belongs in the pantheon of
great Westerns is not demonstrated in
sufficient detail and seems only remotely
related to the original thesis.

3.48   Gehring, Wes D. "*The Electric Horseman*:
          A Contemporary Capra Film." *Journal
          of Popular Film and Television*, 10:4
          (1983), 175-182.

          Gehring argues that there are common
elements and similarly optimistic
messages in both Frank Capra's best-known

films of the 1930s and 1940s and the 1979
Sydney Pollack Western. Unfortunately,
while acknowledging variations in "spirit"
and details, Gehring downplays basic
differences between the films and filmmakers, some of which might be attribu-
table to the changed political climate.
The assertion that *The Electric Horseman*
provides an equivalent to Capra's message
of faith is not convincely argued, and
the differences become more interesting
than the similarities.

3.49   Gomery, Douglas. "*Mise-en-Scene* in John
              Ford's *My Darling Clementine*." *Wide
              Angle*, 2:4 (1978), 14-19.

              This brief analysis of Ford's 1946
Western concentrates on three recurring
objects: buttes, barber poles and cacti.
Gomery argues that these objects reappear
in different shots in balanced and
unbalanced compositions, thereby contributing to the film's "basic antinomy of
stability/disruption." Gomery admits to
the brevity of his analysis and offers it
as just a beginning point for a study of
the complexity of Ford's *mise en scene*.
Includes nine frame enlargements. Part
of a special issue of *Wide Angle* devoted
to the films of John Ford.

3.50   Gomez, Joseph A. "Sam Peckinpah and the
              'Post-Western.'" *American Classic
              Screen*, 4:3 (Spring 1980), 31-34.

              An analysis of Peckinpah's *Junior
Bonner* (1972), which Gomez claims
captures the essence of the director's
philosophy while updating the genre's
conventions. The film's present-tense
setting, the author says, makes it a
"post-Western," and though *Junior Bonner*
is Peckinpah's only gunless Western, it
is consistent with the director's
world view.

3.51   Graham, Don. "The Big Show." *Southwest*

Media Review, 3 (Spring 1985), 26-29.

Article suggests that the setting of
Gene Autry's *The Big Show* (1936) at the
Texas Centennial is just one indication
of the sophistication which sets it apart
from other, more mundane B Westerns.
Treats the film primarily in terms of
self-reflexivity. Article appears in a
special issue of *Southwest Media Review*
examining "Texas Myth in Film."

3.52   ⸺. *"The Great Northfield, Minnesota*
Raid and the Cinematic Legend of
Jesse James." *Journal of Popular*
Film and Television, 6:1 (1977),
77-85.

Examines the revisionist approach
which was central to Philip Kaufman's
1972 film. Graham pays particular attention to Henry King's *Jesse James* (1939),
which Kaufman uses in his opening credits.
He concludes that a "decade" theory of
Westerns is validated by an examination
of the treatment of such material over
time. Suggests that other legend cycles
would be fruitfully illuminated by such
an approach. The James legend was
amenable to radically different uses, and
Graham discusses the elevation of Cole
Younger and the de-mystification of Jesse
in Kaufman's film.

3.53   ⸺. *"High Noon* (1952)." In *Western*
Movies, ed. William Pilkington and
Don Graham. Albuquerque: University
of New Mexico Press, 1979.

This essay discusses the Zinneman
film as a particularly 1950s formulation
of the tensions between individual and
community which are often part of the
Western. Though dated by its political
overtones, Graham argues, its focus on
communal life is the element which
resulted in *High Noon*'s lasting power.

3.54   Greene, Naomi. "Coppola, Cimino: The
                  Operatics of History." *Film
                  Quarterly*, 38:2 (Winter 1984-85),
                  28-37.

              A consideration of *The Godfather* I
          and II, *Apocalypse Now*, *The Deer Hunter*
          and, especially, *Heaven's Gate* (1980) as
          films with melodramatic extremes and
          operatic story forms which alternate
          scenes of spectacle with scenes of
          narration. Greene concludes that such a
          structure breaks down the cause-and-
          effect linearity that characterizes most
          Hollywood movies, thereby destroying the
          general optimism that usually accompanies
          such linearity. The result in all these
          films is a pessimism that parallels the
          post-Vietnam, post-Watergate mood of the
          United States in the late 1970s. In
          Heaven's Gate despair over the American
          past is total: "historical, since an
          almost official slaughter occurs, and
          philosophical, since all idealism is made
          to seem empty." Greene's application of
          aesthetic structure to ideology seems a
          bit facile in the essay but her dis-
          cussion of certain visual motifs in
          Heaven's Gate and her conclusions about
          the film are interesting and provocative.

3.55   Gustafson, Judith. "The Whore with the
                  Heart of Gold: A Second Look at *Klute*
                  and *McCabe and Mrs. Miller*."
                  Cineaste, 11:2 (1981), 14-17, 49.

              Gustafson argues that Alan Pakula's
          Klute and Robert Altman's *McCabe and Mrs.
          Miller* (both 1971) bring to the surface
          the sexual politics behind the "whore-
          with-the-heart-of-gold" stereotype. In
          Altman's film, the author maintains the
          emergence of a distinctly feminist per-
          spective. That the female protagonist
          takes charge and establishes a sense of
          community among her fellow prostitutes
          leads Gustafson to conclude that such a
          display of female self-sufficiency is

more effective because it is posed within
the mythic framework of the Western.

3.56   Hachem, Samir. "Tales from *Silverado*."
        American Cinematographer, 66 (July
        1985), 50-58.

        Hachem's production history of
Silverado (1985) stresses the cinematic
techniques needed in shooting a Western
film, arguing that director Lawrence
Kasdan lets the landscape set the visual
tone and rhythm of the production.
Includes location stills.

3.57   Harvey, Stephen and Marcia Pally. "Hi-Yo
        Silverado, Away." *Film Comment*, 21:4
        (July/August 1985), 20-27.

        Actually three brief articles under
one title. Harvey heaps abuse on three
1985 Westerns, *Rustlers' Rhapsody*, *Pale
Rider* and *Silverado*, even though he had
not yet seen *Silverado*. Harvey also
interviewed one of the stars of *Silverado*,
Kevin Klein. Pally writes admiringly of
another *Silverado* star, Linda Hunt. All
three essays seem to be quick reactions
to the sudden release of new Westerns
rather than ideas carefully conceived.
Of minimal use or value.

3.58   Haver, Ronald. "Preservation: Trail
        Blazing." *American Film*, 11 (May
        1986), 17-19.

        Haver gives a brief production
history of Raoul Walsh's 70mm *The Big
Trail* (1930) on the occasion of the
film's widescreen restoration by the
Museum of Modern Art in New York.
Several production stills, showing the
difference between the 35mm and Fox's
70mm Grandeur versions, are featured,
along with technical details about the
Grandeur process and the Museum of Modern
Art's restoration project.

3.59   Henderson, Brian. "*The Searchers*: An
              American Dilemma." *Film Quarterly*,
              34 (Winter 1980-81), 9-23.

              Henderson's study of John Ford's 1956
          film centers on *The Searchers'* influence
          as a "film myth" on a number of important
          young filmmakers. The movie's effective-
          ness, Henderson argues, stems from its
          power as a myth of race relations, with
          the Indian/white conflict a symbol of
          black/white tensions. *The Searchers*, the
          author suggests, has to do with 1956, not
          the years between 1868 and 1873, the
          years in "history" the story covers.

3.60   Hickman, Larry. "Along the Rio Grande."
              Southwest Media Review, 3 (Spring
              1985), 9-13.

              A nominal Western, D.W. Griffith's
          Martyrs of the Alamo (1915), is examined
          in this treatment of popular myths of the
          Texas/Mexico border. Author sees
          Griffith's use of the Alamo as incidental
          to the film's sexual context, in which
          Anglo-Saxon purity confronts Hispanic
          promiscuity and crudity. The essay is
          part of a special issue of *Southwest
          Media Review* exploring "Texas Myth in
          Film."

3.61   Horowitz, Joseph. "They Shoot Opera
              Singers, Don't They?" *Music Journal*,
              34 (July 1976), 22-23, 51.

              Informal interviews with Bonnie
          Leaders and Noelle Rogers, who play
          Buffalo Bill's opera-singing mistresses
          in Robert Altman's *Buffalo Bill and the
          Indians, or Sitting Bull's History Lesson*
          (1976).

3.62   Jameson, Richard T. "*The Misfits*." *Film
              Comment*, 16:3 (May-June 1980), 46-49.

              This selection from a monograph on
          John Huston briefly describes *The Misfits*

(1961) as "Hustonian."

3.63   ————. "The Sound of One Man Clapping."
              Film Comment, 21:5 (September-October
              1985), 76-78.

              Jameson considers *Silverado* (1985)
              from the perspective of someone who grew
              up watching and loving Westerns. From
              this perspective, Jameson says *Silverado*
              glories in its generic roots and is
              "prodigiously entertaining."

3.64   Kaplan, Frederick I. and William A.
              Vincent. "*The Hired Hand*." *Velvet
              Light Trap*, no. 14 (Winter 1975),
              38-41.

              When *The Hired Hand* was released in
              1971, it was a critical and box-office
              failure. This article, however, argues
              that the film is an artistic success.
              Kaplan and Vincent emphasize how the
              visual qualities of the film complement
              its thematic elements of commitment and
              love. They also praise the film for its
              unusual characterizations and for its
              breaking away from many of the conven-
              tions of the Western genre.

3.65   Kimble, Greg. "*How the West Was Won*--in
              Cinerama." *American Cinematographer*,
              64 (October 1983), 46-50, 89-99.

              Kimble's history of Cinerama high-
              lights *How the West Was Won* (1963) as
              "Cinerama's greatest achievement." The
              article includes budget details and
              production history, along with color
              stills showing the effects of Cinerama on
              the movie image.

3.66   Kleinhans, Chuck. "*Greaser's Palace*:
              Subverting the Western." *Jump Cut*,
              no. 8 (August/September 1975), 11-14.

              Analysis of the techniques used by
              director Robert Downey in his Western

parody, *Greaser's Palace* (1972), through
which "form subverts the content and
thereby presents a political statement."
The techniques are mainly "farce, anti-
conventionality and distanciation."
Kleinhans concludes that although the
film succeeds in attacking the conventional Western and the prevailing
ideology conventional Westerns reflect,
Greaser's Palace fails to provide any
ideological alternatives. The essay is a
thorough and detailed study of the comic
elements of the film. It should be
useful as a study of Western conventions,
comic Westerns or as a good example of a
Marxist critique of the Western genre.

3.67   Lawrence, Floyd B. "The Mythic Waters of
            The Missouri Breaks." *Journal of
            Popular Film and Television*, 5:2
            (1976). Reprinted in *Western
            Movies*, ed. William Pilkington and
            Don Graham. Albuquerque: University
            of New Mexico Press, 1979, pp.
            149-155.

            This short essay treats this 1976
            Arthur Penn film as a "genre Western"
            within the agenda of a monomythical
            approach, a major structuring element of
            which is the symbolic use of water and
            water imagery. Within this agenda, the
            chief cattleman is a detached Olympian,
            the "regulator" Clayton (played by Marlon
            Brando) is a satanic anti-human, and
            Logan (played by Jack Nicholson) a
            warrior hero.

3.68   Lehman, Peter. "Looking at Look's
            Missing Reverse Shot: Psychoanalysis
            and Style in John Ford's *The
            Searchers*." *Wide Angle*, 4:4 (1981),
            65-70.

            A shot-by-shot analysis of the scene
            in *The Searchers* (1956) in which Martin
            Pauly kicks Look, the Indian woman he has
            mistakenly married, down a hill. Lehman

speculates on why there is no reverse
angle shot of Look laying at the bottom
of the hill. He concludes that the
missing shot suggests subconscious guilt
on director John Ford's part for the
mistreatment of Look--Ford did not care
to look upon this callous bit of low
humor. Although Lehman's thesis is
obviously unprovable, it is nevertheless
an interesting discussion of what is an
often criticized scene in the film.
Includes photos of the shots discussed.

3.69   Lovell, Alan. *"The Searchers* and the
        Pleasure Principle." *Screen
        Education*, 17 (Autumn 1975), 53-57.

        A well-done essay which examines *The
Searchers* (1956) from the perspective of
"entertainment," identifying elements
which contribute to the audience's
"psychic" pleasure and interest. Lovell
suggests that pleasure as much as any
socio-political subtext may motivate film
attendance, and makes several theoretical
points which suggest that the pleasure
principle might be a reasonable starting
place for treating film in the classroom.
This article is a bit of a departure from
the other essays on *The Searchers* which
make up this special edition of *Screen
Education* which centers on the film.

3.70   Lusted, David. *"The Searchers* and the
        Study of Image." *Screen Education*,
        17 (Autumn 1975), 14-26.

        Using a group of stills from *The
Searchers* (1956), Lusted draws from
categories developed by Roland Barthes'
"Rhetoric of Image," to suggest a
basically semiological approach to film-
image study in the classroom. Acknowledging some problems with the method,
Lusted argues that it may function best
as an adjunct to other approaches, rather
than being enough of itself. Included in
an issue of *Screen Education* on the film.

3.71   Macklin, F. Anthony. *"Pat Garrett and*
            Billy the Kid." *Film Heritage,* 10
            (Winter 1974-75), 34-37.

            Macklin suggests that Sam Peckinpah's
            1973 film posits Garrett as the arche-
            typal Lawman and Billy as the archetypal
            Outlaw while reflecting parallels in
            authentic source material. In doing so,
            the author argues, Peckinpah manipulates
            Personality over Form.

3.72   Makanna, Phil. "Observations on the
            Making of *The Last Hard Men."*
            Filmmakers Newsletter, 9 (September
            1976), 25-29.

            An on-location discussion of the 1976
            Andrew V. McLaglen movie, Makanna's
            remarks include little if any information
            on the film itself. Emphasis instead is
            on the general problems of location
            shooting.

3.73   Mashiah, Igal I. "Edwin S. Porter's *The*
            Great Train Robbery: A Focus on the
            Origins of Narrative Structure." *Et*
            cetera, 37 (Winter 1980), 355-362.

            A discussion of the fourteen shots in
            The Great Train Robbery (1903) and how
            they function as dramatic and aesthetic
            compositions. Mashiah concludes that
            because dynamic editing and shot variety
            had at the time not been developed,
            Porter compensated by using long shots in
            deep focus and by carefully composing
            action for dramatic emphasis. Although
            the film is not discussed as a Western,
            the discussion offers hints as to why
            Westerns so quickly became popular during
            the earliest days of the narrative film.
            In an era of rather unimaginative use of
            the camera, Westerns, with their emphasis
            on action, offered maximum chances for
            dramatic action within the standard long
            shot.

3.74   McAllister, Nick. "You Can't Go Home:
          Jeremiah Johnson and the Wilderness."
          Western American Literature, 13:1
          (Spring 1978), 35-49.

          Argues that *Jeremiah Johnson* (1972)
          is a tragedy in which the title character
          is a "tragic hero, who carried with him
          into the wilderness his romantic
          illusions and with them the seed of the
          very civilization he sought to repudi-
          ate." That is, Johnson possesses the
          civilized romantic's dream of living a
          peaceful life in a beneficient and
          idyllic nature. The vast and violent
          mountains, however, inevitably destroy
          Johnson's dream. McAllister makes use of
          the literary sources of the film as well
          as parts of the shooting script that do
          not appear in the film itself. The
          analysis of the film is richly demon-
          strated and enlivened by the author's
          obvious love of the mountain environment
          he describes.

3.75   McBride, Joseph. *"The Great Train
          Robbery*: A Critical Symposium."
          American Film, 1 (January-February
          1976), 52-55, 78.

          A series of brief parody-reviews of
          Edwin Porter's *The Great Train Robbery*
          (1903), written in the style of various
          modern movie critics.

3.76   McGee, Rex. "Michael Cimino's Way West."
          American Film, 6:1 (October 1980),
          34-40, 78, 80.

          Article centers on *Heaven's Gate*
          (1980) in production, with vague hints
          about the film's expanding budget.
          Emphasis on Cimino's long obsession with
          making a movie about the Johnson County
          War. Also features some interesting
          color production stills.

3.77   Meier, David. "Taking a Good Look."
            Classic Film Collector, no. 44 (Fall
            1974), 28-29.

            Includes a summary of Thomas H.
            Ince's *On the Night Stage* (1915), William
            S. Hart's first feature film.

3.78   Miller, Gabriel. *"Shane* Redux: *The
            Shootist* and the Western Dilemma."
            *Journal of Popular Film and
            Television*, 11:2 (Summer 1983),
            66-77.

            Draws parallels between *Shane* (1953)
            and *The Shootist* (1976), in terms of
            classical Western archetypes within a
            traditional story of the initiation of
            youth by an older adult. Miller suggests
            that both films center on the tensions
            between masculine impulses for "death-
            bringing and death-giving" and the
            demands of social order and individual
            experience. He argues that neither film
            resolves this issue.

3.79   Mindiola, Tatcho Jr. "El Corrido de
            Gregorio Cortez." *Southwest Media
            Review*, 3 (Spring 1985), 52-56.

            Mindiola argues that a major failing
            in *The Ballad of Gregorio Cortez* (1983)
            is its essentially Anglo bias. Article
            appears in special issue of *Southwest
            Media Review* on "Texas Myth in Film."

3.80   Morsberger, Robert E. "Slavery and *The
            Santa Fe Trail* or John Brown on
            Hollywood's Sour Apple Tree."
            American Studies, 18:2 (Fall 1977),
            87-98.

            An analysis of the 1940 Michael
            Curtiz film with an emphasis on how the
            film distorts history to place blame on
            John Brown for the Civil War, and to make
            all Southerners "wholly sympathetic and
            admirable." Morsberger suggests that

these attitudes are reflective of public
perspectives in 1940 and, perhaps, in
1977, although he makes little effort to
demonstrate such an assumption. For a
similar discussion of this film, see an
earlier article by Linda Pepper and John
Davis (I, 3.93).

3.81   Morse, David. "Under Western Eyes:
        Variations on a Genre." *Monogram*,
        no. 6 (October 1975), 34-39.
        Reprinted in *Passport to Hollywood:*
        Film Immigrants Anthology, Don
        Whittemore and Philip Alan Cecchet-
        tini, eds. New York: McGraw-Hill
        Book Co., 1976, pp. 202-215.

Morse argues that *Dodge City* is a
seminal film in the development of the
Western. The 1939 film, directed by
Michael Curtiz, opened up for the genre
new possibilities of rearticulation and
rephrasing by incorporating virtually all
of the central institutions and icons of
the Western--the stagecoach, the
railroad, buffalo hunters and cattle
drives, lynchings, saloons and tempe-
rance movements, Boot Hill funerals and
barroom brawls. Unlike *Stagecoach*
(1939), which the author claims is a
developmental dead end because it is too
perfect to be expanded upon, *Dodge City*
offered ambiguities which, at the time,
helped point the way toward the future
course of the Western.

3.82   Nachbar, Jack. "*Ulzana's Raid* (1972)."
        In *Western Movies*, ed. William Pil-
        kington and Don Graham. Albuquerque:
        University of New Mexico Press, 1979,
        pp. 139-147.

While in many ways a prototypical
Western, this Robert Aldrich film also
offers a new approach to the classic
dichotomies of the genre. Nachbar
suggests that the central character of
MacIntosh, played by Burt Lancaster, acts

as a symbolic father, mediating between
the platitudes of Eastern Christians and
the savagery of Western Native Americans.
Unfortunately, the promise of the film's
combination of conventional elements and
inventional structure remained unrealized
by other directors of Westerns, or by
Aldrich himself.

3.83   Nowell-Smith, Geoffrey. "Six Authors in
                Pursuit of *The Searchers*." *Screen*,
                17:1 (Spring 1976), 26-33.

            A response to the special issue of
        Screen Education devoted to *The Searchers*
        (1956). Nowell-Smith is disenchanted
        with what he sees as the unacknowledged
        "*auteur*" perspective of most of the con-
        tributors. He argues for a "code-
        centered" approach which treats the film
        as a text of social communication.

3.84   O'Connor, John E. "A Reaffirmation of
                American Ideals: *Drums Along the
                Mohawk* (1939)." In *American
                History/American Film*, ed. John E.
                O'Connor and Martin A. Jackson.
                New York: Frederick Ungar Publishing
                Co., Inc., 1979, pp. 97-119.

            Although the events in the film take
        place during the 1770s, O'Connor argues
        that John Ford's film presents a number
        of values that were also in a number of
        other feature films of the era and that
        collectively suggest American values of
        the 1930s. Among the values discussed
        are patriotism, family life and a
        willingness to persevere through hard-
        ships. Overall, these form a "populist
        view of American society." O'Connor also
        details differences between the film and
        the best-selling novel from which the
        film was adapted. The major changes,
        O'Connor concludes, suggest some of the
        conventions movies had to employ to
        appeal to masses of moviegoers. The
        article is well researched but does not

attempt in-depth analysis of story or
characters.

3.85   O'Donnell, Victoria. "The Great White
           Father and the Native American Son:
           An Oedipal Analysis of *When Legends
           Die*." *Journal of University Film
           Association*, 32:1-2 (Winter-Spring
           1980), 65-69.

           O'Donnell suggests that Jacques
           Lacan's reworking of Freudian psychology
           can provide useful insights into the ways
           in which ethnic minorities are treated
           by Anglo culture and Hollywood films.
           She applies Lacanian analysis and the
           vocabulary of semiotics to Stuart
           Miller's 1972 film as a case study of a
           "healthy" relationship between Native
           Americans and patriarchal White culture.

3.86   Palmieri, Roy. "*Straw Dogs*: Sam Peckin-
           pah and the Classical Western
           Narrative." *Studies in Literary
           Imagination*, 16 (Spring 1983), 29-42.

           Even though *Straw Dogs* (1971) is set
           in contemporary England, Palmieri
           describes how the film utilizes the
           formula for the classical Western as
           defined by Raymond Bellour. Most of the
           article is a Freudian interpretation of
           Straw Dogs rather than a detailing of the
           film as a Western. Nevertheless, at the
           conclusion of the essay, Palmieri is able
           to convincingly conclude that "in *Straw
           Dogs* Peckinpah not only exposes many of
           the simplifications of the classical
           Western narrative but also shows how that
           narrative lies like a time bomb in the
           psyche of the repressed American male."

3.87   Pauly, Thomas H. "Howard Hughes and his
           Western: The Maverick and *The
           Outlaw*." *Journal of Popular Film and
           Television*, 6:4 (1978), 350-368.

           Pauly believes that Hughes found a

major channel of self-expression in
filmmaking, and that *The Outlaw* (1943) is
an important clue to his sensibilities as
well as his business modus operandi.
Calling the film "consistently neurotic,"
Pauly finds its weaknesses are from the
same impulses as its strengths: Hughes'
manipulation of the Western formulas into
a prefiguration of later psychological
and comedic films (particular parallels
are drawn with the 1969 film, *Butch
Cassidy and the Sundance Kid*).

3.88   Perry, Harry F. and Oscar Estes.
            "Shooting *The Vanishing American* for
            Famous Players Lasky." *Classic Film
            Collector*, no. 44 (Fall 1974), 12.

            A light collection of reminiscences
            about the filming of *The Vanishing
            American* (1925), as remembered by
            co-cinematographer Perry.

3.89   Pettit, Arthur G. "The Polluted Garden:
            Sam Peckinpah's Double Vision of
            Mexico." *Southwest Review*, 62
            (Summer 1977). Reprinted in *Western
            Movies*, ed. William Pilkington and
            Don Graham. Albuquerque: University
            of New Mexico Press, 1979, pp.
            97-107.

            According to Pettit, the Mexican
            locale of the majority of the action in
            The Wild Bunch (1969) is the expression
            of director Peckinpah's moral universe.
            Peckinpah's Mexico has two kinds of
            citizens--the vulgar, debased, corrupt
            Mapaches and the loving, dignified, happy
            Villastas. Both groups are placed in
            high contrast to the film's American
            characters. The story is played out
            against the promise of a truly revolu-
            tionized Mexico, a nation which stands
            as the antithesis of the sterility and
            automation of American society.

3.90   Pilkington, William T. "*Fort Apache*

(1948)." In *Western Movies*, ed.
William Pilkington and Don Graham.
Albuquerque: University of New Mexico
Press, 1979.

For Pilkington, *Fort Apache*, while
"Fordian" in many of its values and
visual details, is a transitional film,
standing between the early "simplistic"
view of Native Americans and the distur-
bing portrayal of their culture in *The
Searchers* (1956).

3.91   Place, Janey. "Welcome to Show Busi-
              ness." *Jump Cut*, no. 23 (October
              1980), 21-22.

Place argues that director Robert
Altman employs Bertolt Brecht's method of
"distanciation" in *Buffalo Bill and the
Indians, or Sitting Bull's History Lesson*
(1976). By removing the audience's
emotional involvement with the narrative,
Altman allows the film audience to
intellectually explore how the dominant
ideology of a culture recreates history
to fulfill its own self-image. Show
business is all that is left of history.
Place ends this interesting Marxist
interpretation of the film by saying that
the film succeeds as intellectual social
criticism but, because of distanciation,
it fails as radical popular art.

3.92   "Postscript: The Re-Making of *Ulzana's
              Raid*." *Monthly Film Bulletin*, 49
              (July 1982), 149-151.

Brief study comparing two versions of
Robert Aldrich's *Ulzana's Raid* (1972)
shown in Britain, one released theatri-
cally in 1973 and one shown on the BBC
six years later. The piece uses details
from both to argue that the changes made
in the former (the 1979 showing was with
a U.S. domestic release print) alter many
of the film's themes. First of two parts
(see 3.93).

3.93   "Postscript: The Re-Making of *Ulzana's*
                 Raid." *Monthly Film Bulletin*, 49
                 (August 1982), 182-183.

              The second half of a comparison of
          two versions of *Ulzana's Raid* (1972)
          shown in Britain (see 3.92). Though the
          two versions maintain the same basic
          story, they differ in how they approach
          the complex issue of the Indians'
          "savagery." The ambiguity of the
          Indians' use of violence and of their
          different way of life is watered down in
          the redubbed and re-edited version shown
          in British theatres. An interesting and
          detailed study but of limited value
          because it does not really address the
          issue of why the changes took place.

3.94   Pye, Douglas. "Genre and History: *Fort*
                 Apache and *Liberty Valance*." *Movie*,
                 no. 25 (Winter 1977-78), 1-11.

              In two of John Ford's richest
          Westerns, *Fort Apache* (1948) and *The Man*
          Who Shot Liberty Valance (1962), we see
          the facts of Western history changed to
          legend in order to affirm the ideological
          needs of the East. Pye sees this evolu-
          tion from history to legend as an
          essential characteristic of the Western
          genre itself. In Ford's two films,
          however, this process is seen in much
          more negative terms than in other
          Westerns in which genre conventions
          affirm the coming of Eastern civilization
          to the Western wilderness. According to
          Pye, both *Fort Apache* and *Liberty Valance*
          reveal a historical West with a vital,
          valid community in the process of self-
          destruction. The East, modern civili-
          zation, is less valid and vital, and
          replaces the older Western community with
          legend to justify the change. There is a
          density to Pye's arguments that requires
          close attention, but his thesis contra-
          dicts usual readings of these films in a
          convincing way, and is therefore worth

the attention that must be given them to
be fully understood.

3.95   ———. "*The Searchers* and Teaching the
Film Industry." *Screen Education*, 17
(Autumn 1975), 34-48.

Pye argues that teaching the film
industry is a complex activity, both
practically and theoretically, but one
which can illuminate major cultural
issues. This introductory essay uses *The
Searchers* (1956) as a case study of such
an approach, and examines a variety of
sources ranging from the original story
to reviews of the film's technology.
Part of an issue of *Screen Education*
devoted to *The Searchers*.

3.96 Pym, John and James Ivory. "Almost
Anarchy." *Sight and Sound*, 51:1
(Winter 1981-82), 20-24.

Separate ruminations by each author
about reasons for the critical roasting
and commercial failure of *Heaven's Gate*
(1980). Both authors see merit in the
film and blame part of its failure on
forces outside of the quality of the film
itself. Among these are a desire on the
part of the critical establishment to
attack director Michael Cimino and the
fact that the originality of the film
often contradicts popular story conventions. Includes six photos.

3.97 Rapf, Joanna. "Some Fantasy on Earth:
Doctorow's *Welcome to Hard Times* as
Novel and Film." *Literature/Film
Quarterly*, 13:1 (1985), 50-55.

A comparison between E.L. Doctorow's
novel and the 1967 film directed by Burt
Kennedy. Rapf argues that film adapta-
tions of novels ought to remain true to
the "moral outlook" of the original
source. The film version of *Welcome to
Hard Times* does not do this.

3.98   Reeder, Roberta. "The Mythic Mode:
            Archetypal Criticism and *Red River*."
            Cine-Tracts, 3 (Spring 1980), 58-67.

            Arguing that *Red River* (1948) marks an
            important development in the Western
            genre, Reeder employs the theory of
            archetypes developed by critic Northrup
            Frye in examining the levels of archetype
            in Howard Hawks' movie. The author
            claims that Hawks employs the mythos of
            tragedy--not the mythos of romance--as
            the principal archetypal pattern in the
            film, thus pointing the way for other
            postwar Westerns to follow. The essay
            is part of a special section of *Cine-
            Tracts* on the film, resulting from a 1978
            seminar on semiotics and film.

3.99   Ryall, Tom. "Teaching Through Genre."
            Screen Education, 17 (Autumn 1975),
            27-33.

            The author expands the concept of
            genre to include interrelationships
            between artist, film and audience, as
            well as the commercial and industrial
            context of production. The essay then
            treats *The Searchers* (1956) in terms of
            three principal genre elements: "actua-
            lity," thematic constructions and icono-
            graphy. Emphasizes the ways in which
            genre expectations on the part of the
            audience influence meanings and "readings"
            of the film. Believes "Western" should
            be the start of a genre study rather than
            the conclusion. Included in an issue of
            Screen Education devoted to *The Searchers*.

3.100   "*The Searchers*: Materials and Approaches."
            Screen Education, 17 (Autumn 1975).

            The entire issue of this British
            journal is devoted to essays on *The
            Searchers*. Included are articles by John
            Caughie (3.28), David Lusted (3.70), Tom
            Ryall (3.99), Douglas Pye (3.95), Edward
            Buscombe (3.27) and Alan Lovell (3.69).

A critical review of this effort by
Geoffrey Nowell-Smith was published in
Screen (see 3.83).

3.101   Shor, Francis. "Biographical Moments in
the Written and Cinematic Text:
Deconstructing the Legends of Joe
Hill and Buffalo Bill." *Film &
History*, 14 (September 1984), 61-68.

Shor examines differences and similarities in written and filmic texts to
deconstruct the presentations of biographical "moments," and to reveal our
understanding of the process of history.
Shor discusses Robert Altman's *Buffalo
Bill and the Indians, or Sitting Bull's
History Lesson* (1976) and Don Russell's
book, *The Lives and Legends of Buffalo
Bill*, arguing that Altman's film shows
not only how history becomes myth that
conceals our past but that that conceal-
ment is part of a present rendering of
the past.

3.102   Silverman, Michael. "The Drives and
Cultural Production in *Red River*."
Cine-Tracts, 3 (Spring 1980), 83-87.

Silverman explores *Red River* (1948)
in terms of Freud's concept of "drives,"
arguing that the film works out the
mediation of individual and social drives
toward the consolidation of the West,
traveling from uncertainty to resolution.
The study is included in a special
section of *Cine-Tracts* on the film,
resulting from a 1978 seminar on
semiotics and film.

3.103   Silverman, Stephen M. "Comes a Horseman
to Las Vegas." *American Film*, 4 (May
1979), 16-21.

A standard production history of *The
Electric Horseman* (1979), stressing the
project's emphasis shift from a satire of
Las Vegas to a romantic comedy.

3.104   Simmons, Garner. "The Western: New
            Directors in New Directions." *Film
            Reader*, 1 (1975), 65-70.

            Simmons gives a spirited defense of
            the genre against the "The Western is
            dead" critics by citing the recent works
            of four young directors: Phil Kaufman's
            The Great Northfield, Minnesota Raid,
            Dick Richards' *The Culpepper Cattle
            Company*, Robert Benton's *Bad Company* and
            Stan Dragoti's *Dirty Little Billy* (all
            1972). While each of the films share
            setting, time and iconography with the
            traditional Western, they share with each
            other an "anti-romantic point of view
            with respect to both heroic characteri-
            zation and plot resolution." Simmons'
            analyses are incisive, and his arguments
            against the death of the genre concrete.

3.105   Simon, William. "Liberty Valance Lives."
            Southwest Media Review, 3 (Spring
            1985), 64-69.

            This psychohistorical interpretation
            aligns the major characters in *The Man
            Who Shot Liberty Valance* (1962) with the
            vestigal adolescent pathologies in Ameri-
            can male psyches: the Old West as sexual
            frontier. Author believes the power of
            the Western lies in its function as a
            metaphor, allowing the working out of
            tension without disruption of the social
            order. Essay appears in a special issue
            of *Southwest Media Review* on "Texas Myth
            in Film."

3.106   Simons, John R. "The Tragedy of Love in
            The Wild Bunch." *Western Humanities
            Review* (Spring 1985), 1-19.

            An examination of themes of hetero-
            sexual love, symbolism and sexuality in
            The Wild Bunch (1969). Simons argues
            that director Sam Peckinpah is more
            sensitive to women than is commonly
            assumed.

3.107   Siska, William C. "Formal Reflexivity in
                  Dennis Hopper's *The Last Movie*." In
                  *Explorations in National Cinemas: The
                  1977 Film Studies Annual, Part I,* ed.
                  Ben Lawton and Janet Staiger.
                  Pleasantville, N.Y.: Redgrave Publi-
                  shing Co., 1977, pp. 11-17.

                  Argues that Dennis Hopper's intent in
               The Last Movie (1970) was to turn conven-
               tions of Hollywood films back upon
               themselves, including Western genre con-
               ventions, to make what is in reality an
               experimental film which uses the aesthe-
               tic principles of abstract expressionism.
               Siska concludes that Hopper's film is
               unique because its non-commercial experi-
               mentation was done on a Hollywood budget
               for a Hollywood company.

3.108   Skinner, James M. "The Tussle with
                  Russell: *The Outlaw* as a Landmark in
                  American Film Censorship." *North
                  Dakota Quarterly,* 49:1 (1981), 5-12.

                  A description of the difficulties
               Howard Hughes' famous Western had with
               the Legion of Decency and the Production
               Code Administration Office during the
               1940s. Details of the film itself,
               outside of those most often picked out
               for censoring, are not included. Skinner
               hints that the struggles of *The Outlaw*
               (1943) with Hollywood censorship and its
               consequent success at the box office
               influenced the growing boldness of the
               movies' handling of sexual materials
               during the 1950s and 1960s, but no evi-
               dence is provided for this suggestion.
               Those desiring a presentation of similar
               materials accompanied by a detailed dis-
               cussion of the film itself might better
               spend their time reading an earlier
               article on the film by Thomas Pauly (see
               3.87).

3.109   Sklar, Robert. "*Red River*: Empire to the
                  West." *Cineaste,* 9:1 (Fall 1978),

14-19. Reprinted in *American
History/American Film*, ed. John E.
O'Connor and Martin A. Jackson.
New York: Frederick Ungar Publishing
Co., Inc., 1979, pp. 167-181.

Argues that even though Howard Hawks'
Red River (1948) has been perceived as
just a solid action Western, in actuality
it is full of ideological implications.
The production of the film mirrors the
postwar movie industry. The plot of the
film reflects an economic situation
moving from feudalism to capitalism. And
the justifications offered for the
actions of the main characters reflects
"the basic economic tale of a commodity
finding its outlets to markets." Overall, the film "is about the issues of
empire." All of this is detailed and
adequately demonstrated by Sklar. The
most useful part of the essay, however,
is his discussion of contracts and
compacts within the film and how these
relate to the relationships between men
and women. According to Sklar, Dunson's
recognition of the "contract" between
Matthew Garth and Tess Millay is what
makes Tess' stopping of the fight between
Matt and Dunson at the climax of the
picture logical.

3.110   Strug, Cordell. "*The Wild Bunch* and the
           Problem of Idealist Aesthetics, or,
           How Long Would Peckinpah Last in
           Plato's Republic?" *Film Heritage*, 10
           (Winter 1974-75), 17-26.

Strug deals with the problems some
people have with *The Wild Bunch* (1969)
and its treatment of violence, arguing
that Sam Peckinpah's film is problematic
to some because it undercuts "establishment" violence so well, thus encouraging
identification with hardened killers.
The director's approach is different from
his critics' because, Strug suggests,
Peckinpah stresses violent action, not

violence.

3.111   Thoene, Bodie. *"Stagecoach--A* Legend."
          American West, 23 (May/June 1986),
          38-47.

          On location with the TV-movie
          production of *Stagecoach* (1986), Thoene
          details the events surrounding the
          shooting of John Ford's 1939 *Stagecoach*.
          The article includes production stills
          from both versions.

3.112   Thomson, David. "All Along the River."
          Sight and Sound, 46 (Winter 1976-77),
          9-13.

          In this very personal essay, Thomson
          describes his changing interpretations of
          Howard Hawks' *Red River* (1948), from
          Thomson's first seeing it as a child to
          his teaching the film to skeptical
          students in the 1970s. "Films alter as
          we grow older," Thomson claims, and he
          shows his own perspectives on *Red River*
          changing from a boyhood fascination with
          the John Wayne-Montgomery Clift relation-
          ship to a later *auteur*-ist love of the
          "reality" of the world of Hawks' films to
          a mid-1970s respect for *Red River* as a
          pleasing fantasy of the "mythic love
          between men." By commenting on his
          personal reactions to the film, Thomson
          avoids a single interpretation in favor
          of demonstrating the richness of perspec-
          tive possible from watching *Red River*
          and, by implication, all of the cinema.
          The essay is a rich study of *Red River*
          and a wonderful defense of a life spent
          at the movies.

3.113   Tosi, George. "Geoff Burrowes and George
          Miller: Two Men Behind *Snowy River*."
          Cinema Papers, no. 38 (June 1982),
          206-212, 283.

          An interview with the two men respon-
          sible for the production of the

"Australian Western," *The Man from Snowy River* (1982). Topics discussed include the overall conception of the film, casting, marketing, locations and the relation of the film to the Australian people.

3.114   Truffaut, Francois. "A Wonderful Certainty." *Cahiers du Cinema*, no. 46 (April 1955), trans. Liz Heron. Reprinted in *Cahiers du Cinema, the 1950s: Neo-Realism, Hollywood, New Wave*, ed. Jim Hillier. Cambridge: Harvard University Press, 1985, pp. 107-110.

Truffaut's review of *Johnny Guitar* (1954) depicts Nicholas Ray's film as something other than a standard Western, drawing its analogies from Freud more than from the old West. The French critic-director claims the film is almost the first "psychoanalytical Western."

3.115   Turner, John W. "*Little Big Man*, The Novel and the Film: A Study of Narrative Structure." *Literature/Film Quarterly*, 5 (Spring 1977). Reprinted in *Western Movies*, ed. William Pilkington and Don Graham. Albuquerque: University of New Mexico Press, 1979, pp. 109-122.

Analyzing film narrative in much the same way that fictional narratives are studied, Turner suggests that director Arthur Penn's inability to successfully manipulate the complex structure of the story undermines the success of his visual artistry.

3.116   Vallely, Jean. "The Opening and Closing of *Heaven's Gate*." *Rolling Stone*, no. 336 (Feb. 5, 1981), 33-36, 59.

Recounts the premiere of *Heaven's Gate* in December 1980, the disastrous initial reviews and director Michael

Cimino's decision to pull the picture out
of release and re-edit it. Includes
comments about Cimino and the making of
the film by involved executives and
performers. For another perspective on
the incidents, see Stephen Bach's *Final
Cut* (3.1).

3.117   Watters, Jim. "Return of the Epic
          Western: For $35 Million, Michael
          Cimino makes a panoramic *Heaven's
          Gate*." *Life*, 3:12 (December 1980),
          185-194.

          Photographic essay on shooting of
          Heaven's Gate (1980), highlighting
          Cimino's use of detail ("Details," the
          director claims, "give extra life").
          Brief profile of Cimino includes dis-
          cussion of Cimino's reliance on the
          intensity of place.

3.118   Wegner, Kurt. "Frederic Remington and
          John Ford: Dynamic and Static
          Composition Elements of *Fort Apache*."
          In *Explorations in National Cinemas:
          The 1977 Film Studies Annual, Part I*,
          ed. Ben Lawton and Janet Staiger.
          Pleasantville, N.Y.: Redgrave Publi-
          shing Co., 1977, pp. 27-36.

          Argues that *Fort Apache* (1948) is a
          "screen tragedy" achieved primarily by
          Ford "through the inclusion of dynamic
          and static group elements derived largely
          from the work of Frederic Remington."
          Wegner demonstrates this thesis by
          describing a number of Remington drawings
          and paintings and then showing how some
          of the compositional elements of those
          works occur during the final sequence of
          Fort Apache. This discussion of how
          visual composition can contribute to the
          meaning of the film is interesting but
          the argument suffers from a lack of
          accompanying illustrations from either
          Remington or *Fort Apache*. Only two small
          film stills are included and these are

not discussed.

3.119   Welsh, Jim. "John Ford's *Wagonmaster*:
         Rite of Passage." *American Classic
         Screen*, 4:2 (Winter 1980), 26-30.

         A detailed analysis of Ford's 1950
         movie, which Welsh compares to the direc-
         tor's *Stagecoach* (1939) in structure and
         approach. The key difference between
         the two films, Welsh says, is that *Wagon-
         master* involves a collective, not indivi-
         dual, show of courage--a "democraticized
         heroism" crucial to Ford's depiction of
         the winning of the West.

3.120   Westrum, Dexter. "Jane Russell Doesn't
         Figure: Male Bonding as True Love in
         Howard Hughes' *The Outlaw*." In *Sex
         and Love in Motion Pictures: Procee-
         dings of the Second Annual Film Con-
         ference of Kent State University*,
         ed. Douglas Radcliff-Umstead. Kent,
         Ohio: Kent State University Romance
         Languages Department, 1984, pp. 14-17.

         Westrum argues against reading of
         Hughes' 1943 film as the movie which
         brought sex without love to the Western.
         The "true love" highlighted in *The Outlaw*
         is the relationship between the three
         male protagonists, Billy the Kid, Doc
         Holliday and Pat Garrett, which the
         author claims takes on the aspects of a
         consummated homosexual relationship. For
         a parallel argument, see 3.87.

3.121   Willeford, Charles. "From *Cockfighter* to
         Born to Kill." *Film Quarterly*, 29
         (Fall 1975), 20-24.

         A case-study production history of
         Monte Hellman's *Born to Kill* (1974),
         examining its path from novel to screen.
         The article is written by the author of
         the novel, *Cockfighter*.

WESTERN FILM PERFORMERS

Books

4.1   Autry, Gene and Mickey Herskowitz. *Back
       In the Saddle Again*. New York:
       Doubleday and Co., 1978.

           In this autobiography, Gene Autry
       describes his career as both a singer
       and a singing cowboy in the movies in a
       pleasant, informal manner, often with
       colorful anecdotes. It becomes obvious
       that Autry is prouder of his accomplish-
       ments in the recording studio than on
       the movie set. Although Autry is rarely
       analytical about either his personal
       life or his movies, this book is impor-
       tant to anyone interested in the history
       of Westerns because Autry's emergence as
       a Western star in the mid-1930s ushered
       in basic changes in the B Western
       formula. Includes filmography and
       discography.

4.2   Belafonte, Dennis and Alvin H. Marill.
           The Films of Tyrone Power. Secaucus,
           N.J.: Citadel Press, 1979.

           An affectionate study of Power's
       career which includes a look at his five
       Westerns, with an emphasis on popular
       and critical responses to his work in
       films, radio and television. Also
       features an introductory biographical
       chapter. Includes film credits and
       several stills from each film.

4.3   Belton, John. *Robert Mitchum*. New York:
                 Pyramid Publications, 1976.

                 In this handy and literate career
                 profile Belton argues that Mitchum's
                 screen persona is that of a "romantic
                 cynic," a "lonely adventurer" whose view
                 of life results in an acting style
                 characterized by laconic understatement.
                 This screen personality has evidently
                 lent itself to Westerns since more than
                 one quarter of Mitchum's films have been
                 in the genre. About half of the mono-
                 graph is pictures. Includes one-page
                 bibliography, filmography and index.

4.4   Canutt, Yakima, with Oliver Drake. *The
                 Stuntman: An Autobiography of Yakima
                 Canutt with Oliver Drake*. New York:
                 Walker and Company, 1979.

                 A highly anecdotal, yet extremely
                 entertaining and informative, memoir by
                 the stuntman, chronicling his career.
                 Mixing "rodeo and reels," his work in
                 early silent Westerns elevated him to
                 stardom. Those roles and his later
                 incarnations as stuntman and action
                 director in a variety of productions are
                 organized into a filmography at the end
                 of this volume, which also includes a
                 useful index.

4.5   Cole, Gerald and Wes Farrell. *The
                 Fondas*. New York: St. Martin's
                 Press, 1984.

                 Family biography of Fondas Henry,
                 Jane and Peter in the context of their
                 screen work. Bare, anecdotal mention of
                 the actors' work in specific films.
                 Includes no filmographies and no indexes.

4.6   Dickens, Homer. *The Films of Barbara
                 Stanwyck*. Secaucus, N.J.: The
                 Citadel Press, 1984.

                 An extensive filmography in

chronological order, including her numerous Westerns. Each entry includes production and cast credits, plot synopsis, sample critical quotes, comments about the film in relation to Stanwyck's career and about ten photos.

4.7   Downing, David and Gary Herman. *Clint Eastwood: All-American Anti-Hero*. London: Omnibus Press, 1977.

More than half of this book is photos from Eastwood's films. A first impression, therefore, might be that this monograph is lightweight fare for fans. This is not the case. Although the text is rather brief, the commentary on Eastwood's films is intelligent and analytical. Downing and Herman follow the anti-social Eastwood persona in all of Eastwood's films through 1976, showing how that persona relates to political perspectives of the time and showing how the character evolves. The result is well-argued interpretation as well as useful career data. Includes filmography but, unfortunately, no index.

4.8   Eyles, Allen. *John Wayne*. New York: A.S. Barnes and Co., 1979.

After several early chapters intro-ducing Wayne's career, this book becomes a film-by-film analysis of Wayne's career from *Stagecoach* (1939) through *The Shootist* (1976). On most films, there are several stills and about two pages of discussion which briefly treats the plot and Wayne's role, mentions some produc-tion details and evaluates the quality of the film and Wayne's performance. Although Eyles is obviously a fan, his comments are perceptive and often critical of the films. Also includes an interview with Wayne by Scott Eyman and a detailed filmography. Unfortunately, there is no index.

4.9   Godfrey, Lionel. *Paul Newman, Superstar*.
           New York: St. Martin's Press, 1978.

           Godfrey's lack of critical distance
           from his subject (the actor and his wife
           are dealt with on a first-name basis)
           hampers many of his efforts at analyzing
           the bulk of Newman's work, particularly
           his involvement in several major
           Westerns. Godfrey claims that two of
           Newman's important Western performances,
           in *Hud* (1963) and in *Hombre* (1967),
           combine with his work in *Cool Hand Luke*
           (1967) to fix Newman's screen persona as
           the Great Loner. Also includes brief
           discussions of Newman's work in other
           Westerns. Godfrey's heavy reliance on
           Pauline Kael's critical analysis further
           weakens his conclusions. Includes brief
           filmographies of Newman and wife Joanne
           Woodward.

4.10   Griggs, John. *The Films of Gregory Peck*.
           Secaucus, N.J.: Citadel Press, 1984.

           Includes a brief biographical essay.
           The rest of the book is a movie-by-movie
           description of the films in which Peck
           has appeared, including his eleven
           Westerns. Each entry includes several
           stills, credits and two to four pages of
           discussion. Comments are mainly on
           production details and public reactions.

4.11   Hanna, David. *Four Giants of the West*.
           New York: Belmont Tower Books, 1976.

           Profiles of the life and careers of
           four actors famous for their roles in
           Westerns: Henry Fonda, James Stewart,
           John Wayne and Gary Cooper. The title is
           misleading in that there is no emphasis
           whatsoever on the Westerns of these four
           men. Much of each chapter is gossip
           about their personal lives, making the
           book nearly worthless for those
           interested in Westerns.

4.12   Henry, Marilyn and Ron De Soundis. *The
        Films of Alan Ladd*. Secaucus, N.J.:
        Citadel Press, 1981.

        Examines Ladd's career film by film,
        including *Shane* (1953) and a handful of
        other Westerns.

4.13   Hintz, H.F. *Horses in the Movies*. New
        York: A.S. Barnes and Co., 1979.

        Sketchy but plentiful profiles of
        horse stars and superstars are featured,
        in addition to brief profiles of "no-
        name" movie horses and the actors they
        accompanied, written with the horse lover
        in mind. The author includes a helpful
        (though fan-oriented) summary chapter,
        "The Horse's Contribution to Western
        Movies," as well as chapters on movies
        about horses and training stables. Also
        includes a useful bibliography and an
        abundance of interesting poster and
        still illustrations.

4.14   Horner, William R. *Bad at the Bijou*.
        Jefferson, N.C.: McFarland & Company,
        Inc., 1982.

        A series of interviews with "badman"
        character actors from the 1950s, 1960s
        and 1970s, with the emphasis on the
        dilemma of consistently portraying
        unsavory types. The author's pointed
        position--that the villain in movies,
        particularly in Westerns, helps the
        audience act through their own "dark
        side" catharsis--detracts somewhat from
        the effectiveness of his conversations,
        but the interviews' usefulness comes from
        the actors chosen. Those interviewed
        include Luke Askew, Neville Brand, Robert
        Donner, Jack Elam, Bo Hopkins, L.Q.
        Jones, Strother Martin, Bill McKinney and
        Lee Van Cleef. Also includes 32 pages
        of glossy photos.

4.15   Horwitz, James. *They Went Thataway*.

New York: E.R. Dutton and Co., Inc.,
1976.

After an entertaining first chapter
that recreates the fun of Saturday
matinees with B Westerns during the
1940s, Horwitz devotes the rest of the
book to a brief history of Westerns and
to his experiences of seeking out his
boyhood heroes to find out how they
fared after their careers as screen
cowboys. Included are meetings with
Gene Autry, Sunset Carson, Charles
Starrett, Russell Hayden, Joel McCrea,
Rex Allen, Jimmy Wakely, Duncan Renaldo,
Tim McCoy and Lash Larue. Horwitz
assumes a rather self-conscious pose of
an innocent during most of these
meetings, constantly surprised to find
his former heroes living in different
circumstances than he expected. The book
seems more an exercise in new journalis-
tic stylizing than in useful reporting.
Historical information was derived from
secondary sources and includes a number
of the original errors.

4.16   Johnstone, Iain. *The Man With No Name*.
New York: Morrow Quill Paperbacks,
1981.

A biography of Clint Eastwood to
1980. Much of the research for the book
began with a BBC interview with Eastwood
in 1977. The best parts of the book are
quotes from Eastwood and from his
associates about the production of the
films. The book suffers somewhat from
Johnstone's lack of critical distance.
He is so enthusiastic about Eastwood's
accomplishments, especially as a
director, that his critical comments lack
credibility. Includes a filmography but
does not include a bibliography or an
index. At least one photo is on every
page.

4.17   Kaminsky, Stuart M. *Clint Eastwood*.

New York: New American Library, 1974.

This first career biography of
Eastwood emphasizes Eastwood's films and
his developing star persona rather than
his private life. Research depends
mostly on interviews with Eastwood and
his colleagues and film reviews.
Included is a long interview with
Eastwood and a filmography.

4.18   ————. *Coop: The Life and Legend of
        Gary Cooper.* New York: St. Martin's
        Press, 1980.

A serviceable biography of Cooper
that nicely balances details about the
actor's private life with information
about the production of his 84 films,
including 25 Westerns. Much of the
information is based on interviews with
people who knew and worked with Cooper.
Includes 15 photos, a good bibliography,
a detailed filmography and an index.

4.19   Kobal, John. *People Will Talk.* New
        York: Alfred A. Knopf, 1986.

This book of interviews includes
discussions with four people of some
prominence in the making of Westerns:
performers Joel McCrea and Barbara
Stanwyck and directors Howard Hawks and
Henry Hathaway.

4.20   Kozarski, Diane Kaiser. *The Complete
        Films of William S. Hart: A Pictorial
        Record.* New York: Dover Publica-
        tions, Inc., 1980.

This is a surprisingly informative
volume given its emphasis on photographs.
Over 200 excellent quality stills, some
reproduced for the first time, enhance
Kozarski's literate introduction to one
of the great actors of the silent screen,
whom she contextualizes as an archetypal
Aryan hero. The entries for 69 films

include production and distribution
information, plot synopses, credits and
contemporary reviews.

4.21   Landry, J.C. *Paul Newman*. New York:
            McGraw-Hill Book Company, 1983.

            An illustrated biography of the movie
star reflecting paparazzi sentiments and
ignoring most of the actor's film work.
Scant mention is made of his Westerns,
except where they contribute to his
celebrity status.

4.22   Linet, Beverly. *Ladd*. New York: Arbor
            House, 1979.

            Linet's sympathetic biography of Alan
Ladd emphasizes the actor's insecurities
about his own talent throughout his
career. Specific films, including his
six Westerns, are mentioned only
casually, as they relate to his personal
and emotional life. Much is made of
Shane (1953), as the pinnacle of Ladd's
career, though little other than incidental production information is featured.
Includes filmography.

4.23   Marill, Alvin H. *Robert Mitchum On the
            Screen*. New York: A.S. Barnes and
            Co., 1978.

            A biographical chapter precedes
summaries of and stills from Mitchum's 95
features and B pictures through 1978.
Though the volume's emphasis is on
Mitchum's career, its brief summaries and
cast listings for the actor's early B
Westerns at RKO in particular are useful.

4.24   McBride, Joseph. *Kirk Douglas*. New
            York: Pyramid Publications, 1976.

            McBride's biography of Douglas posits
Champion (1949) as the archetypal Douglas
role, and argues that the actor's sense
of conviction adds to the credibility of

his performances. McBride puts Douglas'
performances into the context of the
actor's developing career and star image.
Douglas' 13 Westerns do not always fit,
but McBride's discussions of them are
generally engaging. Includes a complete
filmography through 1975, along with
numerous photos.

4.25   McCoy, Tim, with Ronald McCoy. *Tim McCoy
        Remembers the West.* Garden City,
        N.Y.: Doubleday and Co., 1977.

        This intriguing and witty autobio-
graphy will delight those who love
informal Western history told mostly as
colorful anecdotes. However, the book is
likely to disappoint those interested in
the history of Western films. McCoy's
fame rests on his status as a major
Western movie hero from 1926 until the
early 1940s. Yet less than one quarter
of this book is devoted to his career in
films and in that section we learn little
about McCoy's films that has not been
previously published elsewhere. McCoy
emerges as an admirable gentleman much
prouder of his years as an authentic man
of the West than of his career as a manufactured hero. Includes a number of
interesting photos and an index.

4.26   Miller, Lee O. *The Great Cowboy Stars of
        Movies & Television.* New Rochelle,
        N.Y.: Arlington House, 1979.

        Miller purports to pay tribute to
Western stars living and dead by tracing
their careers and, where possible,
allowing them a forum to discuss their
work and to air their views on current
movies and television. The author
clearly has pet contentions--particularly
that violence has greatly increased in
the genre, and to its detriment--and
these color his nostalgic summaries and
the comparisons included in them. Some
of the interviews, particularly those

with B-movie performers and with some of
the less-covered television performers
in the genre, are useful as background
material, but this volume is designed
with fans in mind. The filmographic and
videographic information is incomplete
and, in some instances, bare.

4.27   Nicholas, John H. *Tom Mix: Riding Up to
          Glory*. Oklahoma City, Okla.:
          Persimmon Hill, 1980.

          This is mainly a coffee table picture
book with stills of Mix from his films
and public appearances. A number of
newspaper ads for his films are also
included. The accompanying text is a
biographical sketch written from the
perspective of a life-long fan willing
to look beyond Mix's personal weaknesses.
For Nicholas, the son of Greek immigrant
parents, "Tom Mix *was* the dream of
America." Also includes a filmography
of titles and a brief bibliography.

4.28   Parish, James Robert. *The Tough Guys*.
          New Rochelle, N.Y.: Arlington House,
          1976.

          Biographical chapters on seven movie
tough guys, including four who have
appeared in several notable Westerns:
Kirk Douglas, Burt Lancaster, Robert
Mitchum and Robert Ryan. Each chapter
also includes a number of photos and a
detailed filmography. Includes index.

4.29   Parish, James Robert and Don E. Stanke.
          The All-Americans. New Rochelle,
          N.Y.: Arlington House, 1977.

          Detailed career profiles of seven
men who had long Hollywood careers, six
of whom are known for their roles in
Westerns: Gary Cooper, Henry Fonda,
William Holden, Rock Hudson, Ronald
Reagan and James Stewart. Included with
each profile are several stills and an

excellent filmography. Includes index.

4.30   Rainey, Buck. *Saddle Aces of the Cinema*.
        San Diego: A.S. Barnes and Co., 1980.

        Rainey's attempts at profiles and
        complete filmographies addresses its
        subjects as artifacts of a bygone era.
        Despite its nostalgic ring, the book
        includes useful filmographic information
        and illustrations (reprinted movie
        posters and promotion stills) that offer
        insights into the work of the actors
        discussed. These include: Roy Stewart,
        Wally Wales, Tom Mix, Jack Perrin, Rex
        Bell, Harry Carey, Buck Jones, Reb
        Russell, Al Hoxie, Ken Maynard, William
        Duncan, Hoot Gibson, Gene Autry, Fred
        Thomson and Jack Holt. Reissued in 1986
        by Scarecrow Press.

4.31   ————. *The Saga of Buck Jones*.
        Nashville: Western Film Collector,
        1975.

        A short biography of the great
        Western star of the 1920s and 1930s
        written from the perspective of an
        unabashedly adoring fan. Emphasis is on
        brief descriptions of Jones' films.
        About half of the monograph is photos, a
        great many of them interesting repro-
        ductions of original lobby cards. Also
        includes a filmography of the 145 films
        in which Jones appeared between 1918 and
        1942.

4.32   Ricci, Mark, Boris Zmijewsky, et al.
        The Complete Films of John Wayne.
        Secaucus, N.J.: Citadel Press, 1979.

        This book updates the 1970 book by
        the same authors (I, 4.33). Includes
        details of the seven Westerns starring
        Wayne after the publication of the
        original edition.

4.33   Roberson, "Bad Chuck," with Bodie Thoene.

The Fall Guy. North Vancouver,
B.C.: Hancock House, 1980.

The memoirs of a premier Hollywood
stuntman who, in 30 years, worked in
some 250 films, 30 of them as John
Wayne's stunt double. As might be
expected, the book makes little attempt
at analysis. Rather, it is filled with
entertaining stories of dangerous stunts,
crazy practical jokes and high living
off the movie set. Roberson is especially interesting when telling behind-
the-scenes stories about the productions
of John Ford. The book is full of macho
posturing and often reads as exaggeration
rather than simple facts. On this level,
however, it is entertaining reading for
fans of Western films.

4.34   Rogers, Roy and Dale Evans, with Carlton
            Stowers. *Happy Trails.* Waco, Texas:
            Word Books, 1979.

Standard celebrity autobiography,
emphasizing Rogers' and Evans' love of
the West and their Christian faith.
Though the emphasis is on personal lives
over screen work, the authors' anecdotes
cover many of their remembered B Westerns
from 1938 to 1952, as well as some
discussion of Rogers' comeback effort,
Mackintosh and T.J. (1975). Includes
film list and 36 candid photos.
Necessary for anyone looking for inside
glances at the B Western business.

4.35   Rothel, David. *The Singing Cowboys.*
            New York: A.S. Barnes and Co., 1978.

Rothel is a fan first and foremost,
and he uses his love of the topic to his
advantage in this study of popular
singing cowboys. Includes profiles of
Gene Autry, Tex Ritter, Roy Rogers, Eddie
Dean, Jimmy Wakely, Monte Hale, Rex Allen
and a handful of others, with annotated
filmographies for Autry and Rogers.

Though the author's enthusiasm hampers
his objectivity, it also leads him to
present more specific details about the
performers and their films, as well as
first-person interviews and interesting
photos and memorabilia. Also features
selected filmographies for the other
singing cowboys, and a selected bibliography.

4.36   ————. *Those Great Cowboy Sidekicks*.
            Metuchen, N.J.: The Scarecrow Press,
            Inc., 1984.

            Rothel's companion volume to his *The
Singing Cowboys* (4.35) includes extensive
background on the three best-known
sidekicks--Smiley Burnette, George
"Gabby" Hayes and Al "Fuzzy" St. John--
as well as shorter profiles of 36 other
Western film sidekicks. The author's
biography-as-reminiscence methodology,
relying on often lengthy accounts from
co-stars and family members for factual
material, poses some problems, but also
presents some interesting anecdotal
information. Also includes a mine of
reproduced publicity stills and other
Western memorabilia, and--its strongest
asset--useful and often extensive
filmographies of the actors' sidekick
films. In addition, the volume has a
helpful film cross-referencing index.

4.37   St. Charnez, Casy. *The Films of Steve
            McQueen*. Secaucus, N.J.: Citadel
            Press, 1984.

            An extensive filmography in chrono-
logical order of McQueen's films
including his four Westerns. Each entry
includes production and cast credits,
sample review, a two to three page
description of how the film and its
making relates to McQueen's career and
about ten photos.

4.38   Sheperd, Donald and Robert Slatzer, with

Dave Grayson. *Duke: The Life and Times of John Wayne*. New York: Doubleday and Co., 1985.

A tell-all biography written by two specialists in the genre and Wayne's make-up man. The authors are more interested in detailing Wayne's private life than they are in discussing his movies. Those interested in gossip might find this book rewarding, but those interested in Wayne's star persona or his films are likely to be frustrated. Includes a filmography of Wayne's films.

4.39   Stacy, Pat, with Beverly Linet. *Duke: A Love Story*. New York: Atheneum, 1983.

The memoirs of the relationship between the author and John Wayne during the final years of Wayne's life may be of some interest to John Wayne's fans. But it provides no significant insights into Wayne's last films, including his Westerns.

4.40   Swindel, Larry. *The Last Hero: A Biography of Gary Cooper*. Garden City, N.Y.: Doubleday and Co., 1980.

For many, Cooper was the screen's quintessential "man of the West." Swindel's book is a readable and anecdotal account of his life and screen roles, and explores the tensions Swindel finds between Cooper's reticent, almost shy, public persona and the sophisticated background and experiences of his private life. Index and filmography place it above run-of-the-mill "star" biographies.

4.41   Thomas, Tony. *The Films of Henry Fonda*. Secaucus, N.J.: Citadel Press, 1983.

Film-by-film analysis of Fonda's career, including some examination of the actor's changing screen persona. Thomas' introduction, "Henry Fonda--American Original," emphasizes Fonda's versatility and professionalism. Credits and several stills from each film are included.

4.42 ———. *The Films of Ronald Reagan.* Secaucus, N.J.: Citadel Press, 1980.

After a biographical introduction, Thomas presents short descriptions of each of Reagan's 53 films, including his six Westerns. Included for each film are credits, brief discussion and several stills.

4.43 ———. *Gregory Peck.* New York: Pyramid Publications, 1977.

Biography of the actor relies heavily on Peck's remembrances of his varied film roles, including his 11 Westerns. Includes a brief filmography and numerous photos.

4.44 Tibbetts, John C. and James M. Welsh. *His Majesty the American: The Films of Douglas Fairbanks, Sr.* New York: A.S. Barnes and Co., 1977.

Many of the films starring Fairbanks made between 1915 and 1920 were Westerns or featured sequences located in the West. Chapter five traces different attitudes and elements of American culture that comprised Eastern ideas about the West at the turn of the century that the authors argue find expression in Fairbanks' films. Especially important are dime novels, wild west shows and the persona of Theodore Roosevelt, who touted the West as a land of regeneration and rugged masculinity. Unlike most "films of" books, this one attempts to explore in some detail the relationship between its subject and the forces of culture that make the subject's films notable. In the case of Fairbanks' relationship to

American ideas about the West, it
succeeds admirably. Some detailed
attention is given to the films *Wild and
Wooly* (1916) and *Manhattan Madness*
(1916). A filmography, bibliography and
index are included.

4.45   Toffel, Neile McQueen. *My Husband, My
            Friend*. New York: Atheneum, 1986.

A tell-all biography of Steve McQueen
by his first wife. There is very little
information about McQueen's television
Western series, *Wanted, Dead or Alive*,
nor is there any detailing of his roles
in film Westerns. Emphasis is on gossipy
details of McQueen's private life.

4.46   Whitman, Mark. *The Films of Clint
            Eastwood*. New York: Beaufort Books,
            Inc., 1982.

Mostly a collection of closeup stills
of Eastwood from his various films. Also
includes a biographical chapter and a
filmography. The information is
available in more detail elsewhere (see
4.7, 4.16, 4.47).

4.47   Zmijewsky, Boris and Lee Pfeiffer. *The
            Films of Clint Eastwood*. Secaucus,
            N.J.: Citadel Press, 1982.

A film-by-film description of
Eastwood's films to 1980, including 11
Westerns. Each entry includes cast and
production credits, a brief introduction,
a synopsis of the story, several
reviewers' comments and between six and
12 stills. The introduction is a brief
biography written from the perspective of
enthusiastic Eastwood fans.

Articles

4.48   Anderson, Robert. "The Making of a
            Legend: Tom Mix in New Mexico."
            Journal of the West, 16:4 (October

1977), 12-17.

Details Mix's work in one- and two-reel Westerns for Selig Polyscope in Las Vegas, New Mexico in 1915. Emphasis is on the boosterism involved in getting Mix to make films in Las Vegas. The article details no more than a minor event in Mix's film career, but it presents an interesting view of the on-location relationships between local communities and filmmakers during the early years of movie Westerns.

4.49   Basinger, Jeanne. "John Wayne, An Appreciation." *American Film*, 1 (June 1976), 50, 52-53.

A brief survey of John Wayne's career up to *The Shootist* (1976), and an attempt to establish the "idea" of John Wayne.

4.50   Beaver, Jim. "John Wayne." *Films in Review*, 28:5 (May 1977), 257-284.

This essay gives a brief, chatty introduction to Wayne's life and career. Some of his more important films receive a paragraph of text. The filmography following the article lists 156 films, with information on cast, director, year and, in some cases, a short synopsis, as well as eight movies Wayne made before his name change and Western debut in *The Big Trail* (1930).

4.51   ————. "Strother Martin." *Films in Review*, 33:9 (November 1982), 531-538.

A brief biographical essay about Martin, one of Hollywood's finest character actors, who is best known for his role in Westerns as, in Martin's words, "pure prairie scum." Includes a filmography of partial credits of Martin's 60 films.

4.52   Bodeen, DeWitt. "The Farnum Brothers:
        Dustin and William." *Films in
        Review*, 34:9 (November 1983),
        514-528.

        Author traces the careers of two
        major stars of silent film. Dustin
        Farnum made a number of important
        Westerns, including *The Squaw Man* (1914),
        in which he reprised his starring
        Broadway role, and *The Virginian* (1914).
        William Farnum's career spanned 38 years
        and included such Westerns as *Riders of
        the Purple Sage* (1912) and the serial B
        movie *Custer's Last Stand* (1940).
        Filmographies for both actors follow the
        essay.

4.53   ———. "Joel McCrea and Frances Dee."
        Films in Review, 29:10 (December
        1978), 577-596.

        An obsequious essay on McCrea and his
        actress-wife (whom Bodeen appears to
        idolize for putting her family before her
        career). Bodeen suggests that after he
        starred in the 1946 Technicolor version
        of *The Virginian*, McCrea made mostly
        Westerns. Dee had a role in his 1948
        film, *Four Faces West*, which Bodeen
        considers one of the "best Westerns
        either ever made." The article's
        filmography lists 30 Westerns.

4.54   Buckley, Michael. "Henry Fonda." *Films
        in Review*, 33:1 (January 1982),
        26-34.

        Filmographies covering Fonda's first
        62 films are found in the November 1960
        and April 1966 issues of *Films in Review*.
        This article covers the end of Fonda's
        career--from his 63rd film to his 86th--
        during which he made six Westerns.

4.55   ———. "Patrick Wayne, an Interview."
        Films in Review, 26 (October 1985),

466-473.

Interview with Wayne centers on his work in film and television (primarily his non-Western work), his relationship (onscreen and off) with his father John Wayne and his work in the Western satire *Rustler's Rhapsody* (1985).

4.56   ────. "Richard Widmark." *Films in Review*, 37 (April 1986), 222-229; 37 (May 1986), 258-270; (June/July 1986), 322-337.

A three-part essay discussing Widmark's career in film, relying heavily on different interviews with the actor. The third part of Buckley's essay features general reminiscences of Widmark's involvement in several of the 15 Westerns he made during his career, as well as an extensive filmography which describes his roles in the films he appears in.

4.57   Cahill, Tim. "Clint Eastwood: The *Rolling Stone* Interview." *Rolling Stone*, no. 451 (July 4, 1985), 18-23.

An interview in which Eastwood comments on a large number of the films he has appeared in and directed, including his Westerns.

4.58   Christy, Jim. "Monty, Lash and Me." *Take One*, 5:12 (November 1977), 24-25.

Slight remembrance of meeting with Lash LaRue after the cowboy star's run-in with Florida police in 1965. LaRue intimates that he lost the lead role in *Red River* (1948) to Montgomery Clift because of differing sexual proclivities. Strange, but interesting.

4.59   Cocchi, John. "John Wayne." *Films in Review*, 28:7 (August-September

1977), 444-445.

Corrections and additions to Jim
Beaver's Wayne filmography (see 4.50).

4.60   Corneau, Ernest. "A Salute to Gene
            Autry." *Classic Film Collector*, no.
            47 (Summer 1975), 28, x-3.

            An adequate if slightly fawning
outline of Autry's work in popular
music, movies and television. Corneau's
perspective, that the appearance of the
singing cowboy was the second revolution
in Westerns (the first was the coming of
sound), gives his brief portrait an
overblown air.

4.61   Drew, William M. "Esther Ralston."
            American Classic Screen, 5:4 (1981),
            25-32.

            Interview with Ralston touches on
her acting work in silent and sound
features through 1940. Sketchy and
occasionally interesting, the article
contributes anecdotes on Ralston's early
Westerns with Art Acord as well as two
silent Westerns, *The Phantom Fortune*
(1923) and *The Heart Buster* (1924), the
latter with Tom Mix.

4.62   Edgerton, Gary. "A Reappraisal of John
            Wayne." *Films in Review*, 37 (May
            1986), 282-289.

            Looking for the meaning, symbolism
and aesthetic of Wayne's work in films,
Edgerton delivers an apologia for the
Western star's career and his persona.
The author claims that Wayne's screen
image--the prototypical 19th-Century
American Male, self-sufficient and
individualistic--embodies an aesthetic of
action while serving as the ethical and
ideological center of his films. In
particular, Edgerton argues that the
style and ideology of the "John Wayne

movie" are blended in Wayne's last film, *The Shootist* (1976).

4.63   Everett, Eldon K. "Tom Mix, King of the Cowboys." *Classic Film Collector*, no. 45 (Winter 1974), 38-39.

Features the interesting recollections of Ellis Clarke Soper, a cement contracting engineer who hired Mix as a deputy sheriff in 1904. Also includes publicity pictures.

4.64   Firestone, Bruce M. "Kidflicks. The Western Films of Fred Thomson." *American Classic Screen*, 6:2 (1982), 27-30.

A short profile of the life and film career of Fred Thomson, a popular Western hero of the 1920s who is little known today because only two of his 30 films have survived. Firestone emphasizes how the content of Thomson's films was intended to provide moral instruction to young boys. There was an emphasis on action rather than violence, and Thomson's horse, Silver King, was given a prominent role. Includes six photos.

4.65   Goodman, Mark. "The Singing Cowboy." *Esquire*, 84 (December 1975), 154-155, 240, 245-248.

A profile of the career and opinions of Roy Rogers occasioned by the completion of Rogers' first film since 1952, *Mackintosh and T.J.* (1975). Most of the material is available elsewhere but of some interest is data supplied by Rogers' agent Art Rush on Roy's popularity outside of movies and TV.

4.66   Green, Douglas. "The Sons of the Pioneers." *Southern Quarterly*, 22:3

(Spring 1984), 53-65.

Green contends that the Western singing group established the sound, style and repertoire of Western music while also being responsible for impressing the romantic image of the West on the American consciousness. In his history-biography of the group's changing personnel, Green includes some mention of the group's work in movie and TV Westerns. Also featured are a chart of major members from 1933 to the present and an annotated discography.

4.67   Harman, Bob. "A Sagebrush Sweetheart! Claire Rochelle." *Classic Film Collector*, no. 53 (Winter 1976), 25, x-11.

A quick interview-summary of Rochelle's life and career in the film industry, including a filmography of her 14 B Westerns produced in the 1930s.

4.68   Hart, William S. "Living Your Character." *Hollywood Directors 1914-1940*, ed. Richard Koszarski. New York: Oxford University Press, pp. 45-48.

A reprint of a May 1917 article in *Motion Picture Magazine* in which Hart explains some of the specific techniques he employs in his films to create a sense of realism. Includes brief comments on acting style, the use of closeups, the need for realistic sets and Hart's suspicion of elaborate stunts. Also includes a brief discussion of Hart's character in *The Aryan* (1916).

4.69   Hitt, Jim. "The Myth Makers." *True West*, 32:2 (March 1985), 14-21.

A brief overview of the Hollywood period between 1910 and 1915, when real cowboys established screen careers in

Western movies. Included are short
career descriptions of Art Acord, Hoot
Gibson, Tom Mix, Pete Morrison, Neal
Hart and Edmund Cobb. The article is
flawed by a number of incorrect names
and dates.

4.70 ————. "Ronald Reagan: Hero of Old
West Movies." *True West*, 31:8
(September 1984), 12-17.

Brief plot summaries of Ronald
Reagan's six Western films. Hitt
concludes that Reagan's Western persona
was "adequate ... a believable and
likable hero who could, when the need
arose, be tough." For a more detailed
look at Reagan's Westerns, see *The Films
of Ronald Reagan* (4.42).

4.71 Macklin, F. Anthony. "'I Come Ready':
An Interview with John Wayne." *Film
Heritage*, 10 (Summer 1975), 1-33.

Interview with Wayne focuses on his
contributions to his pictures, his view
of the world and his popular image.

4.72 Maynell, Jennifer. "Values and
Violence: A Study of the Films of
Clint Eastwood." *Journal of Moral
Education*, 7 (January 1978),
109-113.

Maynell argues that violence in
Eastwood's films is the result of the
clash between a traditional hero who will
not compromise his values of integrity,
courage, honor and justice and a
viciously corrupt society which no
longer recognizes these values. Most of
the article describes Eastwood's Dirty
Harry films but brief discussions of *A
Fistful of Dollars* (1967) and *High
Plains Drifter* (1973) are also included.

4.73 Mazzoco, Robert. "Supply-Side Star."
New York Review of Books, 29:5

(April 1, 1982), 34-39.

An analysis of the screen persona of
Clint Eastwood and the appeal of this
persona to audiences of the 1970s.
Mazzoco sees Eastwood as a traditional
American rugged individualist hero,
innocent and unchanging, in an era that
has lost faith in liberal solutions for
society's ills. The arguments are
useful and persuasive but are constructed mainly around Eastwood's Dirty
Harry detective character rather than
around his roles in Westerns.

4.74   McBride, Joseph. "Aren't You ... Jimmy
             Stewart?" *American Film*, 1 (June
             1976), 51, 54-56.

A brief examination of Stewart's
career, within the context of his
development as an actor. McBride
briefly touches on Stewart's Western
work with John Ford.

4.75   McDonald, Archie P. "John Wayne: Hero
             of the Western." *Journal of the
             West*, 22:4 (October 1983), 53-63.

An overview of John Wayne's roles as
a Western hero and a description of his
Western heroic persona. In general,
McDonald argues that Wayne is "super-
America, an embodiment of our
nationalism, our jingoistic, self-image
of success, triumph and dominance."
McDonald agrees with other critics that
Wayne's Western characters, beginning
with *Red River* in 1948, often display
fanatic overtones but McDonald is more
sympathetic toward this image than some
other writers. He argues that the later
Wayne hero is also soft-hearted, a
person on a quest for truth. The
article is part of a special issue of
Journal of the West devoted entirely to
the Western film.

4.76   McGilligan, Patrick. "Clint Eastwood."
        Focus on Film, no. 25 (Summer/Autumn
        1976), 13-20.

        An interview with Eastwood shortly
        after he completed his last Western of
        the 1970s, *The Outlaw Josey Wales*
        (1976). Comments in the first half of
        the interview are mainly on Eastwood's
        Westerns.

4.77   Moore, Doug. "Pauline Moore: Girl of
        the Golden West." *American Classic
        Screen*, 4:2 (Winter 1980), 41, 45.

        A sentimental biographical sketch of
        one of Republic Studio's leading Western
        ladies, with the accent on her career in
        Westerns. Though including a certain
        wealth of background material, the
        article's syrupiness saps its usefulness
        (the author, a film professor, also
        happens to be Pauline Moore's nephew).
        Features several photos of minor
        interest from Moore's early films,
        particularly her first B Western, *Wild
        and Wooly*. Part of an *American Classic
        Screen* "Special Western Issue."

4.78   Oney, Steve. "The Last Roundup."
        California Magazine, 7 (November
        1982), 82-89, 156-160, 162.

        Brief career profiles of six B
        Western stars combined with descriptions
        of their then current lives as presented
        in personal interviews. Included are
        Gene Autry, Sunset Carson, Roy Rogers,
        Rex Allen, Gail Davis and Clayton Moore.
        The style is informal but with neither
        the gushing praise of the adoring fan
        nor the condescending irony of the
        cynic, approaches that too often distort
        the information presented in large
        circulation publications.

4.79   Pickard, Roy. "Lee Jay Cobb." *Films in
        Review*, 28:9 (November 1977),

525-537.

Although this essay does not
emphasize Cobb's Western roles, the
filmography at its conclusion includes
10 Westerns in which he had mostly "bit"
parts, from his screen debut in the
Hopalong Cassidy feature *North of the
Rio Grande* (1937) to *The Man Who Loved
Cat Dancing* (1973).

4.80   Podheiser, Linda. "Pep on the Range, or
        Douglas Fairbanks and the World War
        I Era Western." *Journal of Popular
        Film and Television*, 11:3 (Fall
        1983), 122-130.

Author convincingly argues that
silent Westerns have suffered from
critical neglect, and that attention to
early Westerns can illuminate important
matters of genre, formula and film
history. The essay mainly focuses on
Douglas Fairbanks' Westerns as important
transitional films, spoofing stunt-laden
Tom Mix movies and William S. Hart
melodramas. For Podheiser, these films
have a unique contemporary quality,
bringing together the romanticism of the
Old West and the tone of the "modern"
Progressive era. Includes some detailed
analysis of *Wild and Wooly* (1917), *The
Man from Painted Post* (1917) and *The
Mollycoddle* (1920).

4.81   Ponicsan, Darryl. "High Eagle. The
        Many Lives of Colonel Tim McCoy."
        American Heritage, 28 (June 1977),
        52-62.

An interview with McCoy in which the
star of innumerable B Westerns remini-
sces about his career in show business
and discusses his relationship with and
attitudes toward Native Americans.
Includes 10 useful stills. McCoy
includes much of this material in his
autobiography (see 4.25).

4.82   Rainey, Buck. "Hoot Gibson, Cowboy
                1892-1960." *Films in Review*, 29:8
                (October 1978), 471-484.

            An informative introduction to the
        career of a real-life cowboy who became
        a major figure in B Westerns and was a
        star at Universal from 1917 to 1931.
        The article includes a filmography of
        over 210 movies, 195 of which were made
        before 1940.

4.83   ————. "Ridin' and Singin' with Smith
                Ballew." *Filmograph*, 4:4 (1975),
                14-26.

            This biography of former singing
        cowboy Ballew emphasizes the actor's
        diverse background as a musician with
        the bands of Ben Pollack and Hal Kemp
        and as the band leader who gave Glenn
        Miller his break in 1932. Rainey
        includes an anecdotal survey of Ballew's
        film work.

4.84   Rogers, Roy. "Roy Rogers: First Days at
                Republic." *American Classic Screen*,
                4:2 (Winter 1980), 34-36.

            The second King of the Cowboys'
        remembrances of his pre-royalty days in
        the movie business are brief and
        anecdotal, but they do serve as a first-
        person attempt to explain Rogers' gallop
        to stardom. Culled from *Happy Trails*,
        by Rogers and Dale Evans, assisted by
        Carlton Stowers (4.34). Excerpt is part
        of an *American Classic Screen* "Special
        Western Issue."

4.85   Sinclair, Andrew. "The Man on Horseback:
                The Seven Faces of John Wayne."
                Sight and Sound, 48 (Autumn 1979),
                232-235.

            Sinclair claims that Wayne's persona
        has gone through seven public "faces,"
        most of which were informed either by

the powerful machinations of others
(particularly John Ford) or through the
actor's own naive public pronouncements.
Several of Wayne's "faces"--the outlaw
as Galahad, the professional soldier,
the mythic figure brave and lasting unto
death--are imbedded in the Western
genre. Sinclair's analysis is generally
competent, though its complete neglect
of Wayne's pre-Ford work mars its
thoroughness.

4.86   Stark, John. "At 320 Pounds, Divine
               Teams with Tab Hunter to Bushwhack
               Westerns." *People Weekly*, 22:3
               (July 16, 1984), 99-102, 104-105.

            A brief overview of the life and
            career of Divine, the movies' most
            famous transvestite, based on an inter-
            view with Divine on the set of *Lust in
            the Dust* (1985), a parody of spaghetti
            Westerns. Includes six photos.

4.87   Thompson, David. "Richard Farnsworth."
               Film Comment, 19:4 (July/August
               1983), 78-79.

            A brief essay in praise of Richard
            Farnsworth for the grace and dignity he
            brings to the role of Bill Miner in *The
            Grey Fox* (1982).

4.88   Wilson, David. "Kicking Away Gravity:
               The Saga of Four Great Hollywood
               Stuntmen." *American Classic Screen*,
               5:5 (1981), 26-29.

            Sketchy profiles of three recipients
            of the National Film Society's Yakima
            Canutt Award and its namesake--Canutt,
            Harvey Perry, Dave Sharpe and Jock
            Mahoney. Includes brief discussions of
            their work in Westerns, but only within
            the context of their overall careers.

4.89   Wolmute, Roger. "Hoist 'Em, Pards, Lash
               is Back." *People Weekly*, 23:13

(April 1, 1986), 58-60, 63.

A brief overview of the life and
career of Lash Larue, B movie cowboy
hero of the late 1940s and early 1950s,
constructed around an interview with
Larue. Includes four photos.

MAKERS OF WESTERN FILMS

5.1   Anderson, Lindsay. *About John Ford* ...
New York: McGraw-Hill Book Co., 1981.

An affectionate study of Ford's films
which attempts to deal with Ford as a
legend. Anderson's book is centered on a
disconnected series of meeting-interviews
which reveal more about the British
critic-director than they do about Ford.
The author's discussions of Ford Westerns
are limited to *Straight Shooting* (1917),
Fort Apache (1948), *She Wore a Yellow
Ribbon* (1949), *Rio Grande* and *Wagonmaster*
(both 1950). Detailing Ford's films
after 1955, Anderson dismisses the bulk
of them as uneven efforts (excepting
Sergeant Rutledge in 1960 and *The Man Who
Shot Liberty Valance* in 1962) in which
"the poetic flame burns low." Anderson's
celebration of Ford focuses instead on
the director's collaborations with
writers (Dudley Nichols) and actors
(Harry Carey Sr.), his development as
"cine-poet" and his conflicts with studio
management. Although a survey in nature,
the author's study does include a
competent filmography and reproductions
of interviews and correspondence with
Ford's various collaborators, including
Harry Carey Jr., Henry Fonda and Nichols.

5.2   Basinger, Jeanine. *Anthony Mann*.
Boston: Twayne Publishers, 1979.

Argues that Mann's films are about journeys undertaken by a hero in which he crosses a consciousness-evoking landscape and emerges with a new understanding of himself. Examining the important phases of the director's career, Basinger asserts that his Western period (1950 to 1960) represented the full flowering of his film artistry. The author stakes a convincing claim for the existence of multilayered meaning in Mann's ten Westerns, arguing that the films' shifting landscape, narrative line and character development blend together in coherent yet complex unity. Basinger effectively places Mann's Westerns within the context of his work in *films noir* and in period epics. Includes a detailed filmography and a useful bibliography.

5.3   Baxter, John. *King Vidor*. New York: Monarch Press, 1976.

In his introduction to this monograph Baxter argues that Vidor's films are characterized by his use of landscape as metaphor. Unfortunately, he apparently was not very interested in the metaphorical landscapes in Vidor's Westerns because, though they are included, none of the Westerns receives more than a few paragraphs of analysis. Includes a number of good stills, a title filmography of Vidor's films and a two-page selective bibliography.

5.4   Belton, John. *The Hollywood Professionals: Howard Hawks, Frank Borzage and Edgar G. Ulmer*. New York: A.S. Barnes and Co., 1974.

The author's entry has some extensive discussions of Hawks' Westerns, which Belton tries to place within the thematic context of the director's other work. Belton uses Hawks' major Westerns as reflectors of themes important in his overall body of work: *Red River* (1948) reflects the director's comic vision as well as his emphasis on individual perseverance; *Rio Bravo* (1959) embodies a complex interweaving of narratives; *El Dorado* (1967) and *Rio Lobo* (1970) assert the importance of independent action. Also includes a competent filmography.

5.5   Bliss, Michael. *Martin Scorsese and Michael Cimino*. Metuchen, N.J.: The Scarecrow Press, Inc., 1985.

Two chapters of Bliss' study of Cimino's work deal exclusively with *Heaven's Gate* (1980). In "The Beauty of Things That Fade" (pp. 193-239), the author offers a very detailed reading of Cimino's film, claiming it appropriates the best qualities of the director's earlier movies in a subtly effective blend. The second chapter, "The Sabotaging of *Heaven's Gate*" (pp. 240-266), discusses the film's critical and commercial failure. Bliss blames both on the industry's need to keep Cimino in line and on critics' inability to read the film properly. Includes a detailed filmography for both directors.

5.6   Butler, Terence. *Crucified Heroes: The Films of Sam Peckinpah*. London: Gordon Fraser, 1979.

While Peckinpah's films frequently lament the closing of the American frontier, according to Butler, the director's Westerns remain haunted by the frontier as a dynamic concept, "the vitality of Eros, atavistic frenzy, all that is lawless and free." Butler precedes his film-by-film analysis of Peckinpah's work with a chapter comparing the films with others in the genre and with a perceived American tradition. Also includes a detailed filmography.

5.7   Combs, Richard, ed. *Robert Aldrich*. London: British Film Institute, 1978.

This monograph study of director
Aldrich's work argues that the easily
translatable surfaces of his films hide
an inner complexity. In "Robert Aldrich
(1953 to 1961)" (pp. 3-21), Combs argues
that the hero-villain dichotomy is
particularly blurred in Aldrich's
Westerns, where the lyricism of an
idealized past makes even the villains
charming. Both Combs' essay and Tom
Milne's "Robert Aldrich (1962 to 1978)"
(pp. 23-36) frequently discuss aspects of
Aldrich's Westerns within the context of
his other work, in particular *Apache*
(1954), *Vera Cruz* (1954) and *Ulzana's
Raid* (1972). The monograph includes a
lengthy interview with Aldrich, as well
as a definitive filmography through 1977.

5.8   Denton, Clive and Kingsley Canham. *The
             Hollywood Professionals: King Vidor,
             John Cromwell and Mervyn LeRoy.* New
             York: A.S. Barnes and Co., 1976.

Denton discusses Vidor's work in
Westerns as reflective of the crucial
themes in his films. *Northwest Passage*
(1940), according to Denton, reiterates
Vidor's dominant theme of the dynamics of
"leader-against-crowd" relationships;
Duel in the Sun (1946) reflects the
troubles the director experienced with
studio interference.

5.9   Denton, Clive, Kingsley Canham and Tony
             Thomas. *The Hollywood Professionals:
             Henry King, Lewis Milestone and Sam
             Wood.* New York: A.S. Barnes and Co.,
             1974.

Denton's discussion of King's career
includes only slight mention of *Jesse
James* (1939) and *The Bravados* (1958) in
their depiction of the director's
"homespun" style, along with an unclear
filmography (especially before 1921).
Thomas' retelling of Wood's career and
creative frustrations features a brief

note on *Ambush* (1950), as well as a curt listing of his film work.

5.10   Dick, Bernard F. *Joseph L. Mankiewicz*.
        Boston: Twayne Publishers, 1983.

        This overview of the film career of the writer-director includes a brief analysis of Mankiewicz's only Western, *There Was a Crooked Man* (1970), which Dick describes as an exercise in sardonic cynicism. Also includes a chronology of Mankiewicz's career, a selective annotated bibliography, a filmography and an index.

5.11   di Franco, J. Philip, ed. *The Movie World of Roger Corman*. New York: Chelsea House Publishers, 1979.

        Primarily a forum for Corman to discuss his work as director, producer and executive producer of a wide range of low-budget projects, di Franco's book includes general discussion of Corman's 1950s Westerns and of his involvement as executive producer on Monte Hellman's *Born to Kill* (1974). Includes illustrated filmography.

5.12   Dmytryk, Edward. *It's a Hell of a Life But Not a Bad Living*. New York: Times Books, 1978.

        Director Dmytryk's autobiography features detailed accounts of most of his films, including four Westerns: *Broken Lance* (1954), *Warlock* (1959), *Alvarez Kelly* (1966) and *Shalako* (1968). Though his emphasis is on the positive experiences, Dmytryk's production information is forthright and often engaging.

5.13   Ford, Dan. *Pappy: The Life of John Ford*. Englewood Cliffs, N.J.: Prentice-Hall, Inc., 1979.

Written by the director's grandson,
Pappy splits its attention evenly between
Ford's life and his films. Ford,
according to his grandson, was a bene-
volent tyrant with a brutal streak whose
obsessions with the pomp and pride of
military life and with his Irish heritage
had the greatest influence on his work.
Well written and based almost exclusively
on firsthand interviews and family
scrapbook material, *Pappy* discusses in
detail the director's work on most of his
Western films, with the exception of his
work on *How the West Was Won* (1963). The
volume includes several off-camera photos.

5.14   Gallagher, Tag. *John Ford: The Man and*
          His Films. Berkeley: University of
          California Press, 1986.

A major attempt to establish Ford as
one of the great American artists of the
twentieth century. Gallagher admits at
the outset that the purpose of his study
is to "increase appreciation and
pleasure" in Ford's films. To do this,
he has constructed his book as an answer
to criticisms that Ford was shamelessly
sentimental, was a racist, was a
political reactionary and was an
intuitive filmmaker rather than an
intellectual artist. Ford, Gallagher
concludes, was a strong cinematic stylist.
He employed "expressionist" filmmaking
toward an increasingly complex study of
the frustrations of the human inability
to mediate lives lived between the
freedom of chaos and the determinism of
order. If chaos looses violence, order
may lead to repression and racism. The
emphasis of the study is the films
themselves. Biographical comments
present little that is new. Gallagher is
brilliant in detailing films that help
him develop his thesis, but he can be
flat or nearly useless when he analyzes
films he is not interested in. In the
case of Ford's Westerns, for example, *She*

Wore a Yellow Ribbon (1949) merits just
over two pages with the plot quickly
summed up in a footnote, while *The Man
Who Shot Liberty Valance* (1962) receives
an intense analysis of almost 30 pages.
Overall, this is the most detailed
presentation of the entire body of Ford's
films yet published. It presents strong
arguments about both the thematic and
pictorial qualities of individual
pictures and demonstrates how the films,
including the Westerns, are related.
Since Gallagher is mainly interested in
style and themes, however, he is often
confusing on plots. It helps to have
seen the films ahead of reading the book.
Includes an interesting appendix listing
basic financial information about Ford's
films, a detailed filmography, an index
and over 300 frame enlargements.

5.15   Giannetti, Louis. *Masters of the
            American Cinema*. Englewood Cliffs,
            N.J.: Prentice-Hall, Inc., 1981.

        Includes one-chapter career profiles
of eight directors who have made notable
Westerns: John Ford, Howard Hawks,
William Wyler, Fritz Lang, John Huston,
Fred Zinneman, Arthur Penn and Robert
Altman. Chapters include biographical
information and generally reliable
critical comments on the films. These
are good brief introductions to these
directors but, in most chapters, Westerns
are discussed only incidentally.

5.16   Graham, Cooper C., Steven Higgins,
            Elaine Mancini and Loao Luiz Vieira.
            *D.W. Griffith and the Biograph
            Company*. Metuchen, N.J.: The
            Scarecrow Press, Inc., 1985.

        The authors' bookkeeping account of
Biograph's output during Griffith's
tenure as production supervisor (1908-
1913) includes painstaking filmographical
information on each Biograph production

during the period, drawn from original
and secondary sources. In addition to
including information on several of
Griffith's Westerns, the work features an
appendix on the legendary director's *The
Heart of an Outlaw* (1909), which was held
back from release because of the studio's
censorship worries.

5.17   Haskin, Byron, with Joe Adamson. *Byron
                 Haskin*. Metuchen, N.J.: The
                 Directors Guild of America and The
                 Scarecrow Press, Inc., 1984.

This first volume in the Directors
Guild of America Oral History Series
includes some discussion of Haskin's work
on several Westerns, including *Warpath*
(1951), *Denver and Rio Grande* (1952) and
The First Texan (1956). Stressing
production details and Haskin's picture-
making philosophy, the extended interview
does not include a much-needed
filmography for this under-examined
director.

5.18   Horton, Andrew. *The Films of George Roy
                 Hill*. New York: Columbia University
                 Press, 1984.

Horton's basic premise is that there
are ironic subtexts in all of Hill's
films, operating in tension with their
entertainment functions. This perspective informs his chapter on *Butch Cassidy
and the Sundance Kid* (1969), which he
considers a simultaneous parody and
reaffirmation of the Western. For
another study of *Butch Cassidy* as part of
Hill's *oeuvre*, see also 5.39.

5.19   Kagan, Norman. *American Skeptic: Robert
                 Altman's Genre-Commentary Films*. Ann
                 Arbor, Mich.: Pierian Press, 1982.

Kagan argues that each of Altman's
first ten films is a commentary on
established film genres. In chapter

five, he discusses *McCabe and Mrs. Miller*
(1971) as an "anti-genre" film. The
conventions of the Western are defined in
terms of two John Ford films, *My Darling
Clementine* (1946) and *The Man Who Shot
Liberty Valance* (1962). Kagan then
methodically details *McCabe*, showing how
in both characterization and theme,
Altman's film suggests the opposite of
the two Ford Westerns. Too often,
however, Kagan insists on a point rather
than clearly demonstrating it. And
nothing is presented about the overall
place such an approach deserves in the
history of Western films.

5.20   Kass, Judith M. *Robert Altman, American
             Innovator.* New York: Popular
             Library, 1978.

A film-by-film look at Altman's
career, emphasizing the director's
willingness to experiment with generic
conventions and technical aspects despite
continuing commercial failure. Though
Kass praises both *McCabe and Mrs. Miller*
(1971) and *Buffalo Bill and the Indians,
or Sitting Bull's History Lesson* (1976),
she does little more than illustrate her
basic thesis, that Altman is a dedicated
innovator of American film.

5.21   Kern, Sharon. *William Wyler: A Guide to
             References and Resources.* Boston:
             G.K. Hall and Co., 1984.

Includes a biographical overview,
detailed filmography, annotated bibliography, archival sources, film
distributors and indexes. Of particular
interest in the filmography is information
on 30 little-known Westerns Wyler
directed at Universal between 1925 and
1930, including *Hell's Heroes* (1930),
Universal's first sound A Western and one
of a number of filmed versions of Peter
B. Kyne's novel *The Three Godfathers*.

5.22   Kolker, Robert Phillip. *A Cinema of
            Loneliness*. New York: Oxford
            University Press, 1980.

            Kolker's scrutinization of five
            contemporary filmmakers includes chapters
            on two--Arthur Penn and Robert Altman--
            who have worked in Westerns. "Bloody
            Liberations, Bloody Declines: Arthur
            Penn" (pp. 16-68) pays little attention
            to Penn's *The Left-Handed Gun* (1958), but
            briefly examines *Little Big Man* (1970),
            Kolker claims tries to "undo the
            conventions of the Western by exposing
            them as pompous frauds and inhuman
            gestures." The author's "Radical
            Surfaces: Robert Altman" (pp. 270-339)
            features detailed discussions of *McCabe
            and Mrs. Miller* (1971) and *Buffalo Bill
            and the Indians, or Sitting Bull's
            History Lesson* (1976), which center on
            Altman's explorations of the Western as
            the embodiment of myth-as-history and as
            the representation of the use of economic
            power. Includes brief filmographies.

5.23   Kreidl, John Francis. *Nicholas Ray*.
            Boston: Twayne Publishers, 1977.

            Includes a chapter (pp. 43-59) on
            director Ray's *Johnny Guitar* (1954),
            which Kreidl calls "the archetypal Nick
            Ray film" because of its use of color,
            cutting and pacing and because of its
            anti-McCarthy overtones. The author
            compares the film with *Rebel Without a
            Cause* (1955), claiming that although it
            too is heavily allegorical, *Johnny
            Guitar*'s allegory seems more obviously
            contrived. Includes filmography.

5.24   Madsen, Axel. *John Huston*. Garden City,
            N.Y.: Doubleday and Co., 1978.

            A biography with an emphasis on the
            details surrounding the making of
            Huston's films, rather than on analysis.
            Includes one chapter (pp. 183-190) on the

production of *The Misfits* (1961).
Detailing of other Huston Westerns is
very brief. Includes a Huston filmography, a bibliography and an index.

5.25   Mast, Gerald. *Howard Hawks, Storyteller*.
        New York: Oxford University Press,
        1982.

        The author asserts Hawks' role as
storyteller--telling "good stories"--over
his status as *auteur*. Mast dismisses *Rio
Bravo* (1959) and *El Dorado* (1967) because
of unbelievable characterizations,
especially by Dean Martin and Ricky
Nelson in the former and Robert Mitchum
and James Caan in the latter. Mast
devotes a chapter to *Red River* (1948),
Hawks' "genre epic" which the author
presents as an allegory of historical
transition from one kind of law and
virtue to another. Mast claims the 1948
film parallels Homer's *Odyssey* and the
Old Testament.

5.26   McBride, Joseph. *Hawks on Hawks*.
        Berkeley: University of California
        Press, 1982.

        McBride's book, drawn from nine
separate interviews from between 1970 and
1977, touches briefly on Hawks' career as
a maker of Westerns, including brief
chapters on *Red River* (1948) and Hawks'
unintended trilogy, *Rio Bravo* (1959), *El
Dorado* (1967) and *Rio Lobo* (1970).

5.27   McCarthy, Todd and Charles Flynn,
            eds. *Kings of the Bs: Working
            Within the Hollywood System*. New
            York: E.P. Dutton & Co., Inc., 1975.

        Although this anthology of history
and criticism tends to slight the
Western's role in B moviemaking, *Kings of
the Bs* remains the best and most footnoted volume on the world of B movies.
Skewed toward the editors' interests

(particularly *films noirs* and 1960s exploitation pictures), it tends to treat the Western as a minor category. McCarthy and Flynn's "The Economic Imperative: Why Was the B Movie Necessary?" (pp. 13-43) approaches the B Western as part of a larger system of production. Myron Meisel's "Joseph H. Lewis: Tourist in the Asylum" (pp. 81-104) includes discussion of four Lewis Westerns: *A Lawless Street* (1955), *The Seventh Cavalry* (1956), *The Halliday Brand* (1957) and *Terror in a Texas Town* (1958). The only piece in the anthology that stresses the Western is the editors' interview with Joseph Kane (pp. 313-326), which focuses on Kane's work as director and producer of Republic Westerns.

5.28   McKinney, Doug. *Sam Peckinpah*.   Boston: Twayne Publishers, 1979.

Arguing that few people see Peckinpah's films as he intended them to be seen, McKinney purports to sidestep the director's status as legend and to judge his films within the context of Peckinpah's career development. The author asserts that the director's outlook stresses life's constant ambiguity which, while noting the violence inherent in us all, celebrates the capacity for individual action and the importance of commitment. The first major study of Peckinpah's work to be published, McKinney's book draws heavily from Garner Simmons' 1975 doctoral dissertation on Peckinpah's work in Westerns, which has since been published (see 5.40). Includes selected bibliography and a detailed filmography of the director's work in feature-length films through 1978.

5.29   Naha, Ed. *The Films of Roger Corman: Brilliance on a Budget*.   New York: Arco Publishing, Inc., 1982.

Naha's survey of Corman's films
relies heavily on interviews with Corman
and his proteges for background information. Though its emphasis is on
Corman's philosophy of moviemaking, the
work includes production details from
four Corman Westerns: *Five Guns West,*
Apache Woman, Oklahoma Woman (all 1955)
and *The Gunslinger* (1956).

5.30   Niver, Kemp R. *D.W. Griffith: His*
        Biograph Films in Perspective. Los
        Angeles: Locare Research Group, 1974.

A description with stills of 50 films
directed by D.W. Griffith between 1908
and 1912. Included are four Westerns:
The Redman and the Child (1908), *Money*
Mad (1908), *Iola's Promise* (1912) and *The*
Goddess of Sagebrush Gulch (1912).
Emphasis is on the filming innovations in
each film. Includes credits.

5.31   Plecki, Gerard. *Robert Altman.* Boston:
        Twayne Publishers, 1985.

This general introduction to the
films of Robert Altman includes a chapter
on *McCabe and Mrs. Miller* (1971) and a
portion of another chapter on *Buffalo*
Bill and the Indians, or Sitting Bull's
History Lesson (1976). Plecki argues
that the intent of *McCabe* is to strip the
mythology away from the Western.
Similarly, *Buffalo Bill* is essentially an
exploration between image, legend,
history and show business. Also included
are descriptions of background materials
that relate to the films and details
concerning their productions. The book
includes an annotated bibliography and a
detailed filmography.

5.32   Poague, Leland A. *The Hollywood*
        Professionals: Billy Wilder, Leo
        McCarey. New York: A.S. Barnes and
        Co., 1980.

An extensive examination of the films
of Wilder and McCarey, including
competent filmographies and a detailed
discussion of the latter's *Ruggles of Red
Gap* (1935), which the author argues
stresses the interdependence of individuality and community symbolized by the
newly-tamed American West.

5.33   ———. *Howard Hawks*. Boston: Twayne
              Publishers, 1982.

Poague claims that much of the
criticism of Hawks' work has unduly
emphasized a dichotomy between comedy and
adventure and an overall tragic
worldview. Instead, the author examines
the director's films as the opposite,
stating that "the Hawksian world view is
on the whole a comic one regardless of
genre" and that tragedy results when
characters are forced to reject that
comic view of experience. Poague
includes in his discussion of social
groups and society a detailed examination
of *Red River* (1948), which he argues
offers a range of social models and modes
of capitalism as options, stressing the
importance of trusting in the world and
in others as central to Hawksian
societies. The author employs a brief
analysis of *Rio Bravo* (1959) to illustrate the chief inadequacies of
traditional scholarship of the director's
work. Poague's work, while thought-
provoking and on the whole competent, is
weaker when dealing with Hawks'
non-Western action films.

5.34   Rosenthal, Stuart and Judith M. Kass.
              *The Hollywood Professionals: Tod
              Browning and Don Siegel*. New York:
              A.S. Barnes and Co., 1975.

Kass' account of Siegel's career
emphasizes the conflicts he experienced
with studio personnel and actors, as well
as the director's pessimistic (and

misogynistic) outlook. Includes brief
discussions of three Siegel Westerns,
Duel at Silver Creek (1952), *Death of a
Gunfighter* (1969), and *Two Mules for
Sister Sara* (1970), which plant the films
within the aforementioned context.

5.35   Rosenzweig, Sidney. *"Casablanca" and
            Other Major Films of Michael Curtiz.*
            Ann Arbor: UMI Research Press, 1982.

Includes a chapter on Curtiz's
variations on the swashbuckler, arguing
that *Dodge City* (1939), *Santa Fe Trail*
(1940) and *Virginia City* (1940) borrow
much of their style, structure and
characterization from the Hollywood
swashbuckler tradition in general and
from Curtiz's comic swashbucklers in
particular. At the same time, the author
argues that the three films (in varying
degrees) present the Western genre with a
multiplicity of conflict. The chapter,
"Out West and Other Places: Variations on
the Swashbuckler" (pp. 61-75), is
presented as an afterthought to the
book's chapters on Curtiz's earlier
epics. Although a good beginning,
Rosenzweig treats the chapter as if it is
an unfortunately necessary detour.

5.36   Sarris, Andrew. *The John Ford Movie
            Mystery.* Bloomington: Indiana
            University Press, 1975.

Sarris argues that the paradoxes that
critics find in the work of John Ford can
be answered in part by putting the
director's work into the context of
Hollywood moviemaking in general. The
author claims that Ford's work in
Westerns, though within a set of consistent traditions, came to define the
popular understanding of the genre;
Stagecoach (1939), in particular, seems
in its context more the beginning than
the summing up of a tradition. The
inconsistencies between Ford's early

Westerns and those made after 1947,
Sarris argues, stem from the director's
abandonment of "the Tradition of Quality
for a Cult of Personality." Despite the
author's penchant for epithets (Sarris,
for example, calls *The Searchers* a
"lived-in epic"), his analysis puts
Ford's Westerns into the context of both
his career and his world.

5.37   Schickel, Richard. *The Men Who Made the
            Movies.* New York: Atheneum, 1975.

A book interviews of film directors
based on a documentary series Schickel
prepared for public television. Comments
by Howard Hawks, King Vidor, Raoul Walsh
and William A. Wellman include references
to Westerns.

5.38   Seydor, Paul. *Peckinpah: The Western
            Films.* Urbana: University of
            Illinois Press, 1980.

Seydor's critical study of director
Sam Peckinpah's work in Westerns includes
in-depth analyses of six films Westerns:
The Deadly Companions (1961), *Ride the
High Country* (1962), *Major Dundee* (1965),
The Wild Bunch (1969), *The Ballad of
Cable Hogue* (1970) and *Pat Garrett and
Billy the Kid* (1973). Seydor attempts to
place the director's TV and movie
Westerns in conjunction with the major
influences on and sources for Peckinpah's
overall *oeuvre*, while placing his
approach to major themes and conventions
within generic traditions. The author
argues that much of the director's
expressive individualism is linked to an
American tradition of radical thought and
freedom which dates back to the early
nineteenth century. A long, appreciative
analysis of *The Wild Bunch* (1969) is the
most thorough yet published and is the
highlight of the book. Includes
selective filmography and bibliography.

5.39 Shores, Edward. *George Roy Hill.*
    Boston: Twayne Publishers, 1983.

    Part of the Twayne filmmakers series,
this slim volume includes a chapter on
Butch Cassidy and the Sundance Kid (1969)
which argues that Hill uses the Western
genre to illuminate tensions between the
self-conscious "hero" and technological
society. Examples are drawn from the
film to support the author's contention
that Hill finds individuality an
outmoded, weakened stance. In addition
to this chapter, *Butch Cassidy and the
Sundance Kid* is also placed within the
development of Hill's *oeuvre*--
chronologically, stylistically and
thematically. For another study of *Butch
Cassidy* within a context of Hill's other
films, see 5.18.

5.40 Simmons, Garner. *Peckinpah: A Portrait
    in Montage.* Austin: University of
    Texas Press, 1982.

    The author presents the controversial
writer-director's life story (which
concludes before his death) through
production histories of his work in film
and television. Simmons' extensive
reliance on first-person interviews,
ranging from Peckinpah to Don Siegel to
Ben Johnson to studio officials, gives
the work a sense of objectivity. The
director's tradition of conflict with
producers is presented from both sides;
the catastrophic battles surrounding
Major Dundee (1965), for example, are
treated thoroughly and without blame on
either side. Simmons also offers useful
information coming from the director
himself. Though the work stresses
Peckinpah's Westerns, it focuses on
Peckinpah as moviemaker, not as Western
filmmaker.

5.41 Sinclair, Andrew. *John Ford.* New York:
    The Dial Press/James Wade, 1979.

Sinclair's biography of the director is smitten with Ford's legend as the cinematic purveyor of truth about the American West, and the author's analysis is skewed to Ford's mythic status. Still, despite occasional inaccuracies, Sinclair's examination of the director's career does feature some useful insights, including the relationship between *Stagecoach* (1939) and the death of Tom Mix, and the disillusionment Ford experienced while shooting his last "cycle" of Westerns: *The Horse Soldiers* (1959), *Sergeant Rutledge* (1960), *Two Rode Together* (1961) and *The Man Who Shot Liberty Valance* (1962). The book features more than 80 pictures, most of them production stills from Ford's films, and a complete filmography.

5.42   Spoto, Donald. *Stanley Kramer, Film Maker*. New York: G.P. Putnam's Sons, 1978.

This chapter-by-chapter discussion of producer-director Kramer's productions include a brief chapter each on Kramer's two Westerns: *High Noon* (1952) and *Invitation to a Gunfighter* (1964). Emphasis is on production background and evaluation. Analysis is superficial. The book also includes a Kramer filmography and an index.

5.43   Taylor, William R. *Sydney Pollack*. Boston: Twayne Publishers, 1981.

An overview of director Pollack's work through the end of the 1970s. Chapters are structured according to theme rather than according to specific films, which is often the case in the Twayne series. Chapters include a discussion of the visual qualities of Pollack's films, Pollack's images of men, women and villains and the director's "search for an American tradition." References to most of Pollack's films

appear in each chapter, including his
three Westerns: *The Scalphunters* (1968),
Jeremiah Johnson (1972) and *The Electric
Horseman* (1979). The last chapter is an
analysis of *The Electric Horseman* as a
film which incorporates all of Pollack's
visual and thematic preoccupations.
Includes a very brief bibliography, a
filmography and an index.

5.44   Thompson, Frank, ed. *Between Action and
         Cut: Five American Directors.*
         Metuchen, N.J.: The Scarecrow Press,
         Inc., 1985.

Chronological profiles of contract
directors ignored or forgotten in *auteur*
criticism features chapters on three
whose careers included work in the
Western genre: Victor Fleming (5.78),
William K. Howard and Charles T. Barton
(5.135). Also features a separate
filmography section.

5.45   ———. *William A. Wellman.* Metuchen,
         N.J.: The Scarecrow Press, Inc.,
         1983.

A biographical overview of the long
career of one of Hollywood's best action
directors. Emphasis is on details
concerning the actual productions of the
films themselves. Critical or analytical
commentary on the films, including
Westerns, is quite brief. Includes brief
bibliography.

5.46   Tuska, Jon, Vicki Piekarski and Karl
         Thiede, ed. *Close Up: The Contract
         Director.* Metuchen, N.J.: The
         Scarecrow Press, Inc., 1976.

An anthology of career overviews of
ten directors whose careers covered the
studio years of the 1930s and 1940s, nine
of whom worked in Westerns: H. Bruce
"Lucky" Humberstone, William Dieterle,
Joseph Kane (5.124), William Witney,

Lesley Selander, Yakima Canutt (5.144),
Edward Dmytryk and Howard Hawks (5.141).
Each essay, based primarily on first-
person interviews, features a brief
filmography.

5.47   Tuska, Jon, Vicki Piekarski and David
                 Wilson, ed. *Close-Up: The Hollywood
                 Director*. Metuchen, N.J.: The
                 Scarecrow Press, Inc., 1978.

An anthology of career overviews of
nine feature directors, including five
who worked in Westerns: Henry King,
Spencer Gordon Bennet (5.143), William
Wyler, William Wellman and John Huston.
Each essay, based on first-person
interviews, features a film checklist.

5.48   ————. *Close-Up: The Contemporary
                 Director*. Metuchen, N.J.: The
                 Scarecrow Press, Inc., 1981.

An anthology of career overviews of
ten contemporary directors, five of whom
have directed notable Westerns: Sydney
Pollack, Sam Fuller, Sam Peckinpah
(5.142), George Roy Hill and Robert
Altman. Included with each essay is a
brief filmography.

5.49   Wagenknecht, Edward and Anthony Slide.
                 The Films of D.W. Griffith. New
                 York: Crown Publishers, Inc., 1975.

The first chapter of this lavishly
illustrated book traces Griffith's one-
and two-reel films for Biograph (pp.
1-26). Included are brief comments about
Griffith's Westerns, his Indian pictures
and brief descriptions of several
Westerns, including *The Massacre* (1912)
and *The Battle at Elderbush Gulch* (1913),
the *Gulch* section a reprint from Slide's
Early American Cinema (2.16). Also
includes a two-page description with
photos of *Gulch* from *The Biograph*, the
company's selling catalogue. Includes an

appendix listing all films directed by
Griffith.

5.50   Walsh, Raoul. *Each Man In His Time.* New
York: Farrar, Straus and Giroux,
1974.

An anecdotal autobiography of a
Hollywood director whose career spanned
fifty years. Walsh's best work was on
action films, including a large number of
Westerns. The book makes no attempt at
analysis of any of his films, but Walsh
details amusing stories about the making
of such famous Westerns as *In Old Arizona*
(1929), *The Big Trail* (1930), *Colorado
Territory* (1949) and *The Tall Men* (1955).

5.51   Wellman, William A. *A Short Time for
Insanity.* New York: Hawthorn Books,
Inc., 1974.

A free-form autobiography of the
well-known director written as a set of
stream-of-consciousness memories while
Wellman was drugged on pain pills. The
writing is vigorous and anecdotal, and
seems to capture the spirit of the man.
References to the Westerns directed by
Wellman are interspersed throughout the
text, but unfortunately tend to be brief
and of minimal use.

5.52   Willis, Donald C. *The Films of Howard
Hawks.* Metuchen, N.J.: The
Scarecrow Press, Inc., 1975.

A study of the films directed by
Hawks considered on a film-by-film basis.
Part II of the book (pp. 41-72) discusses
each of Hawks' five Westerns. Willis is
perceptive when describing Hawks' *mise
en scene*, but gives little attention to
analyzing thematic materials in the
films. Most of the short chapters are
devoted to evaluation. Willis seems
mainly interested in defending his own
opinions about the performers and the

characters and in arguing with the
evaluative comments of other critics.
This may be entertaining for Hawks' fans,
but it contributes little to either our
appreciation or our knowledge of the
films. The book also includes an
interview with Hawks, a filmography and
an index.

5.53   Wood, Robin. *Hollywood from Vietnam to*
                Reagan. New York: Columbia
                University Press, 1986.

Wood's provocative and insightful
essays on movies in the 1970s and 1980s
includes a chapter on "Two Films by
Michael Cimino" (pp. 270-317). Focusing
his analytic attention on *The Deer Hunter*
(1979) and *Heaven's Gate* (1980), Wood
argues that director Cimino "has
established himself decisively as one of
the American cinema's great architects
and as one of its most authentic formal
innovators." He blames the assault of
Heaven's Gate on critics' and audiences'
unwillingness to accept genuine inno-
vation in Hollywood filmmaking. Wood's
study of Cimino's cinematic reworking of
the Johnson County War uses both the
three-hour, forty-minute and two-and-a-
half-hour versions of the film to
underline its complex design of
immersion, contemplation and reassessment
of actions and subsequent events.

5.54   ————. *Howard Hawks*. London: British
                Film Institute, revised edition,
                1981.

A reissue of Wood's 1968 study of
Hawks' films, in which he places the
director's Westerns within the recurring
thematic framework of Hawks' overall
oeuvre. Although the author keeps intact
his detailed discussions of *Rio Bravo*
(1959), *El Dorado* (1967), *The Big Sky*
(1952) and *Red River* (1948), Wood adds a
chapter of minor revisions made in the

light of changing critical considerations
and changes in the author's personal
perspective; the bulk of these are
complementary rather than contradictory.

5.55   Zucker, Joel S. *Arthur Penn: A Guide to
       References and Resources.* Boston:
       G.K. Hall and Co., 1980.

The core of this useful volume is a
chronologically arranged, 700-item guide
to material about Penn and his work.
Citations for publications in French,
English and Italian are annotated;
material in other languages is merely
listed. Zucker begins the book with a
biography and short critical essay on
Penn's work. In addition to a filmography, he lists reviews of Penn's film
and television efforts.

Articles

5.56   Anderson, Lindsay. "The Method of John
       Ford." *The Emergence of Film Art*,
       ed. Lewis Jacobs. New York: W.W.
       Norton & Company, second edition,
       1979, pp. 230-245.

Anderson, in an essay first published
in *Sequence* (Summer 1950), claims that
Ford's late 1940s work is marked by
"sadly wasteful impatience and lack of
care" which mar the director's overall
contribution to film. Anderson's
discussion includes mention of Ford's
silent Westerns and postwar cavalry
films.

5.57   Appelbaum, Ralph. "Making 'The
       Shootist': An Interview with Don
       Siegel." *Filmmakers Newsletter*, 9
       (October 1976), 28-32.

This interview with director Siegel
emphasizes his background in Westerns.
Production history includes discussion of

actual shooting, editing and shooting on
location.

5.58   Bobrow, Andrew C. *"Hearts of the West*:
        An Interview with Director Howard
        Zieff." *Filmmakers Newsletter*, 9:1
        (November 1975), 27-31.

        This interview touches on Zieff's
        entire career, but centers on his then
        current *Hearts of the West*, a gentle
        comedy about the making of B Westerns
        during the 1930s.

5.59   Bodeen, DeWitt. "Raoul Walsh." *Films in
        Review*, 33:4 (April 1982), 205-219,
        252.

        Walsh directed a number of Westerns
        in a career that lasted from 1913 to
        1964. Walsh's early career, before 1939,
        is given the most attention in this
        typically "talky" and anecdotal article,
        which is followed by a useful filmo-
        graphy.

5.60   Bogdanovich, Peter. "The Cowboy Hero and
        the American West ... as Directed by
        John Ford." *Esquire*, 100:6 (December
        1983), 417-420, 423-425.

        Bogdanovich's affectionate profile of
        Ford is featured in *Esquire*'s "50 Who
        Made the Difference" issue. Bogdanovich
        stresses Ford's importance to the Western
        film genre, but focuses on anecdotal
        history of the director's life and
        worldview.

5.61   Broeski, Pat. "Walter Hill." *Films in
        Review*, 32:10 (December 1981),
        609-612.

        Although this short article is based
        on an interview with Hill about *Southern
        Comfort* (1982), it also contains some
        comments about *The Long Riders* (1980),
        Hill's only Western.

5.62   Budd, Michael. "Genre, Director and
           Stars in John Ford's Westerns: Fonda,
           Wayne, Stewart and Widmark." *Wide
           Angle*, 2:4 (1978), 52-61.

           An attempt to "show how the changes
    in star characterizations are integral to
    the changes in Ford's Westerns
    generally." According to Budd, the line
    of heroic personas moving from Henry
    Fonda to John Wayne to James Stewart and
    finally to Richard Widmark parallels a
    development in Ford's Western heroes from
    heroic isolation to complex solipsism to
    a sociable diminishment of heroic
    qualities to alienated ineffectuality.
    This argument might have been more
    effective if the star personas of the
    four actors had been considered outside
    of Ford's Westerns, which they are not.
    Nevertheless, the persona speculations
    enable Budd to structure a useful
    perspective on the evolution of Ford's
    heroes. The article is part of a special
    issue of *Wide Angle* devoted to the films
    of John Ford.

5.63   ————. "A Home in the Wilderness:
           Visual Imagery in John Ford's
           Westerns." *Cinema Journal*, 16:1
           (1976), 62-75.

           An analysis of visual motifs
    appearing in *Straight Shooting* (1917) and
    all of Ford's sound Westerns, which
    illustrates thematic oppositions between
    wilderness and civilization. Special
    attention is given to Ford's use of door-
    ways, porches and shadings of light and
    dark. *My Darling Clementine* (1946) and
    The Searchers (1956) receive the most
    detailed attention. Although Budd does
    not reach any original conclusions about
    Ford's thematic preoccupations, his essay
    presents a thorough and convincing
    argument about how Ford's films present
    those preoccupations in visual terms.
    The article suffers from a lack of frame

enlargements or stills to accompany the
analysis, but Budd's ability to richly
detail specific moments in the films
nearly replaces the need for visuals.

5.64   Byron, Stuart and Terry Curtis Fox.
            "What is a Western?" *Film Comment*,
            12:4 (July/August 1976), 37-40,
            42-43.

            An interview with director Arthur
            Penn, mostly about his 1976 Western, *The
            Missouri Breaks*. Penn describes the
            making of the film, what he believes the
            film means and the place of the film in
            his overall career.

5.65   Combs, Richard. "Playing the Game, or
            Robert Altman and the Indians."
            Sight and Sound, 48 (Summer 1979),
            136-140.

            An examination of Altman's *Quintet*
            (1977), arguing that the film allows for
            different readings of the director's
            earlier movies, including *Buffalo Bill
            and the Indians, or Sitting Bull's
            History Lesson* (1976). In the Western,
            Combs says, it points to the Indians as a
            "wistful function of Altman's failure to
            reconcile the interior with the exterior
            of his role as public entertainer."

5.66   Coursen, David and Michael Dempsey.
            "John Ford: Assessing the Reassess-
            ment." *Film Quarterly*, 29 (Spring
            1976), 58-62.

            Coursen dismisses Michael Dempsey's
            dressing-down of Ford's filmic vision
            (see 5.68), claiming that factual
            mistakes and facile reasoning cripple
            Dempsey's contentions that Ford's
            sentimentality weakens his intended
            message. Dempsey issues a brief reply,
            reasserting his earlier position.

5.67   Dempsey, Michael. "Invaders and

Encampments: The Films of Philip
Kaufman." *Film Quarterly*, 32:2
(Winter 1978-79), 17-27.

A film-by-film analysis of the five
films Kaufman has directed through 1976,
including his Western about the James-
Younger gang, *The Great Northfield,
Minnesota Raid* (1972). Dempsey perceives
Raid as a comic, "bemused, undoctrinaire
exploration of America's craziest
contradictions." Also includes brief
comments about Kaufman's script for *The
Outlaw Josey Wales* (1976).

5.68   ————. "John Ford: A Reassessment."
Film Quarterly, 28 (Summer 1975),
2-15.

Dempsey claims that at his worst,
John Ford lays his sentiments on too
thickly; the result is visually stunning
but vacuous. This tendency, the author
argues, is not in all but is in too many
of Ford's works. Dempsey's claims are
refuted by David Coursen in the
subsequent volume of *Film Quarterly* (see
5.66).

5.69   "Dialogue on Film: Alan J. Pakula."
American Film, 4:3 (December-January
1979), 33-44.

The director discusses his career as
a director, focusing briefly on *Comes a
Horseman* (1978), categorizing it as one
of his "work" films (along with *Klute* and
All the President's Men).

5.70   "Dialogue on Film: Sydney Pollack."
American Film, 3 (April 1978), 33-48.

Interview with Pollack emphasizes the
director's approach to visual aspects of
his films. Includes a discussion of his
use of shot composition in *Jeremiah
Johnson* (1972).

5.71   Durgnat, Raymond. "Durgnat vs. Paul."
              Film Comment, 14:2 (March-April
              1978), 64-66, 68.

              The final installment of a debate on
            Howard Hawks' status as an *auteur* (see
            5.72 and 5.112).

5.72   ————. "Hawks Isn't Good Enough." *Film
              Comment*, 13:4 (July-August 1977),
              8-19.

              Howard Hawks as an *auteur* has been
            lionized during the last quarter-century
            as one of a handful of great American
            directors. Durgnat confronts this
            reputation and concludes that Hawks does
            not deserve his exalted status in the
            *auteur*ist pantheon. Primarily by
            comparing scenes from certain Hawks films
            with parallel scenes in other movies,
            Durgnat argues that Hawks cannot authen-
            tically present human emotion, that he is
            archaic in his attitudes toward men
            devoted to their work and that Hawks is
            uninterested in presenting the female
            aspects of women. Included in the
            examples detailed are *Red River* (1948),
            The Big Sky (1951) and *Rio Bravo* (1959).
            Whether one agrees with Durgnat depends
            on one's enthusiasm for Hawks' films.
            Durgnat's arguments are persuasive,
            however, and he thereby nicely balances
            much of the gushing praise that
            characterizes most Hawks criticism. For
            a rebuttal of this article, see the
            comments by William Paul (5.112).

5.73   Ellis, Kirk. "On the Warpath: John Ford
              and the Indians." *Journal of Popular
              Film and Television*, 8:2 (1980),
              34-41.

              Argues against the prevalent critical
            opinion that John Ford's Westerns
            featuring American Indians reveal a
            racist mentality. Although a number of
            the films reveal a paternalistic attitude

toward Native Americans, the Indians in
Ford's Westerns are invariably dignified,
skilled and free as well as "savage."
Ellis gives special attention to *The
Searchers* (1956) which, he argues, is a
study of racism as pathology. For a
similar perspective discussed in more
detail, see Tag Gallagher's *John Ford:
The Man and His Films* (5.14).

5.74   Erens, Patricia. "Sydney Pollack." *Film
            Reader*, 1 (1975), 100-104.

The key issues in director Pollack's
work, argues Erens, are the question of
individual responsibility and the
conflict between cultural antagonists.
Interesting analysis of Pollack's films,
though attention to *The Scalphunters*
(1968) and *Jeremiah Johnson* (1972) is not
detailed.

5.75   ─────. "Sydney Pollack: The Way We
            Are." *Film Comment*, 11 (September-
            October 1975), 24-29.

Interview with director Pollack
includes mention of the major themes and
uses of color in Pollack's work,
including *Jeremiah Johnson* (1972).
Pollack discusses the importance of
individual choices in *Jeremiah Johnson*,
and how that theme affected an alternative ending for the film. Article
includes a shorter interview with Robert
Redford, who discusses acting and working
with Pollack on *Jeremiah Johnson* and
other films.

5.76   Eyman, Scott. "I Made Movies: Scott
            Eyman Interviews Henry Hathaway."
            Take One, 5:1 (September-October
            1974), 6-12.

After a laudatory introduction, Eyman
presents his interview with Hathaway as a
monologue, the first part autobiographical and the second part comments

structured around specific films Hathaway
directed. Included in Hathaway's salty
and blunt comments are opinions about a
number of Western performers and remarks
about the making of six of his Westerns.

5.77   Florence, William. "John Ford ... the
            Duke, and Monument Valley." *Arizona
            Highways*, 57 (September 1981), 22-37.

            A description of Monument Valley and
its use in the nine Westerns shot there
by John Ford. Emphasis is on how
Monument Valley was brought to Ford's
attention in 1939 by Valley resident
Harry Goulding. Includes 17 photos of
Monument Valley itself and Ford's films.
The article is weakened somewhat by
several factual errors.

5.78   Gallagher, John A. "Victor Fleming."
            *Between Action and Cut: Five American
            Directors*, ed. Frank Thompson.
            Metuchen, N.J.: The Scarecrow Press,
            Inc., 1985, pp. 6-68.

            Gallagher's profile of Fleming's
career as a contract director pays slight
attention to the director's work on
several silent Westerns, but discusses
little more than tidbits of technical
background on his work on *The Virginian*
(1929), even though Gallagher calls the
film starring Gary Cooper the definitive
screen version of Owen Wister's novel. A
separate filmography (pp. 219-245) is
more useful.

5.79   ————. "William Wellman." *Films in
            Review*, 33:5 (May 1982), 275-298;
            33:6 (June-July 1982), 322-333.

            The author considers Wellman the
director of the first "adult" Western,
The Ox-Bow Incident (1943). Part I
discusses Wellman's personal life as well
as his early career in filmmaking before
his 1923 directorial debut with the

Western *The Man Who Won*. A filmography
is included which lists his acting,
writing and directing credits until 1937.
The second installment chronicles
Wellman's career from 1938 to 1958.
Anecdotes about his work until his death
in 1975 are followed by a filmography for
this period, in which he made a number of
Westerns, including *The Ox-Bow Incident*,
Yellow Sky (1948), *Buffalo Bill* (1944)
and *Westward the Women* (1951).

5.80   Gallagher, John and John Hane. "Penn's
        Westerns." *Films in Review*, 35:7
        (August 1983), 414-427.

        Focusing on *The Left-Handed Gun*
(1958), *Little Big Man* (1970) and *The
Missouri Breaks* (1976) within a context
of *auteur*ism and genre-specific
conventions, authors argue that Penn's
very "contemporary" concerns are
expressed in Western stories about social
outcasts.

5.81   Gallagher, Tag. "Acting for John Ford."
        American Film, 11 (March 1986), 16,
        18, 20.

        The article delivers a brief
recounting of Ford's dealings with actors
and approaches to acting in general.
Includes anecdotal material on *Rio Grande*
(1950) and *The Searchers* (1956).
Excerpted from author's book, *John Ford:
The Man and His Films* (5.14).

5.82   ————. "Brother Feeney." *Film Comment*,
        12:6 (November/December 1976), 12-18.

        A description of the film career of
Francis Ford, John Ford's older brother.
Of particular interest in the first half
of the article is a discussion of
Francis' early years in film as a
director-star of Westerns for Thomas
Ince's Bison studio and for Carl
Laemmle's Universal in 1912 and 1913.

Gallagher argues that these early one-,
two- and three-reel Westerns were
recognized as the best of their era.

5.83   Greco, Mike. "Hard Riding." *Film
            Comment*, 16:3 (May/June 1980), 13-19.

An interview with director Walter
Hill. The first third of the discussion
is about Hill's 1980 film, *The Long
Riders*.

5.84   ————. "Memories of a Texas Childhood."
            American Film, 6:8 (June 1981),
            25-30.

Interview article with Austin
screenwriter Bill Wittliff, stressing his
interest in preserving and presenting
stories and characters of Texas.
Emphasis is on Wittliff's conflicts with
mainstream Hollywood, but also discusses
filmmaking relationship with singer-actor
Willie Nelson, which resulted in
Barbarossa (1980) and an in-progress *Red
Headed Stranger* (1986).

5.85   Handzo, Stephen. "Going Through the
            Devil's Doorway: the Early Westerns
            of Anthony Mann." *Bright Lights*, 1:4
            (Summer 1976), 4-15.

Argues that the post-World War II
Western abandoned the classical Western
of winning the West in favor of "the
losing" of the West, a darker commentary
on American history, and that this change
was spearheaded by director Anthony Mann
in three 1950 Westerns: *The Devil's
Doorway*, *Winchester 73* and *The Furies*.
Contributing to the darker vision of the
West in the three films are stylistic
techniques Mann has used earlier in
several *films noirs* and scripts which
emphasized characters dominated by
uncontrollable compulsions. Most of the
essay is devoted to a detailed analysis
of *The Devil's Doorway*, which Handzo

describes as unique because it questions
the ideal of Manifest Destiny by
"portraying the colonization of the West
from the point of view of the defeated
before the doom of the Indian was
sealed." This is an excellent introduction to Mann's Westerns, showing both
how they fit into Mann's creative
development and how they relate to the
overall history of Westerns.

5.86   Howze, William. "John Ford's Celluloid
            Canvas." *Southwest Media Review*, 3
            (Spring 1985), 20-25.

        An interesting, avowedly preliminary,
examination of connections between John
Ford's *mise en scene* and representations
of both the East and West in paintings by
such artists as Frederick Remington,
William Sydney Mount and Currier and
Ives. Article appears in special issue
of *Southwest Media Review* entitled "Texas
Myth in Film."

5.87   Humphries, Reynold. "The Function of
            Mexico in Peckinpah's Films." *Jump
            Cut*, no. 18 (August 1978), 17-20.

        An analysis of three films directed
by Sam Peckinpah: *Major Dundee* (1964),
The Wild Bunch (1969) and *Bring Me the
Head of Alfredo Garcia* (1974). Humphries
concludes that all three films celebrate
heroic individualism and in doing so they
mask and distort the historical, political and ideological problems of the
United States' relationship with Mexico.
This distortion was not necessarily
conscious on Peckinpah's part, but
represents a general tendency to glorify
individualism within the film medium
itself and within the dominant ideology
of American culture of which Peckinpah is
a participant. This Marxist critique
refuses to allow for irony in the films,
and thus Humphries' comments about
certain scenes in the films seem somewhat

short-sighted. The overall thesis,
however, is well demonstrated by the
accumulated evidence.

5.88   Ince, Thomas H.   "The Early Days at Kay
            Bee." *Hollywood Directors 1914-1940*,
            ed. Richard Koszarski. New York:
            Oxford University Press, 1976, pp.
            62-70.

            A reprint of a March 1919 article in
            Photoplay Magazine, in which the great
            producer recalls the performers who
            worked for him in the first years of
            Hollywood production and recalls details
            about the production of the first
            two-reel Westerns.

5.89   Jameson, Richard T., ed.   "Sam
            Peckinpah." *Film Comment*, 17:1
            (January/February 1981), 33-48.

            This "Midsection" of *Film Comment*
            devoted to Peckinpah's overall body of
            films includes a section on Peckinpah's
            skills as an editor, interviews with two
            regular performers in Peckinpah's films
            (Strother Martin and Warren Oates) and
            analyses of *The Ballad of Cable Hogue*
            (1970) and *Bring Me the Head of Alfredo
            Garcia* (1974).

5.90   Kaminsky, Stuart M.   "The Genre
            Director." *American Film Genres*.
            Chicago: Nelson-Hall Inc., second
            edition, 1985, pp. 171-224.

            Kaminsky's exploration of genre in
            popular filmmaking includes three
            chapters on genre directors, each of whom
            has important work in Westerns.
            Discussing Don Siegel (pp. 171-200), the
            author argues that the director's films
            share cross-genre similarities,
            particularly the emphasis on social and
            emotional schizophrenia. Kaminsky
            asserts that what makes John Ford's
            Westerns (pp. 201-211) so distinctive is

the director's mastery of character type.
In a chapter about Sergio Leone's films
(pp. 213-224), Kaminsky claims the
Italian director's Westerns are comic
nightmares about existence (see 9.4).

5.91   Kloman, Harry and Lloyd Michaels, ed.
        "'A Foolish Optimist': Interview with
        Robert Altman." *Film Criticism*, 7
        (Spring 1983), 20-28.

    This interview with Robert Altman
focuses on the director's technical
handling of and personal approach to
making movies. Contains interesting
anecdotal material about the making of
Altman's two Westerns, *McCabe and Mrs.
Miller* (1971) and *Buffalo Bill and the
Indians, or Sitting Bull's History
Lesson* (1976).

5.92   Lehman, Peter. "An Absence Which Becomes
        a Legendary Presence: John Ford's
        Structured Use of Off-Screen Space."
        Wide Angle, 2:4 (1978), 36-42.

    Argues that film critics should pay
more attention to what is out of the
frame in John Ford's films. To illustrate this thesis, Lehman discusses
off-screen space in three Ford Westerns.
In *The Man Who Shot Liberty Valance*
(1962), the fury of Valance is emphasized
by his entry shots from outside the
frame. In *She Wore a Yellow Ribbon*
(1949), characters staring at an off-
screen Nathan Brittles, emphasizing
Brittles' legendary status. In *The
Searchers* (1956), characters looking
off-screen give added emphasis to the
search for meaning that is central to the
film. Includes 15 frame enlargements.
The article is part of a special issue of
Wide Angle devoted to the films of John
Ford.

5.93   ————. "Howard Hawks: A Private
        Interview." *Wide Angle*, 1:2 (Summer

1976), 28-57.

This rather disconnected interview over the entire body of Hawks' films includes some brief comments about *Red River* (1948), *Rio Bravo* (1959) and *El Dorado* (1967), as well as Hawks' opinions about a number of Westerns made by other directors.

5.94   Lightman, Herb A. "The Film That Took on a Life of Its Own." *American Cinematographer*, 51:11 (November 1980), 1114-1117, 1168-1169, 1181-1188.

This interview with director Michael Cimino stresses the technical aspects of making *Heaven's Gate* (1980), particularly location difficulties and Cimino's unending struggle with studio-enforced deadlines. Considering the almost mythic level of disdain heaped on the film, Cimino's prerelease comments are surprisingly optimistic. The detail-filled interview is featured in an issue of *American Cinematographer* devoted primarily to *Heaven's Gate*.

5.95   Luhr, William. "Howard Hawks: Hawksthief. Patterns of Continuity in *Rio Bravo*, *El Dorado* and *Rio Lobo*." *Wide Angle*, 1:2 (Summer 1976), 10-20.

Luhr demonstrates that although Hawks' *Rio Bravo* (1959), *El Dorado* (1967) and *Rio Lobo* (1970) appear to be repetitious in plot, characters and scenes, a closer examination shows they are essentially different from one another. The thesis is an interesting rebuttal of the critical consensus that emphasizes parallels between the three Westerns. The article is part of a special issue of *Wide Angle* devoted to Howard Hawks and his films.

5.96   Macklin, F. Anthony. "'The Artist and
            the Multitude Are Natural Enemies':
            An Interview with Director Robert
            Altman." *Film Heritage*, 12 (Winter
            1976-77), 1-23.

            Interview with Altman focuses on the
            director's approach to filmmaking and his
            problems in production and at the box
            office. Includes intermittant discussion
            of *Buffalo Bill and the Indians, or
            Sitting Bull's History Lesson* (1976).

5.97   ————. "'Mort Sahl Called Me a 1939
            American': An Interview with Director
            Sam Peckinpah." *Film Heritage*, 11:4
            (Summer 1976), 12-26.

            A loose, rambling interview mainly
            characterized by the ego and cynicism of
            both Peckinpah and Macklin. Of some
            interest is Peckinpah's comments on how
            he believes John Ford's last Westerns
            were failures.

5.98   Marill, Alvin H. "The Films of John
            Huston." *Films in Review*, 36:4
            (April 1985), 215-220.

            A filmography of Huston's work in
            films as a writer, director and actor.
            Includes credits of seven Westerns.

5.99   Mate, Ken and Pat McGilligan. "Burnett."
            Film Comment, 19:1 (January/February
            1983), 58-68, 70.

            Writer W.R. Burnett is best known as
            a crime novelist who wrote *Little Caesar*
            and *The Asphalt Jungle*. Burnett,
            however, wrote the stories and/or screen-
            plays for a number of Westerns as well.
            This anecdotal interview with Burnett
            includes comments about *Law and Order*
            (1932), *The Westerner* (1940) and
            Sergeants 3 (1962). Also included is a
            Burnett filmography.

5.100   McBride, Joseph. "Bringing in the
             Sheaves." *Sight and Sound*, 43:1
             (Winter 1973/74), 9-11.

             On the occasion of John Ford's
             funeral in Los Angeles, the author
             discusses the director's last days.

5.101   McBride, Joseph and Gerald Perry. "Hawks
             Talks: New Anecdotes from an Old
             Master." *Film Comment*, 10:3
             (May/June 1974), 44-53.

             A lengthy interview with Howard Hawks
             during which the director tells stories
             about making his movies and explains his
             attitudes about filmmaking. Includes
             incidental comments about Hawks' four
             Westerns. Of special interest is Hawks'
             detailed answer to the negative comments
             writer Borden Chase made about Hawks and
             the making of *Red River* (1948) (see I,
             5.57). Much of this interview was later
             incorporated into McBride's *Hawks on
             Hawks* (5.26).

5.102   McCarthy, Todd. "John Ford and Monument
             Valley." *American Film*, 3 (May
             1978), 10-16.

             An account of how valley resident
             Harry Goulding led Ford to Monument
             Valley as a shooting locale in the late
             1930s. Detailing the growing icono-
             graphic value of the site, McCarthy
             traces the history of Monument Valley as
             well as its use in Ford's work and in the
             work of others.

5.103   McNiven, Roger. "The Western Landscape
             of Raoul Walsh." *Velvet Light Trap*,
             15 (Fall 1975), 50-55.

             Insightful essay on Walsh's manipu-
             lation of traditionally vast Western
             landscapes for non-traditional purposes.
             Argues that Walsh's landscape is "anti-
             phenomenological," outside the realm of

human presence and therefore all the more
powerful, challenging individuals in
metaphysical ways, as evidenced by the
predominance of "mission" stories in
Walsh's Westerns.

5.104   Miller, Mark Crispin. "In Defense of Sam
          Peckinpah." *Film Quarterly*, 28
          (Spring 1975), 2-17.

          Defending *Bring Me the Head of
          Alfredo Garcia* (1974), Miller argues that
          Peckinpah "cherishes the things we call
          life-affirming." The author discusses
          Ride the High Country (1962) and *The Wild
          Bunch* (1969), asserting the director's
          belief in family and in place, and
          claiming that it is cynicism that leads
          to his highly stylized treatment of
          violence.

5.105   Milne, Tom and Richard Combs. "Kid Blue
          Rides Again." *Film Comment*, 12:1
          (January/February 1976), 54-58.

          An interview with British actor-
          director James Frawley. Most of the
          interview deals with the techniques used
          in and the thematic content of Frawley's
          unusual Western, *Kid Blue* (1973).
          Frawley emphasizes that he intended the
          film to be a satire of traditional
          Westerns and a critical commentary on
          modern America.

5.106   Missiaen, Jean-Claude. "Anthony Mann."
          Trans. Martyn Auty. *Framework*, nos.
          15-17 (Summer 1981), 17-20.

          A 1967 *Cahiers du Cinema* interview
          with Mann, usually limited to anecdotal
          paragraphs on the most important and
          controversial of the director's films,
          including most of his Westerns.

5.107   Mitry, Jean. "Thomas H. Ince: His
          Esthetic, His Films, His Legacy."
          Trans. Martin Sopory with Paul

Attallah. *Cinema Journal*, 22 (Winter
1983), 2-25.

The French film historian presents
Ince as a filmmaker whose aesthetic was
based on finding an equilibrium between
form and content, using plot construction
to expand the movie medium beyond the
constructs of theatrical presentation.
Mitry claims that the producer-director's
Westerns were unlike the majority of his
other works; instead of stressing social
conflict, Ince's Western films serve as
narrative poems, stressing the role of
the geographical and social environments
and reducing drama to "desperate
idealism" and "stark savagery." Included
in this discussion are descriptions of
The Passing of Two-Gun Hicks (1914), *The
Taking of Luke McVane* (1915) and *The
Aryan* (1916), all featuring William S.
Hart. The article also includes a useful
filmography of those of Ince's works that
are still accessible.

5.108   Montgomery, Patrick. "Raoul Walsh Talks
         About D.W. Griffith." *Film Heritage*,
         10 (Spring 1975), 1-4.

Interview centers on Walsh's work
with Griffith on early Westerns and on a
five-reeler, the now lost *The Life of
Villa*.

5.109   Moullet, Luc. "Sam Fuller: In Marlowe's
         Footsteps." Trans. Norman King.
         Cahiers du Cinema, no. 93 (March
         1959). Reprinted in *Cahiers du
         Cinema, the 1950s: Neo-Realism,
         Hollywood, New Wave*, ed. Jim Hillier.
         Cambridge: Harvard University Press,
         1985, pp. 145-155.

Author claims Fuller is Marlowe to
Welles' Shakespeare. Article details
Fuller's career to 1959, discussing the
use of political allegory in *Run of the
Arrow* (1957).

5.110   Murphy, Kathleen and Richard T. Jameson.
           "'You're Goddam Right I Remember.'
           An Interview with Howard Hawks."
           Movietone News, no. 54 (June 20,
           1977), 1-13.

               This 1976 interview with Hawks
           includes some comments by the famous
           director about *Red River* (1948), *Rio
           Bravo* (1959) and *El Dorado* (1967).
           Similar material is included in a
           lengthier interview with Hawks, *Hawks on
           Hawks* (5.26).

5.111   Nolley, Kenneth J. "Printing the Legend
           in the Age of MX: Reconsidering
           Ford's Military Trilogy."
           Literature/Film Quarterly, 14:2
           (1986), 82-88.

               Argues that in an age of possible
           nuclear annihilation it is instructive to
           re-examine John Ford's cavalry trilogy--
           Fort Apache (1948), *She Wore a Yellow
           Ribbon* (1949) and *Rio Grande* (1950)--
           as they relate to possible solutions to a
           search for human community. He concludes
           that the first two films present an ideal
           of a multicultural community of whites
           and Native Americans, but that in *Rio
           Grande*, Ford "abandoned his search for a
           larger human community in favor of a
           simpler and more simplistic nationalism."
           Nolley says his argument is a personal
           reflection about the films, but his
           arguments are persuasive not only in
           their passion but also in their
           detailing.

5.112   Paul, William. "Hawks vs. Durgnat."
           Film Comment, 14:1 (January/February
           1978), 68-71.

               A point-by-point rebuttal of Raymond
           Durgnat's earlier article which
           questioned Hawks' status as a major
           American *auteur* (5.72). For Durgnat's
           comments on Paul's rebuttal, see 5.71.

5.113   Peckinpah, Sam. "Straight Shootin Sam."
          Southwest Media Review, 3 (Spring
          1985), 14-19.

          Record of exchanges between Peckinpah
          and audience after a screening of *The
          Wild Bunch* (1969) and *The Ballad of Cable
          Hogue* (1970), and an interview which also
          took place during the "Texas Myth in
          Film" series at Rice University in the
          spring of 1984. Article appears in a
          special issue of *Southwest Media Review*
          devoted to "Texas Myth in Film."

5.114   Pettit, Arthur G. "Nightmare and
          Nostalgia: The Cinema West of Sam
          Peckinpah." *Western Humanities
          Review*, 29 (Spring 1975), 105-122.

          The first half of this article
          surveys all of Peckinpah's Westerns,
          concluding that Peckinpah's heroes are
          out of sync with changing times. "While
          trying to cope with a West gone mad and
          rotten beyond repair, Peckinpah pines for
          a West that never was, but should have
          been." The second part of the essay
          centers on *The Wild Bunch* (1969) and how
          the film emphasizes a code of loyalty
          that makes its outlaw protagonists the
          best men in a bad world. A final section
          of the article considers and defends
          Peckinpah's use of explicit violence.
          Although Pettit does not present many new
          ideas about Peckinpah's Westerns, his
          analysis of the films is convincingly
          presented and his interpretation of
          certain details in the films is fresh and
          lively.

5.115   ————. "The Polluted Garden: Sam
          Peckinpah's Double Vision of Mexico."
          Southwest Review, 62:3 (Summer 1977),
          280-294.

          An analysis of the Mexico seen in
          Peckinpah's *The Wild Bunch* (1969).
          Pettit concludes that the film presents a

"double vision of Mexico; Mapache's Mexico and Angel's Mexico; the one of madcap music, drunkenness, filth, "dirty" sex and violence; the other of soft music, sobriety, cleanliness, open affections and peace." In a concluding section, Pettit considers Peckinpah's later film set in Mexico, *Bring Me the Head of Alfredo Garcia* (1973), and finds that in the later film the positive alternative of Angel's Mexico has ceased to exist. The article is well written and convincing and is especially useful in explaining how important Mexico is in understanding the moral perspectives in *The Wild Bunch*.

5.116   Phillips, Gene D. "Fred Zinneman: An Interview." *Journal of Popular Film and Television*, 7:1 (1978), 58-66.

Although most of the interview deals with his non-Western work, Zinneman's comments about *High Noon* (1952) and *The Sundowners* (1960) reveal his belief that the genre is a highly stylized form.

5.117   ———. "Hollywood Royalty: Conversations with Henry King." *American Classic Screen*, 5:5 (1981), 14-16, 20-22.

An edited series of conversations in which King discusses his career as a Hollywood director. Includes brief anecdotes on a large number of King's films, including several Westerns.

5.118   Pye, Douglas. "John Ford and the Critics." *Movie*, no. 22 (Spring 1976), 43-52.

Pye argues that several book-length studies of Ford's films published in the mid 1970s suffer from an exclusively *auteur*ist approach to the films. To really get at the complexities of Ford's films, they need to be studied less in

relation to each other and more in
relation to their origins in popular
genres and to how they relate to concepts
of past and present. Pye's examples are
drawn from Ford's Westerns.

5.119   Rafferty, Terrence. "The Paradoxes of
           Home: Three Films by Walter Hill."
           Film Quarterly, 36 (Fall 1982),
           20-32.

           Rafferty argues that the need and the
           personal cost of finding and defending
           home is a prominent theme in director
           Hill's works, including *The Long Riders*
           (1980). In that film, the James Gang
           become outlaws because of their fierce
           attachment to family and to the land.
           The attack on the Northfield bank fails,
           Rafferty claims, because it is a
           symbolic perversion of the outlaws' basic
           values of community and home.

5.120   Roth, Lane. "Folk Song Lyrics as
           Communication in John Ford's Films."
           *The Southern Speech Communication
           Journal*, 46 (Summer 1981), 390-396.

           Roth argues that the songs sung
           onscreen in Ford's films "celebrate
           Ford's ideals of community and nature."
           The songs as they appear in the films may
           be literal celebrations, or they may
           comment ironically. Included in the
           discussion are songs from *Rio Grande*
           (1950) and *The Searchers* (1956). The use
           of music as a ritual of community has
           been written about elsewhere (see, for
           example, Place, I, 5.23) and the article
           sheds no new light on the topic. Also
           disappointing is a lack of commentary on
           the "folk" nature of the songs discussed.

5.121   ————. "Frontier Families: John Ford,
           Sergio Leone." *American Classic
           Screen*, 5:4 (1981), 36-38, 42.

           In-depth analysis of Leone's *Once*

Upon a Time in the West (1969), which
Roth claims shares Ford's central image
of the family as a symbol of community
working together for the future of the
American West. The difference is that
Leone presents the Industrial
Revolution's impact as violently
destructive, while Ford (especially in
How Green Was My Valley) presents it as a
source of gradual disintegration of the
family unit.

5.122 ———. "Ritual Brawls in John Ford's
Films." *Film Criticism*, 7 (Spring
1983), 38-46.

Roth argues that fights in John Ford
films have a salutary function for the
individual as well as for the community,
and thus operate as traditional, socially
sanctioned rituals. Employing anthropo-
logical approaches to ritual study, the
author claims the brawls staged in five
Ford films, including *She Wore a Yellow
Ribbon* (1949) and *The Searchers* (1956),
promote social cohesion and social
integration, while symbolizing support
for order over chaos.

5.123 Routt, William D. "The Old Wild Men of
the Movies." *American Film*, 1:10
(September 1976), 54-59.

The author discusses a discerned
strain of primitivism in American popular
film, particularly in the works of Sam
Fuller, Edgar G. Ulmer, King Vidor, Cecil
B. DeMille and Allan Dwan. Routt's
general approach includes brief mention
of several Westerns.

5.124 Sanford, Harry. "Joseph Kane." *Close
Up: The Contract Director*, ed. Jon
Tuska, Vicki Piekarski and Karl
Thiede. Metuchen, N.J.: The
Scarecrow Press, Inc., 1976, pp.
142-187.

Sanford discusses Kane's career in
the context of the B movie industry,
emphasizing his relationship with
Republic Studios. Though Kane claims he
never thought of himself as a director of
Westerns, the essay stresses his work in
the genre, including an extended
discussion of the problems surrounding
the production of *Dakota* (1945).
Includes a lengthy film checklist by Karl
Thiede.

5.125   Scheib, Ronnie. "Subconsciousness
            Raising." *Film Comment*, 17:1
            (January/February 1981), 24-32.

An analysis of the themes in the
films of scriptwriter Charles Schnee.
Included are comments on the three
Westerns Schnee scripted or co-scripted:
Red River (1948), *The Furies* (1950) and
Westward the Women (1951). "It is in
Schnee's Westerns," Scheib argues, "that
the sense of loss of values outlived and
acts out-of-sync is most powerfully
felt."

5.126   Self, Robert. "Robert Altman and the
            Theory of Authorship." *Cinema
            Journal*, 25 (Fall 1985), 3-11.

Self uses Altman's works, including
*Buffalo Bill and the Indians, or Sitting
Bull's History Lesson* (1976) and *McCabe
and Mrs. Miller* (1971), to illustrate the
problems in employing theories of author-
ships in film. The author argues that
Buffalo Bill enlarges the frame of the
Western conflict between settlers and
Indians to reveal history as contained by
the structures of show business. *Buffalo
Bill*'s representation of the hero
identity in transition, Self claims,
blurs any quest for authorship in the
film.

5.127   Silver, Charles. "The Apprenticeship of
            John Ford." *American Film*, 1 (May

1976), 62-67.

The author's analysis of Ford's work
before 1939 is confusing, and its
treatment of the director's pre-
Stagecoach (1939) Westerns is inconsistent. Treating Ford's silent Westerns
briefly, Silver claims the director's
work is disappointing in comparison to
his post-1939 efforts; at the same time,
he cites *The Iron Horse* (1924) as a
classic and *Three Bad Men* (1926) as
possibly "the greatest Western of the
silent era."

5.128   Simmons, Garner. "Sam Peckinpah's
           Television Work." *Film Heritage*, 10
           (Winter 1974-75), 1-16.

This survey of Peckinpah's work on
television includes a list of the
director's writing and directing credits
from 1955 to 1967, as well as general
discussion of Peckinpah's work on
specific series, including *Gunsmoke*, *The
Rifleman* and *The Westerner*.

5.129   Simon, John. "John Simon on Jan Troell."
           Film Heritage, 9 (Summer 1974), 9-20.

Simon, purporting to discuss *Zandy's
Bride* (1974), picks up Troell's banner
against studio interference. Though the
author attempts to put some of the
Swedish filmmaker's earlier work into
context, he includes very little about
the movies themselves.

5.130   Simonski, Ted. "The Billy Jack Pheno-
           menon: Filmmaking with Independence
           and Control." *Velvet Light Trap*, no.
           13 (Fall 1974), 36-39.

Details the struggle of actor-writer-
director Tom Laughlin to successfully
market the 1971 modern Western, *Billy
Jack*.

5.131   Sragow, Michael. "Don't Jesse James Me!"
             Sight and Sound, 51:3 (Summer 1982),
             194-198.

                  An appreciative overview of the
             career of writer-director Walter Hill.
             Includes a brief commentary on Hill's
             Western, *The Long Riders* (1980). Hill
             himself states the major theme of his
             films: "What I like to do is put
             interesting characters in tough
             situations and force them to make choices
             about conduct." Also discussed is the
             influence on his films of the work of Sam
             Peckinpah and John Ford.

5.132   Starman, Ray. "James Cruze--Cinema's
             Forgotten Director." *Films in
             Review*, 26 (October 1985), 461-465.

                  Well-intentioned profile of director
             Cruze bogs itself down in the fact that
             more than a third of his work is lost and
             untraceable. Useful background infor-
             mation, but scant attention is paid to
             The Covered Wagon (1923), which gave
             Cruze his first critical spotlight.
             Includes production still from the film.

5.133   Sturhahn, Lawrence. "'It's a Long Way
             From Your Heart and On the Wrong
             Side ... '" *North American Review*,
             260 (Spring 1975), 74-80.

                  Argues that *The Wild Bunch* (1969) is
             autobiographical in that it unmasks the
             psyche of its director, Sam Peckinpah.
             The form of the article is short,
             disconnected arguments based mainly on a
             1974 appearance by Peckinpah at the San
             Francisco International Film Festival.
             Included are comments about self-
             indulgence, misogyny and absurdity.
             While critical of many of the implica-
             tions of *The Wild Bunch*, Sturhahn writes
             of the film from the assumption that it
             is a great artistic achievement.

5.134   Thoene, Bodie and Rona Stuck. "Navajo
          Nation meets Hollywood: An Inside
          Look at John Ford's Classic
          Westerns." *American West*, 20
          (September-October 1983), 38-44.

          The authors discuss Ford's use of
          Navajo Indians in each of his Monument
          Valley films, emphasizing the Indians'
          anecdotal experiences over the films
          themselves.

5.135   Thompson, Frank. "Charles T. Barton."
          *Between Action and Cut: Five American
          Directors*, ed. Frank Thompson.
          Metuchen, N.J.: The Scarecrow Press,
          Inc., 1985, pp. 183-216.

          Includes detailed discussion of *Wagon
          Wheels* (1934), Barton's first directorial
          credit, as well as references to six Zane
          Grey projects he filmed for Paramount
          between 1935 and 1938. A separate filmo-
          graphy (pp. 264-295) includes Barton's
          work as an actor, prop boy, assistant
          director, writer and director of film and
          television.

5.136   Thompson, Frank T. "The Wellman
          Westerns: An Appraisal." *American
          Classic Screen*, 4:2 (Winter 1980),
          8-15.

          An examination of William Wellman's
          nine Westerns, with particular attention
          to *The Robin Hood of El Dorado* (1935),
          The Great Man's Lady (1942), *Westward the
          Women* (1951), *The Ox-Bow Incident* (1943),
          Buffalo Bill (1944) and *Track of the Cat*
          (1954). Despite his reputation for male
          bonding films, Wellman made relatively
          few Westerns. Thompson argues nonethe-
          less that his Westerns--particularly
          Robin Hood of El Dorado and *Ox-Bow
          Incident*--contain the finer qualities and
          varied textures of his overall *oeuvre*.
          Includes scattered photos. Part of an
          American Classic Screen "Special Western

Issue."

5.137   Thompson, Richard. "Stocked." *Film
            Comment*, 12:4 (July/August 1976),
            10-21.

            An interview with writer-director
    John Milius covering his career as a
    scriptwriter. Includes some incidental
    comments on two Milius-scripted Westerns,
    The Life and Times of Judge Roy Bean
    (1972) and *Jeremiah Johnson* (1972).
    Milius also describes his passion for *The
    Searchers* (1956).

5.138   Thompson, Richard and Tim Hunter. "Clint
            Eastwood, *Auteur*." *Film Comment*,
            14:1 (January/February 1978), 24-32.

            An interview with Clint Eastwood. Of
    special interest are his comments about
    earlier criticisms of his work by critic
    Pauline Kael and about two Westerns he
    starred in and directed, *High Plains
    Drifter* (1973) and *The Outlaw Josey Wales*
    (1976).

5.139   Thomsen, Christian Braad. "Monte
            Hellman: A Profile." *Take One*, 4:2
            (March 1974), 27-31.

            An interview with director Hellman
    about the making and meaning of his
    films. A substantial amount of the
    interview concerns itself with Hellman's
    two unusual 1965 Westerns, *The Shooting*
    and *Ride the Whirlwind*, which Hellman
    argues are both realistic and mythic.

5.140   Thomson, David. "Niven Busch:
            Sportsman." *Film Comment*, 21
            (July/August 1985), 40-49.

            Interview with novelist-screenwriter
    Busch centers on his conflicts with the
    Hollywood system. Discussion of his
    career includes details of his involve-
    ment in several major Westerns, including

The Westerner (1940), *Duel in the Sun* (1946) and *Pursued* (1947).

5.141   Tuska, Jon. "Howard Hawks." *Close Up: The Contract Director*, ed. Jon Tuska, Vicki Piekarski and Karl Thiede. Metuchen, N.J.: The Scarecrow Press, Inc., 1976, pp. 390-438.

Tuska's review of Hawks' career features a discussion of *Red River* (1948), stressing the director's conscious effort at making the definitive Western film. Includes a film checklist by Karl Thiede.

5.142   ————. "Sam Peckinpah." *Close-Up: The Contemporary Director*, ed. Jon Tuska, Vicki Piekarski and David Wilson. Metuchen, N.J.: The Scarecrow Press, Inc., 1981, pp. 99-133.

The essay details two meetings with Peckinpah and presents an overview of his directing career with some emphasis on *Pat Garrett and Billy the Kid* (1973). The picture of Peckinpah that emerges is of a primitive destroying himself with the same kind of bitterness and self-indulgence that have characterized both the best and the worst of his films. Tuska suggests his great affection for Peckinpah and the overall impression of the director is therefore almost tragic. Includes a brief filmography by Karl Thiede.

5.143   ————. "Spencer Gordon Bennet." *Close-Up: The Hollywood Director*, ed. Jon Tuska, Vicki Piekarski and David Wilson. Metuchen, N.J.: The Scarecrow Press, Inc., 1978, pp. 94-135.

Bennet's work as a director of serials and B features, particularly with cowboy stars like Buck Jones, Ken Maynard, Gene Autry and Bill Elliott, is the focus of this essay. Also includes a film checklist by Vicki Piekarski.

5.144   ————. "Yakima Canutt." *Close Up: The
             Contract Director*, ed. Jon Tuska,
             Vicki Piekarski and Karl Thiede.
             Metuchen, N.J.: The Scarecrow Press,
             Inc., 1976, pp. 262-297.

             A survey of actor-stuntman-director
             Canutt's career which emphasizes its
             growth within the development of the
             Western genre on film. Includes a film
             checklist by Karl Thiede.

5.145   Wegner, Hart. "Frederic Remington and
             John Ford: Dynamic and Static
             Composition Elements of 'Fort
             Apache.'" *Explorations in National
             Cinemas*, ed. Ben Lawton and Janet
             Staiger. Pleasantville, N.Y.:
             Redgrave Publishing Co., 1977, pp.
             27-36.

             Wegner argues that *Fort Apache* (1948)
             "approaches screen tragedy." This is
             accomplished with formal visual
             compositions which were influenced by the
             paintings and drawings of Frederic
             Remington. Although Wegner demonstrates
             his thesis with detailed descriptions of
             several scenes in the film and a number
             of Remington's works, the articles
             suffers from a lack of stills and
             illustrations.

5.146   Willeman, Paul. "Anthony Mann: Looking
             for the Male." *Framework*, nos. 15-17
             (Summer 1981), 16.

             Willeman says that the coherence of
             Mann's Westerns has blinded critical
             approaches to his earlier *films noirs* and
             to his later epics. The common
             denominator, he claims, is a sense of
             spectacle along with a filmmaking style
             which echoes thematic structure.

5.147   Wollen, Peter (Lee Russell). "John

Ford." *New Left Review*, no. 29
(January/February 1965), 69-73.
Reprinted in *Theories of Authorship:
A Reader*, ed. John Caughie. London:
Routledge & Kegan Paul, 1981, pp.
102-108.

Wollen reads the bulk of Ford's work,
particularly his Westerns, as expressions
of Jacksonian populism, a contradictory
blend of liberalism and conservatism.
The author discusses in some detail *Two
Rode Together* (1961) and *The Man Who Shot
Liberty Valance* (1962), arguing that
Ford's later movies reflect an increasing
laziness in style, grounded in part in
the paradoxes Ford intentionally
addresses but cannot resolve. Article
written under a pen name, Lee Russell
(see 2.60).

5.148   Zsigmond, Vilmos. "Behind the Cameras on
         'Heaven's Gate.'" *American
         Cinematographer*, 51:11 (November
         1980), 1110-1113, 1164-1165,
         1172-1181.

The director of photography for
Heaven's Gate (1980) recounts his efforts
to shoot a Western in nongeneric ways,
giving it an epic sweep along the lines
of a David Lean film. Zsigmond's
discussion of the camera work on Michael
Cimino's film offers an unusual critical
perspective on the controversial film,
calling the yet-to-be-released movie a
classic and blaming in-production
difficulties on the studio's impatient
demands for shorter shooting schedules.
Part of an issue of *American Cinematographer* devoted primarily to *Heaven's
Gate*.

WESTERN FILM HISTORY

<u>Books</u>

6.1 Bataille, Gretchen M. and Charles L.P.
Silet, ed. *The Pretend Indians:
Images of Native Americans in the
Movies*. Ames: The Iowa State
University Press, 1980.

An anthology of articles and film
reviews about films featuring Native
American characters. Sections include
media stereotyping of Native Americans,
images of Indians in early films, general
articles on movie images of Indians in
later films, a section of photographs and
a section of reviews of selected films.
Also includes an excellent, annotated
bibliography and an index. There is an
annoying sameness to much of the
material--a tendency to condemn narrow,
inaccurate stereotypes of Native without
a careful detailing of the images' subtle
differences or of the differing
intentions of such stereotyping. The
result, however well intentioned, is too
often sermonizing rather than insightful
analysis. Several useful essays, and the
fact that this is the only general
anthology on the subject, make the book
important for anyone interested in images
of Native Americans in the mass media.

6.2 Bell, Geoffrey. *The Golden Gate and the
Silver Screen*. Cranbury, N.J.:
Associated University Presses, Inc.,
1984.

Within this excellent history of
silent filmmaking in the San Francisco
Bay area is a gem of a chapter on the
Western unit of the Essanay Film Manu-
facturing Company, the makers of many
silent Westerns, including the "Bronco
Billy" series. In addition to its
informative text, this book includes an
appendix which lists the titles and
production data of silent films produced
in northern California (including four
pages of Bronco Billy listings) and an
appendix listing the personnel of the
Essanay Western unit.

6.3   Berkofer, Robert F., Jr. *The White Man's
           Indian*. New York: Alfred A. Knopf,
           Inc., 1978.

This book is generally recognized as
the single best overall history of Native
American stereotyping by whites yet
published. The book includes examples in
all mediated forms and shows how these
images relate to legal policies
concerning Native Americans.
Unfortunately, the study includes only a
few pages on images of Indians in films,
and even these pages are rather superficial. Includes index.

6.4   Biskind, Peter. *Seeing Is Believing*.
           New York: Pantheon Books, 1983.

Biskind's provocative study of the
social and political tensions in 1950s
Hollywood films includes in-depth
examinations of several Cold War Westerns.
In "Cochise, Si! Geronimo, No!: The
Limits of Tolerance" (pp. 228-245),
Biskind analyzes three American Indian-
focused features--*Broken Arrow* (1950),
The Searchers (1956) and *Apache* (1954)--
arguing that each represented 1950s
approaches to the race issue, with *The
Searchers* offering a right-wing view and
Broken Arrow and *Apache* taking left-
center positions. The author also

explores the two-front fight for control
against extremists on the one hand and
for control of the center on the other in
My Darling Clementine (1946) and *High
Noon* (1952), and the feminization of the
American male hero in *Red River* (1948).
Superbly written and well reasoned,
Biskind's book is essential for a
contextualization of 1950s Westerns.

6.5   Brownlow, Kevin. *The War, The West, and
          The Wilderness*. New York: Alfred A.
          Knopf, Inc., 1979.

The middle section of this study of
location shooting during the silent film
years (pp. 221-399) describes the making
of a number of silent Western fictional
and documentary films. Brownlow details
films not described in other histories of
Westerns, including films featuring
Buffalo Bill, the lawman Bill Tilghman,
and outlaws Al Jennings and Emmett
Dalton. Also of special interest are
chapters in which Brownlow suggests that
Native Americans were pictured more
complexly in early films than recent film
criticism suggests and a chapter on a
lost film, *Sundown* (1924), a documentary-
drama which records with unusual realism
the last days of the western cattle
empire. Brownlow constructs all these
and other material around a thesis that
even though silent Westerns were not
realistic depictions of the old West, the
use of genuine locations and the employ-
ment of actual cowboys and historical
characters gave a number of silent
Westerns an unusual aura of authenticity.
The text is accompanied by dozens of
excellent photos. Included at the end of
the volume is a very useful list of
sources for rental, purchase or study of
the films discussed. Includes an index.
Overall, an invaluable resource for the
study of silent Westerns.

6.6   Cary, Diana Serra. *The Hollywood Posse.*

Boston: Houghton Mifflin Co., 1975.

An informal history of the men who
played bit parts and did stunts for the
low-budget Westerns of the 1920s, 1930s
and 1940s, told by the daughter of one of
these performers. Cary stresses the
authenticity of these men, pointing out
that most of them had been working
cowboys before drifting to Hollywood.
The emphasis is on anecdotes rather than
careful research, and for that reason the
book's primary appeal may be to fans of B
Westerns. The book, however, may also be
of interest to those considering the
Hollywood filmmaking process and to those
interested in the overall history of
Westerns. By emphasizing non-featured
performers, Cary provides information on
a group of Western performers not found
elsewhere.

6.7   Cline, William C. *In the Nick of Time:*
             Motion Picture Sound Serials.
             Jefferson, N.C.: McFarland and
             Company, Inc., 1984.

This survey of movie serials produced
from 1930 to 1956 is more informational
than critical. In looking at the history
of sound serials, Cline focuses more on
creators (with chapters on writers,
technicians and directors) and character
types (sections on who played the heroes,
sidekicks, villains and henchmen) than on
specific genres. One chapter, "The Six
Faces of Adventure," breaks the more than
225 serials surveyed into formulas,
including the Western. Also includes a
thorough filmography of film chapterplays
released between 1930 and 1956, including
principal creators, performers and
chapter titles. Includes 32 pages of
publicity pictures and posters.

6.8   Cocchi, John. *The Westerns: A Picture*
             Quiz Book. New York: Dover
             Publications, Inc., 1976.

Interesting for the trivia, and for
its 238 still photos. Made marginally
useful by its performer and film indexes.

6.9   Cross, Robin. *The Big Book of B Movies,
        or How Low Was My Budget.* New York:
        St. Martin's Press, 1981.

A description of low-budget films
arranged by genre, including a section
(pp. 70-87) devoted to B Westerns. About
two-thirds of the chapter is 30 stills
from Western films. The pages of
description include some interesting
information about certain specific films,
but topics discussed seem arbitrarily
chosen and are not arranged in logical
order.

6.10   Dippie, Brian W. *Custer's Last Stand:
        The Anatomy of an American Myth.*
        Missoula, Mont.: University of
        Montana Publications in History,
        1976.

Dippie tries to show how the familiar
concept of Custer's Last Stand is
"largely a creation of nonhistorical
materials, of popular culture which ...
feeds upon fact and fancy, history and
legend." In his ruminations on how
different forms of popular culture
approach the Last Stand and the Custer
myth, Dippie devotes separate chapters to
poetry, painting and fiction, but then
lumps theatre, traveling shows (including
Buffalo Bill's Wild West Show),
festivals, television and film into one
chapter (pp. 89-124). The movies, he
argues, offer three different "Custers":
one who goes to a heroic death due to the
fault of others (epitomized in *They Died
With Their Boots On*, 1941), a one-
dimensional villain (*Little Big Man*,
1970) and a complex, tragic hero (*Custer
of the West*, 1968). Dippie claims that
the natural repetitiveness of the movies'
accounts of Little Big Horn is

intentional, so that the "sensation of
deja vu is expected, even encouraged."
Useful in its field, though the study
does tend to give more weight to other
media.

6.11   Edmonds, I.G. *Big U: Universal in the
            Silent Days.* New York: A.S. Barnes
            and Co., 1977.

Scattered information predominates
this studio history, but rare production
stills and contemporary promotional
material provide fertile sources of
information. Survey history includes
brief discussion of Universal's Western
stars during the silent era, including
Hoot Gibson, Art Acord, Jack Hoxie and
Josie Sedgwick, as well as an account of
the collaborative efforts of John Ford
and Harry Carey, Sr.

6.12   Etulain, Richard W., ed. *Journal of the
            West*, 22:4 (October 1983).

A collection of eight articles about
the history of Western films and Western
film analysis. Emphasis is on the
development of Westerns as reflections of
the cultural preoccupations of their
respective eras. See 6.61, 6.62, 6.63,
6.70 and 6.75.

6.13   Graham, Don. *Cowboys and Cadillacs: How
            Hollywood Looks at Texas.* Austin:
            Texas Monthly Press, 1983.

A chatty, personable and informative
look at the image of Texas, as a landscape and a state of mind, at the hands
of the American film industry. Well
illustrated with black-and-white photos,
the book also includes an iconoclastic,
chronological filmography of movies with
Texas elements.

6.14   Green, Douglas B. *Country Roots: The
            Origins of Country Music.* New York:

Hawthorne Books, Inc., 1976.

Includes a chapter on "Singing
Cowboys: Back in the Saddle Again" (pp.
87-108) which argues that although
singing cowboys have been generally
degraded by historians of the Western
genre, they filled an influential role in
country music. The singing cowboys'
frequent appearance in B films in the
1930s and 1940s, according to Green, gave
the music dignity in the face of its
"hillbilly" image while spreading the
music nationwide. Though fan-oriented,
Green's essay offers a good introduction
and includes interesting still photos.

6.15   Hurst, Richard Maurice. *Republic
Studios: Between Poverty Row and the
Majors*. Metuchen, N.J.: The
Scarecrow Press, Inc., 1979.

Hurst's very general study of
Republic argues that the studio's B
movies influenced audiences and rein-
forced predominantly Midwestern and
"Bible Belt" values, but is unclear as to
what those values are. The book's
treatment of Republic Westerns is limited
to descriptive surveys of the studio's
principal "cowboy" series--The Three
Mesquiteers, Gene Autry and Roy Rogers.
Also included are lists of the films made
in each of the three series.

6.16   Hyams, Jay. *The Life and Times of the
Western Movie*. Kent, England:
Columbus Books, 1983.

This coffee table book is mainly
notable for over 200 stills, a number of
them in color. The text is a rather
informal history of American Westerns
with an emphasis on specific films rather
than trends or directors. Hyams' usual
method in each chapter is to describe the
plots of about 50 Westerns from a decade.
Most of the details concern the plot,

although Hyams occasionally throws in a
bit of historical background. Analysis
is nearly nonexistent. B Westerns are
not included. The book is not a very
useful history of Westerns. It is,
however, attractively packaged and does
describe a number of Westerns not
detailed in the more complete histories
by Fenin and Everson (I, 6.27) and by
Tuska (6.28). It may therefore be
enjoyed as a pleasant diversion or as an
occasionally useful supplement. Includes
an index.

6.17   Kinnard, Roy. *Fifty Years of Serial
                 Thrills*. Metuchen, N.J.: The
                 Scarecrow Press, Inc., 1983.

             Kinnard uses his serial filmography
in two ways: first, to summarize some of
the representative serials produced in
the sound era; and second, to attack
efforts toward imposing the "camp"
aesthetic onto serials and B movies.
Useful for its filmographic information,
organized by studio (Mascot, Republic,
Columbia, Universal), the book only
summarizes one Western serial in any kind
of depth--*The Phantom Empire* (1935),
which Kinnard calls "the screen's only
musical science-fiction Western." Also
includes an incomplete listing of silent
serials and useful title and name
indexes.

6.18   Malone, Bill C. *Country Music U.S.A.*
                 Austin: University of Texas Press,
                 revised edition, 1985.

             Malone's detailed history of country
music includes a chapter on "The Cowboy
Image and the Growth of Western Music"
(pp. 137-175), in which he argues that,
through Gene Autry and those who followed
his success in 1930s B Westerns, hillbilly music had a new medium through
which to popularize itself. The B movie
image of the singing cowboy, equally able

with both gun and guitar, also helped
romanticize the cowboy and shaped the
public idea of western music. Malone's
examinations include cowboy singers who
made their reputations on and off the
screen. This probably is the most
detailed discussion of the topic in
print. For a shorter version of the same
argument, see Malone's *Southern Music,
American Music* (Lexington: University
Press of Kentucky, 1979).

6.19   May, Lary. *Screening Out the Past: The
Birth of Mass Culture and the Motion
Picture Industry*. Chicago: The
University of Chicago Press, 1983.

May's controversial (and mistake-
ridden) study of early Hollywood includes
a look at "Revitalization: Douglas
Fairbanks, Mary Pickford, and the New
Personality, 1914-1918" (pp. 96-146),
which features discussions of the
changing image of the cowboy in William
S. Hart's films and the promise of
reinvigoration in Fairbanks' Westerns.
Though the rest of May's book is plagued
with inaccuracies, this section is
insightful and clear.

6.20   McGee, Mark Thomas. *Fast and Furious:
The Story of American International
Pictures*. Jefferson, N.C.: McFarland
and Company, Inc., 1984.

McGee's discussion of the most
prominent of the rapid-fire independent
production companies to spring up in the
1950s includes incidental production
information about and stills from several
Westerns made by the company, including
Five Guns West (1955), *Gunslinger* (1956),
Apache Woman (1955) and *Oklahoma Woman*
(1956), all directed by Roger Corman.

6.21   Parks, Rita. *The Western Hero in Film
and Television*. Ann Arbor: UMI
Research Press, 1982.

In the first half of this monograph,
Parks traces the Western genre from its
origins in history and mythic archetypes
into various American literary forms.
The second half is devoted to the
development of the history of the form in
movies and television. The chapter on
film is an historical overview with more
detailed attention given to the Westerns
of John Ford and Sam Peckinpah. The
television chapter places TV Westerns
within the development of other television programming and gives some
specialized attention to *Gunsmoke* and
Bonanza. Parks' research ended in 1973,
and so was almost ten years out of date
by the time it was published. The book
also suffers from chronological errors
throughout and a failure to cite specific
episodes in the television chapter.
Parks also tends to rely on secondary
sources for historical information
instead of doing original research. The
first half of the book, however, does
provide a solid introduction to the genre.

6.22   Sarf, Wayne Michael. *God Bless You,*
                  Buffalo Bill. New York: Fairleigh
                  Dickinson University Press, 1983.

A study of the differences between
historical incidents and characters in
the old West and their dramatization in
Westerns. Included are chapters on
lawmen, gunmen, outlaws, Butch Cassidy,
Custer, Buffalo Bill, Indians and other
minorities. Sarf is critical of the
tendency to glorify Westerners whose
deeds were in reality motivated by greed
or insanity, but he is equally critical
of recent revisionism that shows
Westerners as worse than they really
were. All of this is expressed with
humor and good writing. But Sarf never
establishes why Westerns have a responsibility to historical fidelity. The
book therefore suffers in places from
sarcasm seemingly for its own sake and

overall from a lack of a thesis beyond
what is quite obvious in the first place.
Includes an annotated bibliography. For
a more in-depth condemnation of Westerns
for their historical inaccuracies, see
Jon Tuska's *The American West in Film*
(7.15).

6.23   Savage, William W. *Singing Cowboys and*
        All That Jazz. Norman, Okla.:
        University of Oklahoma Press, 1983.

        A history of popular music in Okla-
homa which includes a look at the role of
singing cowboys in popular culture.
Savage claims that in the 1930s and 1940s
there existed a symbiotic popularity
between the music and B Westerns. The
focus is on some minor performers and
songwriters from Oklahoma who were
involved in films.

6.24   Silver, Charles. *The Western Film.* New
        York: Pyramid Publications, 1976.

        This brief history of the Western is
about half still photos. As a result,
commentary on specific films is quite
brief, rarely more than a single
paragraph. Comments show a decided slant
toward the Westerns of John Ford and for
classic Westerns. Includes a brief
bibliography, filmography and index.

6.25   Spoto, Donald. *Camerado: Hollywood and*
        the American Man. New York: New
        American Library, 1978.

        This study of the masculine image in
American film includes a brief discussion
of the Western genre, in which he claims
that the Western's appeal for men is in
the hero's independence and his own
physicality, while women are drawn to the
genre's idea of the civilizing domes-
ticity of women in the story form. Spoto
does not do much to support these points,
particularly in his slight examinations

of *Red River* (1948), *High Noon* (1952) and
The Alamo (1960).

6.26   Stedman, Raymond William. *Shadows of the
            Indians: Stereotypes in American
            Culture*. Norman, Okla.: University
            of Oklahoma Press, 1982.

            An examination of the primary stereo-
            types of Native Americans that have
            appeared throughout American history in
            all types of popular culture, including
            movies. Stedman's generalizations are
            well proven and are presented in a lively
            fashion that makes the book appealing to
            general readers as well as scholars.
            There are a number of factual errors in
            the book's details, however, and the tone
            of the book sometimes becomes
            unfortunately condescending toward the
            popular artifacts being discussed. Of
            special interest is Stedman's demon-
            stration that so-called sympathetic
            treatments of Indian characters in books,
            on stage and in the movies are often just
            as stereotyped as more negative
            portrayals. Includes dozens of useful
            illustrations, a literary/historical
            chronology, bibliography and general and
            title indexes.

6.27   Tuska, Jon. *Billy the Kid: A Bio-
            Bibliography*. Westport, Conn.:
            Greenwood Press, 1983.

            Most of this book is a concise
            biography of Billy the Kid and a
            discussion of earlier works about the Kid
            purporting to be historically accurate.
            Also included, however, are a chapter on
            fiction about Billy, another chapter
            about Billy the Kid in the movies and a
            last chapter evaluating critical analyses
            of the Kid as a figure in history and
            legend. The chapter on Billy in the
            movies (pp. 162-187) is chronological and
            mainly details the various plots. A
            filmography is included at the end of the

chapter. Tuska's commentaries on the
critical analyses of Billy the Kid
narratives in either fiction or film are
based on his insistence that the primary
responsibility of the creator of
narrative is to be historically accurate.
In this way, Tuska's attitude is in
fundamental opposition to the book on
Billy the Kid by Stephen Tatum (9.17).
Also includes an historical chronology of
events in the life of Billy the Kid and
an index.

6.28   ———. *The Filming of the West*. Garden
City, N.Y.: Doubleday and Co., 1976.

A detailed history of the Western
film from the beginning through the early
1970s. Tuska's method was to select 100
of what he considers the greatest
Westerns and to write of the overall
history of the genre from the perspective
of these 100 films. Emphasis is on plot
summary and detailing of production
backgrounds. More than half the book is
devoted to B Westerns and to biographical
details about B Western stars. There are
a number of flaws in this book. There
are needless digressions, and some of the
details are uselessly trivial. Tuska's
limiting himself to 100 films means that
a number of important or popular Westerns
such as *The Magnificent Seven* (1960) and
The Searchers (1956) receive little or no
mention at all. Tuska's love of earlier
films also seems to make him over-
critical of modern Westerns. There is
little attempt to place the films within
their cultural context. Despite these
flaws, this, along with Fenin and
Everson's *The Western: From Silents to
the Seventies* (I, 6.27) is one of the two
essential histories of the genre. Tuska
spent years interviewing performers and
technicians as well as studying the films
themselves. The result is details about
the films and the industry that produced
them that are not available in any other

book. Includes index.

6.29   ————. *The Vanishing Legion: A History
            of Mascot Pictures 1927-1935.*
            Jefferson, N.C.: McFarland and
            Company, Inc., 1982.

An expanded version of a series of
articles Tuska wrote for *Views and
Reviews* between 1971 and 1973 (I, 6.127).
Until it merged into Republic Pictures in
1935, Mascot produced mainly serials,
including about a dozen Westerns.
Emphasis was on action over plot, a
formula that made Mascot second only to
Universal as a producer of popular
serials during the period. Tuska
describes how the studio reflected the
personality of owner Nat Levine. A
typical chapter outlines the career of
the stars of a particular serial,
discusses the production of the serial
and outlines the plot. Tuska uses
concepts of psychologist Carl Jung to
explain the meaning of the chapterplays,
but unfortunately makes little attempt to
discuss their thematic implications in
relation to the specific times in which
they were produced. Western stars
profiled include Rin Tin Tin, Jack Hoxie,
Harry Carey, Ken Maynard, Gene Autry, Tom
Mix and John Wayne. Of special interest
is Tuska's description of *The Phantom
Empire* (1935), Gene Autry's first
starring vehicle, and *The Miracle Rider*
(1935), Tom Mix's last film. Includes 39
rarely reproduced stills, an index and a
filmography of all Mascot serials and
features. Overall, an invaluable history
of one of the important B studios. For
another history of Mascot with an
emphasis on stills, see *Next Time Drive
Off the Cliff* (I, 6.28).

6.30   Willoughby, Larry. *Texas Rhythm, Texas
            Rhyme.* Austin: Texas Monthly Press,
            1984.

Survey of the history of Texas music
includes a chapter on "The Singing
Cowboys" (pp. 25-35), in which Willoughby
argues that the combination of the music
and the fixed stereotype on film has
permitted the romantic image of the
cowboy to endure.

Articles

6.31   Anderson, Robert. "The Role of the
        Western Film Genre in Industry
        Competition, 1907-1911." *Journal of
        the University Film Association*, 31:2
        (Spring 1979), 19-26.

        Anderson argues that the Western film
played an important role in weaning
nickelodeon film audiences away from
foreign-made films at exactly the moment
of foreign film proliferation in the
United States. Westerns in 1907 and 1908
emphasized local color to differentiate
themselves from European one-reelers. By
1909, Westerns shot in the East were
imitating those shot on location in the
West. By 1910 and 1911, the Western had
established itself as a "fully articulated genre." Most of the information in
this article was gathered from trade
journals of the period. The result is an
emphasis on film industry developments
and minimal information about the Western
films themselves. No attempt is made to
detail and interpret any Westerns of the
era. Within this structure, however,
Anderson has carefully researched his
arguments. The essay should be of
interest to those looking either at
Western film history or at the history of
the American film industry.

6.32   Armitage, Shelley. "Rawhide Heroines:
        The Evolution of the Cowgirl and the
        Myth of America." *The American Self:
        Myth, Ideology and Popular Culture*,
        ed. Sam B. Girgus. Albuquerque:
        University of New Mexico Press, 1981,

pp. 166-181.

Although the passive "sunbonnet
woman" is the dominant image of the women
of the West, there were also women who
fully participated in the physical
activities of the settlement of the
Western frontier usually associated with
men--riding, roping, shooting, etc.
Armitage traces these "cowgirls" through
their historical origins and through
their presence as heroines in a number of
popular culture formats, including dime
novels, hardcover fiction, rodeos, Wild
West shows and the movies. The overall
perspective provided is informative and
useful. Unfortunately, the material on
the movies is brief and rather superficial.

6.33   Bataille, Gretchen and Charles L.P.
            Silet. "The Entertaining
            Anachronism: Indians in American
            Film." *The Kaleidoscopic Lens: How
            Hollywood Views Ethnic Groups*, ed.
            Randall M. Miller. Englewood Cliffs,
            N.J.: Jerome S. Ozer, Publisher,
            1980, pp. 36-53.

Argues that movies' stereotyped
presentations of American Indians have
been more damaging than those in print
media because they developed concrete
images. The authors' tracing of the
roots of the Indian stereotype is fairly
general, and their analysis inconsistent,
based in part on the authors' strong
personal views.

6.34   Bergan, Ronald. "The Decline of the
            Western." *Films and Filming*, no. 345
            (June 1983), 2-5.

Bergan attempts to trace the entire
history of the sound Western in about two
pages of text. Needless to say, his
argument that the Western "declined"
after 1956 is superficial. The

subheading of the essay and three still
photos suggest the article is mainly
about *Heaven's Gate* (1980), but the film
is only mentioned in the last two
sentences.

6.35 ————. "The Other Side of the Western."
Films and Filming, no. 350 (November
1983), 13-16.

This rather flat attempt at whimsy
briefly describes a number of Westerns
that are "oddball" members of the genre.
Categories include Westerns with women
protagonists, comedies and singing
Westerns. Bergan does little more than
mention titles.

6.36 Blumenberg, Richard M. "The Evolution
and Shape of the American Western."
Wide Angle, 1:1 (Spring 1976), 39-43,
46-47, 49.

A brief history of the movie Western,
with an emphasis on how the films were in
part shaped by the available technology
and common filming techniques of their
eras. The article suggests that such an
approach may indeed be valuable, but the
essay is much too brief and sketchy to be
any more than a starting point.

6.37 Buscombe, Edward. "Painting the Legend:
Frederic Remington and the Western."
Cinema Journal, 23:4 (Summer 1984),
12-27.

An attempt to describe the influence
of painters of the West, especially
Frederic Remington, on the establishment
of Western films as an important
Hollywood genre. Buscombe describes how
in the late nineteenth century Remington
and other magazine illustrators began to
paint and draw images of the West
centered on moments of climactic action.
These images were widely reproduced and
prepared Americans even more than photos

of the West for the genre conventions
audiences quickly accepted in Western
films. Thus, Western films of the
twentieth century adapted visual motifs
and images already well established by
Remington and others as early as 1880.
Buscombe presents a good argument for
including Remington as an important
influence on the Western. Unfortunately,
the article suffers somewhat from a
failure to connect Remington directly to
early Western films. Comparisons are
mainly with the cavalry trilogy of John
Ford, which didn't begin until 1948.

6.38   Churchill, Ward, Mary Anne Hill, et al.
           "Examination of Stereotyping: An
           Analytical Survey of Twentieth-
           Century Indian Entertainers." *The
           Pretend Indians: Images of Native
           Americans in the Movies*, ed. Gretchen
           M. Bataille and Charles L.P. Silet.
           Ames: The Iowa State University
           Press, 1980, pp. 35-48.

        Argues that anti-Indian stereotyping
began in the nineteenth century as a
support for manifest destiny and has
continued in all of the mass media of the
twentieth century, including the movies.
The second half of the essay is made up
of brief profiles of several Native
American performers, a few of which have
appeared in Westerns. Generalizations in
this essay tend to be oversimplifications
of images of Native Americans which
earlier scholarship had already
established.

6.39   Dixon, Wheeler. "PRC: The Unknown
           Studio." *Films in Review*, 35:7
           (August/September 1984), 405-410.

        This overview of the 1940s Poverty
Row studio is a call for a more detailed
study of the topic. Includes some
details of cost-cutting methods used in
the production of PRC Westerns. For a

more detailed history and analysis of
Producers Releasing Corp., see Dixon's
book, *Producers Releasing Corporation*
(1.15).

6.40   Etulain, Richard W. "Changing Images:
            The Cowboy in Western Films."
            Colorado Heritage, 1 (1981), 37-55.

            Etulain outlines the history of the
Western genre through the changing image
of the movie cowboy. Fairly general,
Etulain's study focuses on major
performers as important symbols,
particularly Broncho Billy Anderson,
William S. Hart, Tom Mix, Gary Cooper,
the singing cowboys and John Wayne.

6.41   Everett, Eldon K. "Son of Gower Gulch."
            Classic Film Collector, no. 44 (Fall
            1974), 26-27.

            The second of two in-depth looks at
the filmmaking careers of turn-of-the-
century outlaws. Article focuses on
Emmett Dalton (of the Dalton Gang) and Al
Jennings, with detailed emphasis on the
production history of Jennings' only
starring feature, *Beating Back* (1913).
Includes photo.

6.42   Everson, William K. "The Sun Valley
            Western Film Conference." *Films in
            Review*, 27:8 (October 1976), 477-483.

            An anecdotal review of the conference
which included academics and Hollywood
luminaries.

6.43   ————. "The Western." *American Silent
            Film*. New York: Oxford University
            Press, 1979, pp. 138-159.

            This chapter from Everson's history
of silent movies in American provides a
brief and serviceable overview of
Westerns from 1898 until the introduction
of sound. Unfortunately, no stills are

included to illustrate the text. For a
more complete history of the era with
useful stills, see Everson and Fenin's
*The Western: From Silents to the
Seventies* (I, 6.27) and Tuska's *The
Filming of the West* (I, 6.48).

6.44   Foote, Cheryl J. "Changing Images of
             Women in the Western Film." *Journal
             of the West*, 22:4 (October 1983),
             64-71.

             Despite the title of this article,
Foote's brief overview of images of women
throughout the history of Westerns shows
that a vast majority of Westerns have
portrayed women characters as either
"good" women who are "civilizers and
culture-bringers to a raw frontier" or
"bad" women who are mainly objects of
sexual gratification. Foote also shows,
however, that Westerns of the 1970s and
1980s such as *Tom Horn* (1980), *Comes a
Horseman* (1978) and *Heartland* (1980) show
women as complex, often independent
characters rather than as merely symbolic
stereotypes. The article is part of a
special issue of *Journal of the West*
devoted to the Western film (6.12).

6.45   Graham, Don. "Remembering the Alamo: The
             Story of the Texas Revolution in
             Popular Culture." *Southwestern
             Historical Quarterly*, 89:1 (July
             1985), 35-66.

             Arguing that for most Americans the
Alamo is the complete expression of the
history of the Texas revolution, the
article traces its use as historical
occurence and icon in various popular
expressions, including films from the
epic *Martyrs of the Alamo* (1915) to the
revisionist satire of *Viva Max* (1969).
For another interpretation of the Alamo
as a film icon, see Brian Huberman and Ed
Hugetz's "Fabled Facade" (6.48).

6.46   ————. "A Short History of Texas in the
              Movies: An Overview."
              Literature/Film Quarterly, 14:2
              (1986), 70-81.

              How the movies have portrayed Texas,
              mostly in Westerns. Graham good-
              naturedly shows how many movies about
              Texas are obviously filmed elsewhere.
              Thus, Texas is a mythical place in films,
              the history of which is suggested by the
              developments in *Red River* (1948), *Giant*
              (1956) and *Hud* (1962). Some detailed
              discussion is also given to a 1936 Gene
              Autry Western, *The Big Show*, which uses
              the Texas Centennial Exhibition as the
              central location for the story. These
              materials are presented in greater detail
              by Graham in his book, *Cowboys and
              Cadillacs* (6.13).

6.47   ————. "When Myths Collide." *Texas
              Monthly*, 14 (January 1986), 42, 98.

              Argues that the theme of *Giant* (1956)
              and *Hud* (1962) is traditional cattle-
              ranching pitted against the modern oil
              industry. Jett Rink in *Giant* is
              paralleled by Hud in *Hud*; both represent
              the amoral yet lucrative oil business.
              Both of these characters are echoed by
              J.R. Ewing in the television series
              Dallas. Mythically, the two movies and
              the TV series represent the inevitable
              triumph of oil. "Oil is king, and money
              is the sole measure of value."

6.48   Huberman, Brian and Ed Hugetz. "Fabled
              Facade." *Southwest Media Review*, 3
              (Spring 1985), 30-34.

              A review of the changing ways in
              which the Alamo has been used as a filmic
              icon over the years. Argues that the
              power of its image centers on its incar-
              nation as a "democratic gesture."
              Article appears in a special issue of
              Southwest Media Review examining "Texas

Myth in Film." For another study of the
Alamo as a film icon, see Don Graham's
"Remembering the Alamo" (6.45).

6.49   Hutton, Paul. "Billy the Kid as Seen in
            the Movies." *Frontier Times*, 57:3
            (June 1985), 24-29.

            A brief overview of the more than 40
films featuring the character Billy the
Kid. Hutton very briefly sums up the
historical career of the Kid and attempts
to place the changing image of the Kid in
a cultural context. The essay is
accompanied by ten film stills. Those
looking for a much more detailed study of
the Billy the Kid films should look at
the book-length studies by Stephen Tatum
(9.17) and Jon Tuska (6.27).

6.50   ————. "The Celluloid Custer." *Red
            River Valley Historical Review*, 4:4
            (Fall 1979), 20-43.

            Through a survey of movies about
Custer and his Last Stand, Hutton
concludes that "the image of Custer on
film has been based on a flexible myth
that changed in response to changing
social values. Whether Custer's image
was depicted in a positive or negative
light, it invariably bore little resem-
blance to historical fact." According to
Hutton, most films about the Last Stand
produced between 1909 and the 1950s
depict Custer in heroic terms. Later
films, however, show him in an
increasingly uncomplimentary fashion
until, by 1970, he is pictured as cruel,
egomaniacal and even insane. The essay
seems well researched and the discussions
of the films are clear and useful.
Hutton does not, however, relate the
films to American cultural preoccupations
in any more than familiar and rather
obvious ways.

6.51   ————. "Celluloid Lawman: Wyatt Earp

Goes to Hollywood." *American West*,
21 (May-June 1984), 58-65.

The author dispenses with issues of
fact and fiction, emphasizing instead
Earp's relationship with Hollywood and
the latter's shifting interpretations of
the legendary lawman. In addition to
discussing Earp's input in John Ford's
My Darling Clementine (1946), Hutton
examines the fictional and "biographical"
presentations of the former Marshal of
Tombstone, including: *Law and Order* (1932
and 1953), *Frontier Marshall* (1934 and
1939), *Tombstone* (1942), *Gunfight at the
O.K. Corral* (1957), *Warlock* (1959), *Hour
of the Gun* (1968) and *Doc* (1971).
Article also features several stills from
the films mentioned.

6.52   ————. "Custer as Seen in Hollywood
              Films." *True West*, 31:6 (June 1984),
              22-28.

A brief overview of the changing
image of George Armstrong Custer as
pictured in films from 1909 until the mid
1970s. The article is illustrated with
ten film stills. For a more complete
discussion of the movie Custer by the
same author, see "The Celluloid Custer"
(6.50).

6.53   ————. "From Little Bighorn to Little
              Big Man: The Changing Image of a
              Western Hero in Popular Culture."
              Western Historical Quarterly, 7
              (January 1976), 19-45.

Hutton argues that tracing the
popular image of George Armstrong Custer
through history reveals a partial
reflection of American opinions and
values. Hutton briefly details nine
features and two serials that center on
Custer from 1932 to 1970, with John
Ford's *Fort Apache* (1948) the first
"anti-Custer film." For other surveys of

Custer films, see 6.10, 6.50 and 6.52.

6.54   Jefchak, Andrew. "Prostitutes and
        Schoolmarms: On Women in Western
        Films." *American Renaissance and
        American West*, ed. Christopher S.
        Durer, Herbert R. Dieterich, et al.
        Laramie: University of Wyoming, 1982,
        pp. 133-140.

        Using the women characters from four
Westerns as examples--Dallas and Lucy
from *Stagecoach* (1939), Amy and Helen
from *High Noon* (1952), Etta from *Butch
Cassidy and the Sundance Kid* (1969) and
Mrs. Miller from *McCabe and Mrs. Miller*
(1971)--Jefchak argues that throughout
the history of Western movies there has
been no essential change of status in
roles and functions of women. Even
though Western men have significantly
evolved, women continue to "suppress the
need for self-discovery because they are
essentially too busy hoping against hope
that *he* will come out alive." To reach
these conclusions, Jefchak tends to oversimplify the women characters he
describes. As a result, his thesis,
although interesting, seems somewhat
forced upon the materials he describes.
The essay is part of the published
proceedings of the second University of
Wyoming American Studies Conference.

6.55   Jones, Daryl E. "The Earliest Western
        Films." *Journal of Popular Film and
        Television*, 8:2 (1980), 42-46.

        A brief description of films produced
by Edison in the late nineteenth century
that may be seen as establishing the
visual roots of the later Western genre.
Most of these films are short documentaries of Western locales and customs,
but two, *Poker at Dawson City* and *Cripple
Creek Bar-room Scene*, both made in 1898,
contain minimal dramatic content and
therefore may lay claim to being the

first Westerns. Includes a checklist of
pre-1900 prototype Western films in the
Library of Congress Paper Print
Collection.

6.56   Judson, William. "Buffalo Bill and the
Wild West: The Movies." *Buffalo Bill
and the Wild West*, ed. The Brooklyn
Museum. Pittsburgh: University of
Pittsburgh Press, 1981, pp. 68-83.

A tracing of the figure of Buffalo
Bill from early documents showing the
Wild West Show during the 1890s and early
1900s, through films in which Cody
participated until his death in 1917 and,
finally, through the films in which
Buffalo Bill appears as a character.
Judson argues that history has been
largely ignored when Cody has been
depicted in the movies. Instead, he is
almost always presented as a conventional
Western hero. Cody remains a mythical
hero on screen until the 1970s. The
essay includes a chronology of Buffalo
Bill on film, with partial screen
credits. Of special interest are 32
stills from the films described. The
booklet in which the essay appears was
meant to accompany an exhibition of
posters and other Buffalo Bill materials
that was shown in art museums in 1982.

6.57   Kaufmann, Donald L. "The Indian as Media
Hand-Me-Down." *Colorado Quarterly*,
23 (Spring 1975), 489-504. Reprinted
in *The Pretend Indians*, ed. Gretchen
M. Bataille and Charles L.P. Silet.
Ames: The Iowa State University
Press, 1980, pp. 22-34.

Describes the negative stereotypes of
Native Americans as seen in movies and
television as having earlier origins in
popular fiction and drama of the nineteenth century. This is a rather
superficial overview of the topic, made
annoying by its smug assumption that it

is saying something that is new. For a
more detailed and balanced perspective on
this topic, see Robert F. Berkofer's *The
White Man's Indian* (6.3).

6.58   Keshena, Rita. "The Role of American
            Indians in Motion Pictures."
            *American Indian Culture and Research
            Journal*, 1 (1974), 25-28. Reprinted
            in *The Pretend Indians: Images of
            Native Americans in the Movies*, ed.
            Gretchen M. Bataille and Charles
            L.P. Silet. Ames: Iowa State
            University Press, 1980, pp. 106-111.

            A condemnation of the narrow stereo-
            typing of Native Americans in Hollywood
            films, mostly Westerns. Keshena argues
            that commercial considerations rather
            than social responsibility led to early
            portrayals of Indians as brutal or
            stupid. More recent films showing
            Indians as good guys are just as
            inaccurate and created for the same
            commercial reasons. Some detailing of
            the 1974 Western *Billy Two Hats* is
            presented as evidence of Hollywood's
            indifference toward portraying Native
            American people accurately. At the end
            of the essay, Keshena calls for the
            increased involvement of Indians in the
            filmmaking process as the only logical
            solution to the problem. The overall
            article is harmed somewhat by a tone of
            smug condescension.

6.59   Knies, Donald V. "The Aging Hero in the
            Changing West." *West Virginia
            University Philological Papers*, 26
            (August 1980), 66-73.

            An analysis of three films Knies
            perceives as a kind of trilogy about the
            aging Western hero: *Ride the High Country*
            (1962), *Hud* (1962) and *The Shootist*
            (1976). All three deal with aging
            Western heroes living their final days in
            a Western environment that is

increasingly institutionalized. Each man
attempts to pass on his older values of
individualism and personal integrity to a
younger man, but with differing degrees
of success. Thus, the heroic impulse of
Western fiction and films of earlier eras
is shown as being in jeopardy as the West
modernizes. The analysis of each film is
carefully reasoned, but the article seems
overly cautious about its conclusions,
stating only what are already familiar
arguments about these films.

6.60   Lamb, Blaine P. "The Convenient Villain:
        The Early Cinema Views the Mexican-
        American." *Journal of the West*, 14:4
        (1975), 75-81.

        Lamb argues that in pre-feature
American films, Mexican-Americans are
nearly always stereotyped as conniving,
untrustworthy and crooked. Although a
number of examples are cited, the
evidence is weakened by being gathered
from plot summaries in *Moving Picture
World* rather than actual viewing of the
films. In the second half of the
argument, Lamb mentions a number of films
in which Mexican-Americans are pictured
sympathetically and even heroically, thus
further qualifying his argument that
Mexican-Americans were almost invariably
stereotyped as villains. Little attempt
is made to explain why certain stereotyped images of Mexican-Americans
predominated in early movies.

6.61   Lenihan, John H. "Classics and Social
        Commentary: Postwar Westerns, 1946-
        1960." *Journal of the West*, 22:4
        (October 1983), 34-42.

        A cultural analysis of postwar
Westerns describing how the films of the
era reflected "psychological and social
themes." Major developments include
Western heroes more flawed than their
predecessors and an exploration within

Westerns of American racial attitudes.
Overall, "one cannot help noticing how
many of these allegedly escapist enter-
tainments were preoccupied with America's
failures and weaknesses." The essay is
essentially a highlighting of arguments
Lenihan makes in much greater detail in
his book, *Showdown: Confronting Modern
American in the Western Film* (7.7). The
article is part of a special issue of
Journal of the West devoted to Western
films (6.12).

6.62   Marsden, Michael T. "The Rise of the
            Western Movie: From Sagebrush to
            Screen." *Journal of the West*, 22:4
            (October 1983), 17-23.

An overview of the development of
Western films from their origins in stage
melodramas during the 1800s through the
era of silent films. Although Marsden
provides no new historical details, the
essay will be useful to some readers
because it attempts to put the
development of Western movies into a
broader cultural perspective. Marsden
describes how the Western falls within a
traditionally American love for didactic
melodrama and how it represents
traditional attitudes toward middle-class
values, and mixed emotions about the
Western landscape. The article is part
of a special issue of *Journal of the West*
focusing on Westerns (6.12).

6.63   Nachbar, Jack. "Horses, Harmony, Hope
            and Hormones: Western Movies, 1930-
            1946." *Journal of the West*, 22:4
            (October 1983), 24-33.

A diverting and informational overview of Westerns of the period,
describing the "rebirth" of Westerns in
the sound era, a rejuvenation largely
tied to the double feature as a marketing
device. According to Nachbar, this
period marked the last major expression,

in both A and B Westerns, of the
traditional mythic and democratic under-
pinnings of the genre. Westerns of the
1930s and the years of World War II,
Nachbar claims, reflect populist values,
but the immediate postwar years saw the
development of sexual and psychological
themes. Part of a special issue of
Journal of the West devoted to Western
films (6.12).

6.64   Nelson, Richard Alan. "Mormons as Silent
        Cinema Villains: Propaganda and
        Entertainment." *Historical Journal
        of Film, Radio and Television*, 4:1
        (March 1984), 3-14.

        An overview of silent anti-Mormon
        films made in the United States and
        Europe. Includes a description of two
        1918 Westerns adapted from Zane Grey
        novels, *Riders of the Purple Sage* and *The
        Rainbow Trail*.

6.65   Oshana, Maryann. "Native American Women
        in Westerns: Reality and Myth." *Film
        Reader*, 5 (1982), 125-131.

        White misrepresentations of Native
        American cultures and the distinctively
        different gender roles in those cultures
        have reduced most depictions of Native
        American women to ridicule. Oshana
        surveys the different roles women
        fulfilled in major tribes, and then skims
        recurring Western themes relating to
        Native American women: the inevitable
        conflicts stemming from miscegenation,
        Indian women sacrificing themselves for
        their white-male betters and the effects
        of Indian captivity on women. The
        author's survey of films dealing with
        Indian women is brief, and its lengthier
        analyses (discussing, for example, *Duel
        in the Sun*, 1946 and *The Searchers*, 1956)
        reveal few surprises.

6.66   Pauly, Thomas H. "The Cold War Western."

Western Humanities Review, 33 (Summer 1979), 257-273.

Pauly argues that Westerns changed in the post-World War II decade from the affirmative, clearly motivated stories most of them were before the war. These postwar Westerns mirrored the "disillusionment, confusion and anxiety" of their audience. Before 1950, successful films such as *My Darling Clementine* (1946) and *Red River* (1948) suggest that the use of violence may be an indication of psychosis. After 1950, Westerns tended to feature aging heroes whose use of righteous violence toward a successful end may soon no longer be possible. The essay concludes with a detailed treatment of public anxieties reflected by the two most famous Westerns of the early 1950s, *High Noon* (1952) and *Shane* (1953). Pauly's sample of films is perhaps too small to justify the broad conclusions he draws from them. No B Westerns or low-budget films are even considered, even though these comprised the largest number of Westerns released during the period. On the other hand, Pauly draws imaginative conclusions and points out notable relationships between Westerns not often compared. The article is an important starting point for the cultural study of Westerns of the era and its conclusions deserve to be tested with further research.

6.67   Peary, Gerald. "Collector's Choice: Westerns." *American Film*, 8:10 (September 1983), 72-76.

Summary reviews of ten diverse Westerns available on videocassette. General material, but the author attempts competently to place them within the traditions and evolutions of the movie Western.

6.68   Price, John A. "The Stereotyping of

North American Indians in Motion
Pictures." *Ethnohistory*, 20 (Spring
1973), 153-171. Reprinted in *The
Pretend Indians*, ed. Gretchen M.
Bataille and Charles L.P. Silet.
Ames: Iowa State University Press,
1980, pp. 75-91.

A superficial overview of the history
of American movies that have featured
Native Americans as important characters.
Price tends to only consider whether or
not the films were pro- or anti-Indian
until the end of the article, when he
calls for films about Native American
cultures outside of the plains and the
southwest. Topic headings include silent
films, sound serials, the 1930s and
1940s, the shift to pro-Indian films in
the 1950s, the breaking down of stereotypes in a few movies in the 1970s,
interracial sexual relations, the need
for Indian actors and the documentary
movie. In none of these sections are any
films or characters discussed in detail.

6.69   Rainey, Buck. "The 'Reel' Cowboy: Myth
        Versus Realism." *Red River Valley
        Historical Review*, 2:1 (Spring 1975),
        25-63.

This review of the history of the
cowboy image in film stresses the
contrived reality of the B Western hero.
Rainey argues that the cowboy's romantic
symbolism in American history was
"perpetuated, perfected, and extended" by
movie portrayals, and to such an extent
that the average person cannot differentiate between the image's reality and its
status as myth. The author's historical
overview of the movie cowboy hero is
included in a special issue of *Red River
Valley Historical Review* exploring "The
Cowboys." The entire issue has been
reprinted as *The Cowboys: Six Shooters,
Songs and Sex* (ed. Charles Harris and
Buck Rainey; Norman, University of

Oklahoma Press, 1976).

6.70   Robertson, Richard. "New Directions in
            Westerns of the 1960s and 70s."
            Journal of the West, 22:4 (October
            1983), 43-52.

            An overview of major thematic trends
            in Western movies from *Sergeant Rutledge*
            (1960) through *Heaven's Gate* (1980).
            Robertson describes these trends as being
            primarily an exploration of racism, an
            increased emphasis on sex and violence,
            the struggles of aging Western heroes
            living past the era of the open frontier
            and "a general loss of confidence in the
            ability of law and civilization to affect
            social justice." All of these trends are
            related to general cultural preoccu-
            pations of the two decades. The article
            is part of a special issue of *Journal of
            the West* devoted to the Western film
            (6.12).

6.71   Silet, Charles L.P. and Gretchen M.
            Bataille. "The Indian in Film: A
            Critical Survey." *Quarterly Review
            of Film Studies*, 2:1 (February 1977),
            56-74.

            Centrally concerned with lack of
            accuracy in portrayals of Native
            Americans in popular culture. Takes
            basically historical approach. Includes
            bibliography of material on Native
            Americans in film.

6.72   Steckmesser, Kent L. "The Three Butch
            Cassidys: History, Hollywood,
            Folklore." *American Renaissance and
            American West*, ed. Christopher S.
            Durer, Herbert R. Dieterich, et al.
            Laramie: University of Wyoming, 1982,
            pp. 149-155.

            Argues that Butch Cassidy did not
            become a nationally famous outlaw-hero
            until the release of the hugely

successful film *Butch Cassidy and the
Sundance Kid* in 1969. This film both
whitewashed the historical Butch Cassidy
and led to revisionist history perceiving
Butch more sympathetically, as well as
establishing details of Cassidy's life
with folkloric origins. All of this
change from the actual life of Cassidy
suggests the popular audience prefers
nostalgia and fantasy to reality in the
country's historical personalities. The
essay is part of the published
proceedings of the second University of
Wyoming American Studies Conference.

6.73   Steiner, Stan. "Real Horses and Mythic
        Riders." *American West*, 18:5
        (September/October 1981), 54-59.

        A sketch of the recent Santa Fe
Western Film Festival panels. Steiner
sides with the real-life cowboys, who
argue the movie Western is basically a
lie. Includes quotes from actors and
directors involved with the genre, who
participated in several festival panels.

6.74   Waldman, Diane. "What Do Those Birds in
        Hollywood Have That I Don't?: Early
        Filmmaking in Colorado." *Velvet
        Light Trap*, no. 22 (1986), 3-15.

        A description of filmmaking in
Colorado during the silent era. The
earliest films were short documentaries
about Indians, the scenery or rodeos. By
1910, important early production
companies such as Selig and Essanay were
making Westerns in Colorado. After 1913,
however, small, local companies made
feature films, mostly Westerns, but
neither the companies nor the films were
successful on a national level. Information about Westerns is sketchy and not
the central emphasis of the article.

6.75   Welsh, Michael. "Origins of Western Film
        Companies, 1887-1920." *Journal of*

the West, 22:4 (October 1983), 5-16.

An overview of the development of the
Western film from Wild West shows to Tom
Mix. Emphasis is on developments in
California beginning in 1908. All of
Welsh's information appears to have been
derived from secondary sources. As a
result, the information tends on one hand
to be already familiar and on the other
hand to be wrong. The essay may be
useful as a general description of major
trends, but those needing reliable
details are advised to look elsewhere.
The essay is part of a special issue of
Journal of the West devoted to Western
films (6.12).

6.76   Woll, Allen L. "Bandits and Lovers:
            Hispanic Images in American Film."
            *The Kaleidoscopic Lens: How
            Hollywood Views Ethnic Groups*, ed.
            Randall M. Miller. Englewood Cliffs,
            N.J.: Jerome S. Ozer, Publisher,
            1980, pp. 54-72.

            Tracing the history of the treatment
            of Hispanics in popular films, Woll only
            deals with Westerns briefly, emphasizing
            instead Warner Bros.' social issue films
            (*Bordertown*, *Juarez*), Lupe Velez' Mexican
            Spitfire series and Carmen Miranda.

THEORIES OF WESTERN FILMS

<u>Books</u>

7.1   Armes, Roy. *Film and Reality: An Historical Survey.* Baltimore: Penguin Books, 1975.

      An introduction to film history, organized around how groups of films do or do not approximate reality. A short chapter on the Western (pp. 141-149) is included in a section on how Hollywood films, for mainly commercial reasons, create worlds of illusion rather than reality. Since the chapter includes both historical details and an attempt to define the main conventions of the genre in less than ten pages, the results are understandably superficial.

7.2   Braudy, Leo. *The World in a Frame: What We See in Films.* Garden City, N.Y.: Anchor Press, 1976.

      In this intriguing examination of popular film, Braudy argues that the Western continues the tradition of the pastoral novel in literature, in which contemporary conflicts are resolved without the interference of complicated urban experience. By defining a special place--the nineteenth-century American West--the Western can address threatening issues in nonthreatening ways. The frontier location of the Western, Braudy claims, is less often physical than it is the audience's sense of what is and what is not historically true.

7.3   Calder, Jenni. *There Must Be a Lone
           Ranger: The American West in Film and
           Reality*. New York: Taplinger, 1974.

           This thematic study attempts to
           describe some of the mythic elements in
           Westerns, both novels and films. The
           arguments fail, however, for two reasons:
           there are a huge number of factual
           errors; and, in her descriptions of a
           number of Westerns, Calder treats fiction
           as if it is historically correct.

7.4   Cawelti, John G. *Adventure, Mystery, And
           Romance*. Chicago: University of
           Chicago Press, 1976.

           This important theoretical work about
           the relationship of popular story forms
           and the cultures out of which they arise
           is essentially a fleshing out of concepts
           Cawelti originally developed in *The Six-
           Gun Mystique* (I, 7.6). The main cultural
           purposes of story formulas, according to
           Cawelti, are: to affirm existing
           interests and attitudes; to resolve
           tensions and ambiguities of conflicting
           attitudes or interests; to safely explore
           the boundaries between what is culturally
           allowable and what is forbidden; and to
           allow for the assimilation of changing
           patterns of cultural values. Chapter
           eight (pp. 192-259) describes these ideas
           as applied to the popular Western
           formula. The emphasis of the chapter is
           on how the Western has evolved from the
           novels of James Fenimore Cooper through
           the novels of Zane Grey and the films of
           William S. Hart, through the filmed
           Westerns of the 1970s, which Cawelti sees
           as moving away from earlier optimistic
           views of America toward a more pessimis-
           tic perspective dominated by an obsession
           with violence. Cawelti's arguments are
           weakened somewhat by a general ignoring
           of industrial imperatives which, in some

cases, have as much to do with the look
of a formula as audience expectations.
He also ignores data which might identify
levels of popularity. Nevertheless, the
book has become a standard reference for
anyone discussing formula storytelling in
the United States, and those interested
in doing scholarly research on the
Western should not ignore it.

7.5 ————. *The Six-Gun Mystique.* Bowling
Green, Ohio: Bowling Green State
University Popular Press, second
edition, 1984.

This updating of the important first
edition of Cawelti's monograph (I, 7.6)
reprints the original essay, bibliographies and filmographies and adds an
introductory essay and additional
bibliographical and filmographic
materials. In the introduction, Cawelti
discusses important books about the
Western published since 1970 and details
what he perceives as the major reasons
for the decline of the popularity of the
Western since 1970. Cawelti concludes
the Western has lost most of its
popularity because the West is becoming
like the rest of the country, because we
spend more time in the West, because
other, more contemporary genres have
replaced it, because the Western has
begun to parody itself and because we
have come to recognize moral ambiguities
in the genre such as sexism and racism.

7.6 French, Philip. *Westerns.* New York:
Oxford University Press, second
edition, 1977.

With the addition of minor corrections, this is the same as the first
edition of French's book first published
in 1973 (I, 7.9A). In an "afterword,"
French updates his discussion of recent
Westerns by discussing the films released
between 1973 and 1976.

7.7   Lenihan, John H. *Showdown: Confronting
            Modern America in the Western Film.*
            Urbana, Ill.: University of Illinois
            Press, 1980.

            An examination of how Western movies
            reveal changing American beliefs and
            values between the end of World War II
            and the late 1970s. Focusing on A
            Westerns, Lenihan analyzes the films as
            they relate to attitudes about the Cold
            War, about racism, about social
            alienation and about general social
            attitudes of the complacent 1950s and the
            anti-establishment 1960s and 1970s.
            Lenihan suggests that the Westerns reveal
            a common American consciousness about
            problems and contradictions in American
            life that previously have been thought to
            be the exclusive domain of the intelli-
            gensia. The method employed in the book
            is to provide multiple Westerns as
            examples. As a result, commentaries on
            specific films are short, usually less
            than a page, but Lenihan's citing of
            numerous films for evidence tends to make
            his arguments convincing. The emphasis
            is on American culture of the period,
            however, so those whose main interest is
            in extended discussions of the films
            themselves are likely to be disappointed.
            Weaknesses with Lenihan's methods include
            a failure to base any of his discussion
            on the degree of popularity of specific
            films or types of films and a tendency to
            relate certain films to specific
            historical events when evidence for such
            a relationship is minimal. Overall, this
            is an important addition to scholarship
            relating Westerns to American culture,
            and an essential resource for those who
            need a broad perspective on the subject.

7.8   McConnell, Frank. *Storytelling and Myth-
            making: Images from Film and
            Literature.* New York: Oxford
            University Press, 1979.

Establishes four types of storytelling as a means of comparing film
stories with fiction in various eras:
epic (the hero founds a civilization),
romance (the hero establishes codes of
conduct), melodrama (the hero seeks an
understanding of the workings of a
civilization) and satire (the hero
reveals the weaknesses of a civilization).
Several of the examples cited, especially
in the first two categories, are Western
films. McConnell's structuring is
interesting as a perception of how
certain Westerns relate to non-Western
novels and films.

7.9   Nichols, Bill, ed. *Movies and Methods:*
        An Anthology. Berkeley: University
        of California Press, 1976.

Nichols' anthology of film criticism
includes reprints of three essays dealing
with the Western, each of which is noted
in its earlier form in volume one of this
bibliography: Andre Bazin's "The
Evolution of the Western" (I, 7.3), Alan
Lovell's "The Western" (I, 7.76) and Greg
Ford's "Mostly on *Rio Lobo*" (I, 3.52).

7.10   Ray, Robert B. *A Certain Tendency of the*
        Hollywood Cinema, 1930-1980.
        Princeton: Princeton University
        Press, 1985.

Ray examines the history of American
film in the sound era in terms of formal
and thematic paradigms, which he argues
have shaped popular understandings and
expectations of the moviegoing experience. Contending that Hollywood's
conservative politics necessitated the
formal paradigm of invisible style and
thematic paradigms which stress conflict
resolution through mediation, the author
depicts American cinema in near-
monolithic terms. Although this view
hampers his examination of some of
Hollywood's exceptional "moments"--films

which in some way violate aspects of this
conservative process--Ray's study offers
much toward an understanding of the
relationship between Hollywood's general
ideology and its stylistic paradigm. The
framework of the Western, he argues,
promotes many of Hollywood's principal
thematic paradigms; *Shane* (1953) effectively summarizes this framework,
blending such themes as the confrontation
between outlaw and official heroes and
the reluctant hero's progression from
moral detachment to physical involvement.
Using Jim Kitses' system of opposing
values (as developed in *Horizons West* in
1969) as his theoretical base, Ray claims
postwar Westerns suggest the period's
revisionist anxiety. Includes extensive
discussion of *The Man Who Shot Liberty
Valance* (1962) as one of two films (Frank
Capra's 1946 *It's a Wonderful Life* is the
other) which the author claims represent
postwar American moods and Hollywood's
controlled responses to them. Ray first
draws parallels between *My Darling
Clementine* (1946) and *Casablanca* (1943),
highlighting the use of love triangles
featuring grey but still defined
"opposing" heroes, and then draws
connections between *Clementine* and
Liberty Valance, including a shot-by-shot
examination of the latter's gunfighting
sequence.

7.11   Reader, Keith. *Cultures on Celluloid*.
            London: Quartet Books, 1981.

            A study of how America, France, Great
Britain and Japan "depict themselves"
through their own movies. The introduction includes a rather superficial
analysis of *The Searchers* (1956), which
asks more questions about the meaning of
the film than it answers. Part I of the
book includes a section comparing the
Western and the gangster movie as
reflecting agrarian and urban attitudes
in America during the 1930s (pp. 41-50).

Reader relies on Will Wright's *Sixguns and Society* (7.17) for his discussion of Westerns and concludes that what Westerns of the 1930s suggest is white male superiority over Indians, women and blacks, hardly a surprising or original concept. Includes an unannotated bibliography, a filmography with partial credits and an index.

7.12　　　Schatz, Thomas. *Old Hollywood/New Hollywood: Ritual, Art, and Industry.* Ann Arbor, Mich.: UMI Research Press, 1983.

Schatz contends that classical Hollywood film genres confront cultural contradictions, resolving them in favor of the community and in turn ritualizing collective cultural ideals. In his analytical framework, Schatz divides the various genres into those which operate in determinate and in indeterminate space, and between those which function as rites of order and as rites of integration. The Western, he argues, functions within finite, contested space, in which conflicting forces of social order and anarchy are locked in epic struggle. The series of oppositions inherent in the genre are embodied in its individualistic hero, who helps impose order in the name of civilization. In his analysis of the functions of genre in the "New Hollywood," Schatz argues that genre filmmaking has operated within a growing tension between its classical mythmaking function and a modernist impulse for demystification. The "New Hollywood" Western, the author claims, continues the surface structure of the genre while repeatedly undercutting its spirit and form. Schatz's approach to the Western genre is treated in more depth in *Hollywood Genres* (10.4), but his conclusions here are solidly based.

7.13　　　Solomon, Stanley J. *Beyond Formula:*

American Film Genres. New York:
Harcourt Brace Jovanovich, Inc.,
1976.

An examination of film genres as
works of art rather than as cultural
artifacts, the approach used, says
Solomon, by those who study genres as
popular culture. Solomon's central
premise is "the most generic works--the
most 'typical' works--of a significant
genre are, artistically and intellectually, the best works of that genre."
In a chapter on the Western (pp. 11-58),
Solomon briefly describes a number of the
important conventions in Westerns and
then goes on to describe how these
conventions are successfully employed in
eight Westerns: *Stagecoach* (1939),
Winchester 73 (1950), *Shane* (1953),
Johnny Guitar (1954), *The Searchers*
(1956), *Comanche Station* (1960), *The Wild
Bunch* (1969) and *Butch Cassidy and the
Sundance Kid* (1969). The discussions of
these films are useful but, since they
are only about four pages in length each,
tend to be rather forgettable.

7.14   Tudor, Andrew. *Image and Influence.* New
         York: St. Martin's Press, 1975.

A study of the relationship between
society and culture and the movies.
Chapter 8, "Cinema and Society: Popular
Genres" (pp. 180-220), speculates on the
thematic structure and possible social
meanings of three popular film genres:
Westerns, gangster movies and horror
movies. Tudor sees Westerns working out
their individual stories within two major
polarities: wilderness and civilization,
and individual and community. Tudor
stresses that the Western is the most
pliant of genres because of the vast
potential between these sets of polarities. Near the end of the chapter, Tudor
concludes that Westerns, along with
gangster movies and horror movies,

reflect a justification for violence,
male domination and self-interest as
justifiable means of establishing an
acceptable social order. Genres do not
create these values; people do. Tudor's
method is reasoned and informative. Much
of the chapter is spent discussing both
the strengths and weaknesses of other
critical perspectives on these three
genres.

7.15   Tuska, Jon. *The American West in Film:*
       Critical Approaches to the Western.
       Westport, Conn.: Greenwood Press,
       1985.

Tuska describes his methodology in
this study of the meaning of Westerns as
"defantasization," a process of searching
out the implications of films Tuska sees
as distortions of history for purposes of
imposing ideological values on their
audiences. To do this, he presents four
different approaches: the structure of
different types of Westerns, *auteur*
studies of six directors, a comparison
between the real and reel lives of six
Western legends, and an analysis of the
stereotyping in Westerns of women and
Indians. The overriding assumption in
all of these sections is that in ignoring
or changing known historical facts about
the West, Western filmmakers have perpetuated a perspective on American history
that defends white, capitalist, racist
and sexist values at the expense of
ethics and human values. In making these
arguments, Tuska rejects the perspectives
of almost all academic writers on culture
and Westerns, a polemic position both
maddening and refreshing. There are
glaring weaknesses in the book, among
them a mostly unnecessary mania for
quoting foreign cultural historians and a
tendency to automatically assume the most
negative possible interpretation of a
film. Tuska also tends to repeat himself
so often about the evilness of

stereotyping women and Indians that the
effect of his generally valid arguments
on this topic tends to be lost. On the
other hand, Tuska has read widely and has
seen seemingly every Western ever made.
His views, however overstated or
eccentric, deserve serious attention.

7.16   Wood, Michael. *America in the Movies*.
            New York: Basic Books, 1975.

A witty and insightful set of speculations about the cultural implications
of American movies mostly released
between 1946 and the end of the 1950s.
In the second chapter (pp. 24-50), Wood
discusses the movies' preoccupation with
the romantic image of the isolated
individual. Westerns are especially
suited for presenting this image, he
concludes, because of "those vast, empty
landscapes--all invitations to
loneliness.... In these solitary spaces
neither self nor society has any claims
on you." Wood offers no extended
examples, but what convinces us of his
ideas about Westerns is his finding
similar patterns in other types of movies
as well as Westerns themselves.

7.17   Wright, Will. *Sixguns and Society: A
            Structural Study of the Western*.
            Berkeley: University of California
            Press, 1975.

A study of sound Westerns as American
"myths" of the twentieth century. Using
methods of myth study developed by
Kenneth Burke, Vladimir Propp and Claude
Levi-Strauss, Wright attempts to describe
the plot structures of the most popular
Westerns of different eras and to explain
what these structures reveal about the
prominent patterns of beliefs of American
society during each period. Wright
argues that four different plots charac-
terize the most popular Westerns: the
classical plot (1931-1955), in which a

lone gunfighter hero saves a community;
the vengeance variation (early 1950s to
about 1960), in which a gunfighter seeks
revenge because society has failed to
provide justice; the transition plot
(early 1950s), in which a gunfighter and
the heroine defend society but are
rejected by it; and the professional plot
(1958-1970), in which a group of professional fighters take jobs for money.
Wright concludes that the reasons for
this evolution are best explained by
economic changes in American life: the
change from "a competitive, market
society to a planned, corporate economy"
dominated by specialist experts.
Selected films receive detailed attention
as examples of overall structures.
Although Wright says that his descriptions and conclusions are based on
objective, scientific principles, his
methodology proves to be more personal
than scientific. The movies he includes
are those that grossed at least $4
million, according to *Variety*, but no
inflation factor is included. Wright's
relating the films to economic
developments is intriguing, but seems
based on his own interests rather than
any scientific necessity. Also, a number
of the analyses of specific films are
based on Wright's need to place them
within categories that fit his thesis
rather than on consistently applied
principles. Despite these major flaws,
the book has become one of the most cited
studies of Westerns yet published.

Articles

7.18   Amelio, Ralph J. "Bonanzaland Revisited:
          Reality and Myth in the Western Film."
          See, 4:1 (1970), 24-28.

          Argues that the appeal of the Western
          is a combination of realistic and mytho-
          logical elements. Realistic elements

include violence and the exploitation of
Indians. Romantic elements include the
splendor of nature and the glorification
of individualism. Most of these ideas
are handled in greater detail elsewhere,
but Amelio is unusual in arguing that the
Western's appeal is on both the realistic
and mythic levels.

7.19   Cawelti, John G. "*Chinatown* and Generic
         Transformation in Recent American
         Films." *Film Theory and Criticism*,
         ed. Gerald Mast and Marshall Cohen.
         New York: Oxford University Press,
         third edition, 1985, pp. 503-520.

In a 1978 essay, Cawelti claims that
major traditional film genres like the
detective story and the Western have, for
varying reasons, undergone significant
changes. Using a detailed analysis of
Chinatown (1974) as a beginning, he
develops four modes of generic transformation: humorous burlesque, evocation of
nostalgia, demythologization of generic
myth and affirmation of myth as myth. In
his well-defined yet speculative
arguments, Cawelti draws insightful
details from several 1960s and 1970s
Westerns.

7.20   ————. "The Gunfighter and the Hard-
         Boiled Dick: Some Ruminations on
         American Fantasies of Heroism."
         American Studies, 16 (Fall 1975),
         49-64.

Cawelti compares the heroes of the
Western and the hard-boiled detective
story, tracing the developments in both
formulas which reveal shared cultural
roots. Cawelti includes general material
to show the two genres' similar
approaches to shared themes, such as the
role of the dynamic individual within
society and the primacy of continual
social progress and self-improvement.

7.21   ————.   "Myths of Violence in American
              Popular Culture." *Critical Inquiry*,
              1:3 (March 1975), 521-541.

              Cawelti argues that Americans have
         traditionally believed in "the moral
         necessity of violence," and that this
         belief is expressed in a number of
         popular story formulas, including
         Westerns. Within these story formulas,
         five different "myths" reappear, all of
         which justify violence: the myth of
         "crime does not pay," which emphasizes
         violence as righteous justice; the myth
         of the "vigilante," which justifies the
         use of private violence because the
         socially sanctioned forces of law and
         order are ineffective; the myth of
         "equality through violence," which allows
         a rise in socio-economic status through
         the application of violent skills; the
         myth of "regeneration through violence,"
         which offers violence as a means of moral
         purification. Cawelti suggests these
         categories offer a beginning place for
         the discussion of violence in the
         American imagination.

7.22   Churchill, Ward. "Film Stereotyping of
              Native Americans." *Book Forum*, 5
              (1981), 370-375.

              Argues that three primary factors
         result in the negative stereotyping of
         Native Americans in the movies: limiting
         portrayals of Native Americans to the
         period of time between 1825 and 1880;
         presenting native cultures only as they
         relate to Euro-American culture; and
         reducing the many different Native
         American cultures to a single, polyglot
         image. The results of these factors,
         Churchill argues, "is a necessary
         ingredient in the maintenance of a
         contemporary Euro empire on the North
         American continent." Churchill's ideas
         are presented with passion, but his
         arguments are weakened by a lack of

detailed examples. Only *A Man Called
Horse* (1970) receives any detailed
attention.

7.23   Countryman, Edward. "Westerns and United
              States' History." *History Today*, 33
              (March 1983), 18-23.

                  Westerns, Countryman argues, draw
              their strength from cultural preoccu-
              pations with the conquering of the
              American continent. Their historical
              strength comes not from focusing on past
              events, but is derived from the awareness
              they generate of the historical process.
              Also, by examining the same historical
              problems from changing points of view,
              films in the genre form part of the
              cultural history of their own time.
              Using the imposing presence of Frederick
              Turner's "frontier thesis" as his
              nucleus, Countryman examines several
              major Westerns from different periods
              (and with special attention paid to John
              Ford's films), using them to reflect
              understandings of changes in American
              appreciation of its past.

7.24   Durgnat, Raymond and Scott Simmon. "Six
              Creeds That Won the Western." *Film
              Comment*, 16:5 (September/October
              1980), 61-68, 70.

                  A description of how six important
              American patterns of belief are present
              in Westerns: Puritan Calvinism, Hobbesian
              and Rousseauian views of nature,
              Jeffersonian and Jacksonian democracy,
              social Darwinism, populism and Manifest
              Destiny. In different sections of the
              essay, these terms are defined and
              several Westerns are detailed as
              examples. Obviously, a number of these
              beliefs contradict one another. The last
              section of the article discusses how
              Westerns are able to embrace such contra-
              dictory beliefs. No attempt is made to
              present these patterns of beliefs or

their presence in Westerns in great
detail. Nevertheless, the essay is an
essential starting point for anyone
interested in the relationship between
Westerns and American culture.

7.25   Harrington, John. "Understanding
        Hollywood's Indian Rhetoric."
        Canadian Review of American Studies,
        8:1 (Spring 1977), 77-88.

Without excusing Hollywood's mostly
negative stereotyping of Native
Americans, Harrington points out that in
most Westerns Indians serve an allegori-
cal purpose. In early Westerns, Indians
symbolized evil; in more recent Westerns,
Indians usually represent good.
Harrington calls for more accurate
portrayals of different Native American
cultures and for more individualizing of
Indian characters as ways to portray
Native Americans responsibly on film
without violating narrative necessities.
Three Westerns are briefly but insight-
fully discussed as examples: *Little Big
Man* (1970), *Ulzana's Raid* (1972) and
When the Legends Die (1972).

7.26   Jordan, Roy A. "Myth and the American
        West." *American Renaissance and
        American West*, ed. Christopher S.
        Durer, Herbert R. Dieterich, et al.
        Laramie: University of Wyoming, 1982,
        pp. 141-148.

Argues that the Western is America's
epic poem of its own cultural identity
and that changes in the movie Western
formula "are vital in maintaining the
flexibility of that myth in a modern
age." These arguments have been common
in scholarly writing about Westerns for a
long time, reflected by Jordan's
footnotes, which are all from secondary
sources. Part of the published
proceedings of the second University of
Wyoming American Studies Conference.

7.27   Karp, Walter. "What Westerns are All
                About." *Horizon*, 17:3 (Summer 1975),
                38-39.

            Briefly argues that one of the hidden
            meanings of Westerns is "nothing less
            than the shared American understanding of
            politics." In the Western, lawlessness
            and disorder stems not from "the people's
            licentiousness" but "is the direct result
            of lawless rule, and it stems from
            usurpation." Karp's argument is
            interesting but, because of the brevity
            of the essay, his concept is presented
            generally rather than from specific
            examples.

7.28   Lehman, Peter, Edward Mitchell and Loren
                Hoekzema. "American Film Genre: An
                Interview with John Cawelti." *Wide
                Angle*, 2:2 (1978), 50-57.

            Cawelti, author of two important
            books about the Western genre, *The Six-
            Gun Mystique* (7.5) and *Adventure, Mystery
            and Romance* (7.4), speculates about genre
            studies, including Westerns, as a means
            for cultural analysis.

7.29   Levitin, Jacqueline. "The Western: Any
                Good Roles for Feminists?" *Film
                Reader*, 5 (1982), 95-108.

            Arguing that most theoretical studies
            of the Western dismiss the problem of the
            female spectator, Levitin attempts to
            analyze the roles of women in several
            Westerns, particularly in psychological,
            social and mythic terms. Examinations of
            Stagecoach (1939), *Arizona* (1940), *Johnny
            Guitar* (1954), *Hannie Caulder* (1971) and
            Comes a Horseman (1978) reveal the
            continued subservient and symbolic nature
            of the woman in the Western film.
            Levitin briefly presents Mae West's two
            "Westerns," *Klondike Annie* (1936) and *My
            Little Chickadee* (1940), as the only
            American-made Westerns that "bear the

stamp of a woman's point of view, and the
only ones that deal with the West from
the perspective of women's power." The
essay is essential reading for anyone
interested in images of women in Western
films. Analyses of the films are
interesting and persuasive and the
conclusions are provocative.

7.30   Mahan, Jeffrey H. "Once Upon a Time in
         the West." *Explor*, 7 (Fall 1984),
         70-83.

         The essay was written for Christian
clergy, suggesting that they seek an
understanding of popular culture artifacts instead of condemning them
automatically because the artifacts seem
to violate Christian values. Mahan
divides the Western into two categories:
the "classic" Western as defined by John
Cawelti, Robert Warshow and Will Wright,
which emphasizes the values of
civilization, and "The Modern Manifesta-
tion," which stresses the values of
individualism in a corrupt civilization.
Both of these are important because
Westerns are "myths" which express the
deepest beliefs we have about our past.
"Classic" Westerns seem to separate
Christianity from what is necessary for
the establishment of society. "Modern"
Westerns often link the church to the
social corruption that the films
criticize. Overall, the article is a
worthy addition to the small number of
essays that consider the Western film in
a religious context. It is also a
provocative presentation of how
traditional Westerns are fundamentally
different from the modern Westerns that
began to appear in the second half of the
1960s. Included is a brief analysis of
Sam Peckinpah's *Pat Garrett and Billy the
Kid* (1973).

7.31   Marsden, Michael T. "Western Films:
         America's Secularized Religion."

Movies as Artifacts, ed. Michael T.
Marsden, John G. Nachbar and Sam L.
Grogg Jr. Chicago: Nelson-Hall Inc.,
1982, pp. 105-114.

The Western formula is a secular
ritual celebrating American progress.
Within this ritual, the Western hero acts
as a "hero-priest-messiah." Marsden
shows parallels between Christ and a
number of Western heroes from the silent
era through the late 1970s. In the main,
the essay is an updating of Marsden's
"Savior in the Saddle," first published
in 1973 (I, 7.91).

7.32   McMurtry, Larry. "Pencils West: Or, a
            Theory for the Shoot-'Em-Up."
            American Film, 2 (December 1976),
            6-7, 80.

McMurtry disagrees with Will Wright's
myth approach to the Western (as outlined
in *Sixguns and Society*, 7.17), arguing
against Wright's structuralist analysis
of the genre. In its place, McMurtry
offers Northrup Frye's theory of
fictional modes as a more encompassing--
and more flexible--base from which to
explore the genre.

7.33   Mulvey, Laura. "Mulvey on *Duel in the
            Sun*." *Framework*, nos. 15-17 (Summer
            1981), 12-15.

The subtitle of this article, "After-
thoughts on 'Visual Pleasure and
Narrative Cinema' inspired by *Duel in the
Sun*," suggests the overall direction of
this interesting essay. In her earlier,
quite famous article, Mulvey argues that
the visual structure of most Hollywood
movies reflected a masculine or
patriarchal viewpoint on the part of the
audience. In this essay, Mulvey
considers this concept and its effect on
women film viewers who identify with
these masculine viewpoints. Pearl in

Duel in the Sun (1946) represents this
perspective because she is drawn to men
who symbolize two sides of her: a
feminine side that represents social
order and a masculine side that is
erotic. Her destruction by the masculine
side suggests Freud's conclusion that the
latent masculine side of a woman's psyche
must finally be repressed. "In this
sense ... the female spectator's phantasy
of masculinization is always to some
extent at crosspurposes with itself,
restless in its transvestite clothes."
Two of the photos that illustrate the
essay are from *The Man Who Shot Liberty
Valance* (1962), which is also discussed
in the article, are incorrectly identified as stills from *Duel in the Sun*.

7.34   Nichols, Bill. "Style, Grammar and the
        Movies." *Film Quarterly*, 28 (Spring
        1975), 33-49. Reprinted in *Movies
        and Methods: An Anthology*, ed. Bill
        Nichols. Berkeley: University of
        California Press, 1976, pp. 609-628.

        Nichols argues for a better under-
standing of the important questions in
film scholarship, in particular the roles
played by technical questions regarding
framing (who does it, how is it done) and
temporal sequence, narrative and the
ideological and historical contexts
involved. As his exemplary texts, the
author uses two John Ford films: *Young
Mr. Lincoln* (1939) and *My Darling
Clementine* (1946).

7.35   Palmer, R. Barton. "A Masculinist
        Reading of Two Western Films: *High
        Noon* and *Rio Grande*." *Journal of
        Popular Film and Television*, 12:4
        (Winter 1984/1985), 156-162.

        From a theoretical base in Lacan and
deconstructivism, this essay offers a
provocative and interesting treatment of
two important Westerns. Focusing on *High*

Noon (1952) and *Rio Grande* (1950) as
"masculine" texts, Palmer offers an
alternative to both mainstream and
feminist readings of the Western genre.

7.36   Pye, Douglas. "Genre and Movies."
               Movie, no. 20 (Spring 1975), 29-43.
               Reprinted in *Film Genre: Theory
               and Criticism*, ed. Barry K. Grant.
               Metuchen, N.J.: The Scarecrow Press,
               Inc., 1977, pp. 195-211.

        Pye argues that generic approaches to
film often center on the misconception
that a genre is essentially definable,
and that therefore genre criticism is
made up of defining criteria. Using
Northrup Frye's *The Anatomy of Criticism*
as his theoretical framework, Pye traces
the development of the Western genre from
James Fenimore Cooper and the dime novel
to Frederic Remington and the film
Western. Pye then presents the Western
genre as a central model for the whole of
genre criticism because of its accessible
prehistory and the continuity of its
traditions.

7.37   Randisi, Jennifer. "The Rangers of the
               Mind: Roy Rogers, King of the Cowboys
               and the Western Tradition."
               Southwest Media Review, 3 (Spring
               1985), 2-8.

        An apologia for musical Westerns.
Using *The Bells of Saint Angelo* (1947) as
a central example, the author ties its
themes and images to the politics of the
period. Randisi argues that the
specificity of visual details which made
such films accessible to and popular with
audiences of the time are the "kiss of
death" to any possibility that these
movies might participate in the Western
genre's ability to embody a transcendant
mythos. An unusually perceptive analysis
of a B Western, this essay is part of a
special issue of *Southwest Media Review*

entitled "Texas Myth in Film."

7.38   Rohdie, Sam. "Who Shot Liberty Valance?
          Notes on Structures of Fabrication in
          Realist Film." *Salmagundi*, no. 29
          (Spring 1975), 159-171.

          Rohdie uses the lies told in John
          Ford's *Fort Apache* (1948) and *The Man Who
          Shot Liberty Valance* (1962) as examples
          on which to speculate about truth and
          falsity in narrative films in general.
          No in-depth analysis of the films
          themselves is intended, although some
          differences in the conclusions in the two
          films is briefly discussed at the end of
          the essay. Most of the speculations are
          based on theories in Roland Barthes'
          writings and Freudian concepts of
          fetishism.

7.39   Ross, T.J. "Death and Deliverance in the
          Western: From *The Virginian* to *The
          Man Who Shot Liberty Valance*."
          Quarterly Review of Film Studies, 2:1
          (February 1977), 75-87.

          Ross argues that typology of Western
          characters is neither simple nor
          straightforward. Nuances of characteri-
          zation shade meaning in subtle and
          important ways, expanding the genre's
          nature. The essay centers on discussion
          of hero and sidekick in several films
          from *The Virginian* (1929) to *The Missouri
          Breaks* (1976) as illuminating complex
          issues of personality and culture.

7.40   Roth, William. "Where Have You Gone, *My
          Darling Clementine*." *Film Culture*,
          nos. 63-64 (1977), 153-163.

          A brief description of some of the
          conventions of the Western genre--the
          hero, the land, Indians, women and the
          outlaw--leads to the conclusion that
          Westerns are about "the Promethian mode
          of perception," "that of a human body

trying to transcend itself." Roth
concludes that this mode of perception is
acceptable during certain historical
periods, but is no longer useful.
Therefore, the Western has ceased to be a
viable American epic. *Cheyenne Autumn*
(1964) is offered as one of two examples.
While these speculations about the
contemporary relevance of the Western are
unusual and provocative, Roth weakens his
arguments by providing little or no
evidence for his initial generalizations
about the conventions in Westerns.

7.41   Rushing, Janice Hocker. "The Rhetoric of
            the American Western Myth."
            Communication Monographs, 50 (March
            1983), 14-32.

Uses Western films to establish a
context for explaining the cultural
significance of the fad for Western chic
in the early 1980s. Rushing argues that
myths, ideally, present cultural values
in a state of dialectical tension. Only
Westerns of the 1950s did this. The
others fail as myths because they emphasize one side of the opposition between
individualism and community. Recent
Westerns *Urban Cowboy* (1980) and *Comes a
Horseman* (1978), as well as the imagery
of the Reagan presidency and the fad of
wearing Western clothing, are a "pseudo-
synthesis" that "obscure the fact that
the qualities are indeed contradictory."
This interesting thesis is weakened by a
rather superficial detailing of earlier
examples in Western films and by a
failure to show 1980s trends in Westerns
are more false in resolving ideological
tensions than Westerns of earlier
decades. While Rushing centers her
thesis on a dialectic pattern of conflicting values, she never considers a
Marxist position which might well find
more "pseudo-synthesis" throughout the
history of Western films than she is
willing to admit.

7.42   Ryall, Tom. "The Notion of Genre."
         Screen, 11:2 (March/April 1970),
         22-32.

         Uses the Western as the main example
to discuss the main elements in American
film genres. According to Ryall, genres
are familiar patterns made up of a
"complex of basic material or subject
matter, of thematic preoccupations and of
iconographical continuity." The article
also advises against the evaluation of
specific genre items based on a "classic"
model and briefly discusses the
implications of the genre discussion as
it relates to the teaching of American
film.

7.43   Sarris, Andrew. "Death of the Gun-
             fighters." *Film Comment*, 18:2
         (March/April 1982), 40-42.

         Speculations about the end of the
Western genre with *Barbarosa* (1982),
offered as an example of why Westerns are
no longer capable of reaching a mass
audience. Sarris concludes that Westerns
are no longer popular because urban
violence has become so omnipresent that
the frontier violence in Westerns no
longer seems relevant.

7.44   Self, Robert T. "Ritual Patterns in
             Western Film and Fiction." *Narrative
         Strategies*, ed. Syndy M. Conger and
         Janice R. Welsch. Macomb, Ill.:
         Western Illinois University, 1980,
         pp. 105-114.

         Describes the popular Western genre
as a story form that poses a conflict
between the forces of civilization and
wilderness, with a resolution in favor of
either side possible. When a Western
story in fiction or film emphasizes
ambiguity rather than resolution, the
intended audience for the story is
usually more elite than those for clearly

resolved Western stories, but even these
elite stories rely on genre conventions
of the popular Western to successfully
communicate with their audience. The
main example used is Robert Altman's
*Buffalo Bill and the Indians, or Sitting
Bull's History Lesson* (1976). The essay
is an interesting speculation of how a
popular genre can appeal to different
types of audiences.

7.45   Siegal, Mark. "Western Film: Romance
            Narrative in the American Tradition."
            *American Renaissance and American
            West*, ed. Christopher S. Durer,
            Herbert R. Dieterich, et al.
            Laramie: University of Wyoming, 1982,
            pp. 157-165.

Argues that criticisms that Western
films are unrealistic fail to consider
these films within their proper artistic
context. Westerns, says Siegal, like
most of the great novels of American high
culture, are romances as defined by
Richard Chase in his book, *The American
Novel and Its Tradition* (1957).
Romances, according to Chase, emphasize
action and plot over complex characterization, and they allow for highly colored
renderings of reality for the purpose of
establishing ideological contradictions
and paradoxes. Whereas the essay is
useful in establishing a context for
interpretation and in part answers some
modern critics who perceive Westerns as
simplifying cultural contradictions, the
arguments it presents are weakened by a
failure to establish any historical
relationships between Western movies as
"classic" American novels. The essay is
part of the published proceedings of the
second University of Wyoming American
Studies Conference.

7.46   Simmons, Garner. "The Generic Origins of
            the Bandit-Gangster Sub-Genre in the
            American Cinema." *Film Reader*, 3

(1978), 67-79.

Simmons argues that films that make up the bandit-gangster sub-genre (such as *Bonnie and Clyde*, *High Sierra*, *Gun Crazy*) share a stronger generic bond with the Western than with the gangster movie. Using Jim Kitses' analysis of opposing cultures in the Western (in *Horizons West*, 1969; I, 7.10), Simmons claims the protagonists of the bandit-gangster pictures emphasize honor, reject civilization and incorporate women as full partners in their escape into the wilderness.

7.47   Sonnichsen, C.L.   "The West That Wasn't."
        American West, 14 (November-December
        1977), 8-15.

Presents the standard "truth versus legend" dichotomy of the West in his survey of the treatment of the old West in fiction, film and television. Sonnichsen concludes that the Western owes its popularity to Americans' need to believe in their own "heroic" past; the Western functions as an American mythology.

7.48   Tatum, Stephen.   "The Western Film Critic
        as 'Shootist.'"   *Journal of Popular
        Film and Television*, 11:3 (1983),
        114-121.

Discusses the "death" of the Western by examining critical responses from the 1950s to the 1980s in order to expose changes in the audience's expectations of and demands on the genre. Tatum concludes that most criticisms of modern Westerns are based on the assumption that "classical" models are an ideal form and that any deviation from these means an inferior genre film. Tatum rejects this assumption as a misunderstanding of how genres evolve. The author also offers interesting insights into the roles of what he calls "genre critics."

7.49   Walker, Michael. "Melodrama and the
                 American Cinema." *Movie*, nos. 29-30
                 (Summer 1982), 1-38.

        Walker transposes Robert Heilman's
     model of melodrama as a world of external
     division (distinguishing it from
     tragedy, in which the division between
     good and evil is internalized) to
     American cinema, splitting melodrama into
     forms of action and forms of passion.
     Westerns, he argues, are included in the
     former, primarily because in them
     conflicts between good and evil are
     resolved through action.

THESES AND DISSERTATIONS
ON WESTERN FILMS

8.1   Arnett, Robert. The Searchers:
        Rhetoric/Film/Argumentation. M.A.,
        Washington State University, 1983.

8.2   Bentley, Robert. *Trends in the Western
        Genre Film: 1959-1972*. M.A.,
        University of Texas, 1977.

8.3   Black, Louis. *A History of the B Movie,
        with an Emphasis on Economic Factors*.
        M.A., University of Texas, 1980.

8.4   Budd, Michael. *A Critical Analysis of
        Western Films Directed by John Ford
        From* Stagecoach *to* Cheyenne Autumn.
        Diss., University of Iowa, 1975.

        See 5.62 and 5.63.

8.5   Cody, Diane. *The Star Personality: A
        Study of Four Western Stars*. Diss.,
        University of Michigan, 1977.

8.6   Desser, David. *The Influence of American
        Popular Formulas on the Samurai Films
        of Akira Kurosawa*. Diss., University
        of Southern California, 1981.

        See 9.2 and 9.25.

8.7   Falkenberg, Pamela. *Rewriting the
        "Classic Hollywood Cinema": Textual
        Analysis, Ironic Distance, and the
        Western in the Critique of Corporate*

Capitalism. Diss., University of Iowa, 1983.

See 3.41.

8.8   Gagnier, Chris. *The Code of Honor of the Western: An Analysis of the Theme in Selected Western Films.* M.A., California State University at Fullerton, 1974.

8.9   Gallagher, Thomas. *The Movies of John Ford.* Diss., Columbia University, 1978.

8.10   Jesionowski, Joyce. *A Visual Narrative: Structure in D.W. Griffith's Biograph Films (1908-1913).* Diss., Columbia University, 1981.

8.11   Karp, Alan. *The Films of Robert Altman.* Diss., University of California at Los Angeles, 1980.

8.12   Kiley, Cheryl. *The Career and Films of Dudley Nichols.* Diss., St. Louis University, 1982.

8.13   Lau, Kwok Wah. *A Relational Approach as Applied to Two Specific Films:* The Shootist *and* The Battle of Algiers. M.A., Bowling Green State University, 1981.

8.14   Lehman, Peter. *The Search For a Balance between East and West: An Analysis of John Ford's* Fort Apache *and* She Wore A Yellow Ribbon. M.A., University of Wisconsin, 1973.

See 3.68, 5.92, 5.93 and 7.28.

8.15   Lenihan, John. *Western Movies: A Study of American Popular Culture and Society Since 1945.* Diss., University of Maryland, 1976.

See 6.61 and 7.7.

8.16   Libott, Richard. *Themes and Resonances
        in the Films of Arthur Penn.* M.A.,
        University of California at Los
        Angeles, 1972.

8.17   Mass, Roslyn. *Values in Film: A
        Comparison of Selected American
        Western Films of the 1940's and
        1970's.* Diss., New York University,
        1978.

8.18   Matta, Ricardo Mendez. *A Survey and
        Analysis of the Films of Sam
        Peckinpah.* M.A., Ohio State
        University, 1983.

8.19   Merlock, Raymond. *From Flintrock to
        Forty-Five: James Fenimore Cooper and
        the Popular Western Tradition in
        Fiction and Film.* Diss., Ohio
        University, 1981.

8.20   Money, Mary. *Evolution of the Popular
        Western in Novels, Films and
        Television, 1950-1974.* Diss.,
        University of Texas, 1975.

8.21   Murphy, Kathleen. *Howard Hawks: An
        American Auteur in The Hemingway
        Tradition.* Diss., University of
        Washington, 1977.

        See 5.110.

8.22   Nachbar, John. *Published Materials on
        Western Movies: Annotated Guide to
        Materials in English.* Diss., Bowling
        Green State University, 1974.

        See Volume I and 1.67, 3.82, 6.63 and
        10.9.

8.23   Parks, Rita. *Mass Media Mythology: The
        Western Hero in Film and Television.*
        Diss., Northwestern University, 1974.

        See 6.21.

8.24   Peyton, Robert. *Western Justice: The*
            Politics of Fenimore Cooper, Owen
            Wister, and the Western Movies.
            Diss., University of California at
            Berkeley, 1980.

8.25   Pisioni, Susan. *Religious Motifs in John*
            Ford's Sound Films. M.A., University
            of Southern California, 1978.

8.26   Place, Janey. *John Ford and a Semiology*
            of Film. Diss., University of
            California at Los Angeles, 1975.

8.27   ————. *The West of John Ford.* M.A.,
            University of California at Los
            Angeles, 1973.

            See I, 5.23; and 3.91.

8.28   Plecki, Gerard. *The Films of Robert*
            Altman. Diss., University of
            Illinois at Champaign-Urbana, 1979.

            See 5.31.

8.29   Reider, Richard. *The Use of Ritual as a*
            Primary Element in the Films of John
            Ford. M.A., University of Southern
            California, 1981.

8.30   Roman, Brenda. *The Portrayal of Indians*
            in American Silent Films. M.A.C.,
            University of North Carolina at
            Chapel Hill, 1976.

8.31   Roth, Lane. *Film Semiotics Put to*
            Empirical Test: Leone's Western
            Trilogy. Diss., Florida State
            University, 1976.

            See 5.120, 5.121, 5.122, 9.12 and
            9.38.

8.32   Sack, Chuck. *The Films of Robert Altman.*
            M.A., University of Kansas, 1976.

8.33   Schneider, Diana. *The Clothing of the*

"*Wild West*": *Evolution of Costumes in Western Films*. M.A., University of New Orleans, 1981.

8.34   Seydor, Paul. *Sam Peckinpah, the American Aspect: A Study of His First Five Films*. Diss., University of Iowa, 1977.

See 5.38.

8.35   Siminoski, Ted. *Sioux vs. Hollywood: The Image of Sioux Indians in American Films*. Diss., University of Southern California, 1979.

See 5.130.

8.36   Simmons, Louis. *The Cinema of Sam Peckinpah and the American Western: A Study of the Interrelationship Between an Auteur Director and the Genre in Which He Works*. Diss., Northwestern University, 1975.

See 3.104, 5.40, 5.128 and 7.46.

8.37   Spence, Stephen. *George Roy Hill: Study of an American Director*. M.A., University of Southern California, 1983.

COMPARATIVE STUDIES

<u>Books</u>

9.1   Bondanella, Peter. *Italian Cinema: From
        Neo-Realism to the Present.* New
        York: Frederick J. Ungar Publishing
        Co., 1983.

        In addition to passing speculations
        on the influence of Westerns on two neo-
        realist directors (Germi and DeSantis),
        the author devotes a chapter to Sergio
        Leone and the phenomenon of the
        "spaghetti Western" as influenced by and
        influencing American Westerns.

9.2   Desser, David. *The Samurai Films of
        Akira Kurosawa.* Ann Arbor, Mich.:
        UMI Research Press, 1983.

        This study of the samurai film is
        sprinkled with references to Westerns,
        both as a parallel genre and as an
        inspiration for Kurosawa's work. Of
        particular interest is Desser's final
        chapter, "Implications for Further
        Study," which includes a short but
        interesting discussion of the relation-
        ship between *The Wild Bunch* (1969) and
        Seven Samurai (1954).

9.3   Frayling, Christopher. *Spaghetti
        Westerns: Cowboys and Europeans, From
        Karl May to Sergio Leone.* London:
        Routledge and Kegan Paul, 1981.

Although he ties together the decline of Westerns in the United States and the rise of Western film production in Europe, Frayling fails to provide a compelling argument for either phenomenon within his assertions about film and the production and reaffirmation of social ideologies. Occasionally so "transdisciplinary" as to obscure the point, this Marxist-influenced volume still has much to recommend it. Frayling's book is a detailed, and nicely illustrated, examination of a much-neglected area: non-American Westerns with an emphasis on Italian "spaghetti Westerns." He begins by detailing the transformation of the story of Sutter's discovery of gold in California by the American popular press and compares versions found in a French novel, a Nazi propaganda film, an Eisenstein screenplay and a classic American Western. Other chapters include discussions of the "code" of the West and the manipulations of its American meanings in Italian hands; Karl May's impact on the European view of the Old West; an analysis of the studio system responsible for "spaghetti Westerns"; a "reading" of the political subtexts in European Westerns; and an extensive discussion of Sergio Leone's contribution to the genre, including a detailed treatment of *Once Upon a Time in the West* (1970). This volume's usefulness is enhanced by its appendices: a filmography; a tantalizingly short introduction to the implications of the editing of Leone's Westerns; and a short essay on the impact of Italian Westerns on the American-made ones that followed. Those interested in Italian Westerns might also find Roth's *Film Semiotics, Metz and Leone's Trilogy* (9.12) and Staig and Williams' *Italian Western: Opera of Violence* (9.15) worth investigating.

9.4   Kaminsky, Stuart M. *American Film Genres*. Chicago: Nelson-Hall Inc., second edition, 1985.

Kaminsky's important study of popular film genres includes a brief comparative study of the Western and the samurai film (pp. 63-72). The jidai-geki, Kaminsky asserts, deals with cultural myth in ways different from the Western because (unlike the Western) the Japanese story form goes beyond the limitations of acceptable possibility to meet audience expectations. See also 5.90.

9.5   Kirkley, Donald H., Jr. *A Descriptive Study of the Network Television Western During the Seasons 1955-56-- 1962-63.* New York: Arno Press, 1979.

A 1967 Ph.D. dissertation, Kirkley's study traces the development of the Western genre in literature, film and radio as a sort of prelude to the television Western. The author surveys critical reaction to the genre, and then briefly describes the Westerns aired each television season. Kirkley then breaks down the genre into standard conventional elements, with particular emphasis placed on the categorization of heroes within the TV Western. Competent, but dated.

9.6   Kittredge, William and Steven M. Krauzer, ed. *Stories into Film.* New York: Harper & Row Publishers, Inc., 1979.

A collection of nine short stories which were made into movies, including Ernest Haycox's "Stage to Lordsburg" (the basis for the 1939 *Stagecoach*) and Dorothy H. Johnson's "The Man Who Shot Liberty Valance" (the beginnings of the 1962 film of the same name). Each story is prefaced with general comments from the editors, comparing the original story and its realization on film. "Liberty Valance" is also preceded by a brief remembrance from Johnson of the story's transition from page to screen, including

some of the original piece's mistakes.
The introductory essays emphasize the
changes made in the translation process,
although in fairly vague terms.

9.7   MacDonald, J. Fred. *Don't Touch That
           Dial!: Radio Programming in American
           Life from 1920 to 1960.* Chicago:
           Nelson-Hall Inc., 1979.

MacDonald's thematic and generic
history of radio programming includes a
chapter on radio Westerns. Tracing the
radio Western from its beginnings as a
primarily adolescent-oriented genre to
the development of the "adult" Western,
the author relates the drift toward
realism in the radio Western to postwar
cultural anxieties and similar developments in the movie Western. In addition
to in-depth examinations of several
different series, MacDonald stresses the
juvenile Western hero's role as teacher.
By emphasizing the Western heroes as
champions of the oppressed, communicators
of morality and as representatives of
peace-loving civilization, the author
argues, radio Westerns set themselves up
as transmitters of societal standards.
MacDonald's book is the only real attempt
at a scholarly approach to radio
programming, and his conclusions are well
supported.

9.8   ———. *Who Shot the Sheriff?: The Rise
           and Fall of the Television Western.*
           New York: Praeger Publishers, 1987.

An examination of the growth of the
popularity of television Westerns during
the 1950s, and their decline in the 1960s
and 1970s. MacDonald's monograph carefully documents this rise and fall with
statistical tables and brief examples.
The concluding section, an explanation
for the growth and decline of the TV
Western, argues that the genre itself
could no longer reflect the

preoccupations of the late 1960s and
1970s. In addition, the militarism,
racism and sexism in most television
Westerns no longer was acceptable to the
post-Watergate generation. Includes
bibliography and index.

9.9   Osgood, Dick. *WYXIE Wonderland (An
         Unauthorized 50-Year Diary of WXYZ
         Detroit)*. Bowling Green, Ohio:
         Bowling Green University Popular
         Press, 1981.

A personal history of the Detroit
radio and television station which
created *The Lone Ranger*, *The Green Hornet*
and *Sergeant Preston of the Yukon*,
Osgood's book includes anecdotal
background material on the development of
The Lone Ranger and its spinoffs in
Republic serials, cartoons, comic books,
novels and other merchandise.

9.10   Pettit, Arthur G. *Images of the Mexican
         American in Fiction and Film*.
         College Station, Texas: Texas A and M
         University Press, 1980.

A description of the most common
stereotypes of Mexicans in popular
literature and Hollywood films. In an
initial chapter on film, Pettit shows how
stereotypes in films from the 1890s until
the end of World War II were at least as
old as the nineteenth century dime
novels. Films in this chapter receive
little individual attention, and Westerns
are not central. In another chapter,
Pettit discusses movies featuring Mexican
characters made from 1946 until the end
of the 1960s. Most of the films in this
section are Westerns. *Viva Zapata!*
(1952) and *The Wild Bunch* (1969) are
discussed in detail. The book is well
researched and Pettit clearly demonstrates the lingering presence in popular
culture of such stereotypes as the
greaser clown, the bandito and the dark

lady. No effort is made, however, to
explore the implications of these stereotypes in books and movies. Includes a
good bibliography and an index.

9.11   Pronzini, Bill and Martin H. Greenburg,
           ed. *The Reel West*. Garden City,
           N.Y.: Doubleday & Company, Inc.,
           1984.

A compendium of ten short stories
which are, solely or in part, the
original sources for Western movies. *The
Reel West* is a random collection, chosen
more for enthusiast-related reasons than
for scholarly purposes. The collection
includes: Bret Harte's "Tennessee's
Partner" (the basis of the 1955 film of
the same name); Stephen Crane's "The
Bride Comes to Yellow Sky" (*Face to Face*,
1952); O. Henry's "A Double-Dyed
Deceiver" (*The Texan*, 1930); James Warner
Bellah's "Massacre" (*Fort Apache*, 1948);
John M. Cunningham's "The Tin Star" (*High
Noon*, 1952); Steve Frazee's "My Brother
Down There" (*Running Target*, 1956);
Elmore Leonard's "Three-Ten to Yuma" (the
1957 movie of the same name); Dorothy M.
Johnson's "The Man Who Shot Liberty
Valance" (the 1962 film of the same
title); Frank Gruber's "Town Tamer" (the
1965 movie of the same name); and Jack
Schaefer's "Jeremy Rodock" (*Tribute to a
Bad Man*, 1956). The brief introductions
make little attempt at evaluation or
commentary, and give no insight into the
transitions the stories made from
original source to final product.

9.12   Roth, Lane. *Film Semiotics, Metz, and
           Leone's Trilogy*. New York: Garland
           Publishing Inc., 1983.

Published as part of a series of
dissertations on film, this book has much
to recommend it to anyone with an abiding
interest in Sergio Leone or semiotics.
Roth's "close reading" of Leone's *Dollars*

trilogy is instructive even if the reader
is unfamiliar, or uninterested, in Metz's
theories. Roth "translates" the films'
screenplays into visual units as he
explores the manipulation of symbols in
the three films.

9.13   Rothel, David. *Who Was That Masked Man?*
              New York: A.S. Barnes and Co.,
              revised edition, 1981.

              Rothel traces the origins and
development of the Lone Ranger in its
many media manifestations: radio; movie
serials and features; television, both
live and animated; comic books and comic
strips; and even radio cereal premiums.
The entire history of the use of the
character is chronicled from its initia-
tion as a radio concept in 1932 to the
latest Lone Ranger feature film in 1981.
The approach is from the perspective of a
fan, so the emphasis is on a gathering of
information rather than a commentary on
themes or meanings. Rothel relies on
interviews with those involved with
producing Lone Ranger stories and on a
huge group of stills that comprises more
than half of the book. Overall, the most
complete description of the Lone Ranger
available. Includes a brief bibliography
and an index.

9.14   Savage, William W., Jr. *The Cowboy Hero:*
              His Image in American History and
              Culture. Norman, Okla.: University
              of Oklahoma Press, 1979.

              After an introductory chapter in
which he criticizes other historians for
sloppy research about the history of the
West, Savage takes up the image of the
cowboy in a number of popular culture
manifestations--movies, clothing styles,
records and advertising. Unfortunately,
Savage commits the same sins of which he
initially accuses other historians. He
is constantly cynical about the products

in popular culture and this cynicism
leads him to constantly condemnatory conclusions which are, for the most part,
either insufficiently demonstrated or
simply wrong. This is the worst kind of
popular culture research--a book with
pretensions of making a serious,
scholarly contribution but which, in the
final analysis, is sloppy, superficial
and insensitive. Includes a "cowboy
chronology" of popular cowboy images, a
brief biographical note and an index.

9.15   Staig, Lawrence and Tony Williams.
         Italian Western: The Opera of
         Violence. London: Lorimer Books,
         1975.

         This book is particularly valuable
for its emphasis on the place of music in
"spaghetti Westerns." The authors'
intriguing discussion of Ennio
Morricone's music in Sergio Leone's films
makes its point with examples known to
most Americans interested in the genre.
Readers interested in the "spaghetti
Western" should see the entries for
Frayling (9.3) and Roth (9.12) for other
book-length treatments of the subject.

9.16   Striker, Fran, Jr. *His Typewriter Grew*
         Spurs. Runnemede, N.J.: Quest Co.,
         1983.

         A very affectionate biography of Fran
Striker by his son. It is general
knowledge that Striker wrote most of the
radio scripts for *The Lone Ranger* and
other radio favorites. Striker Jr.
documents that Striker was actually the
inventor of the "masked rider of the
plains," and had a great deal to do with
movie serials, books, comic strips and
books, the television series and feature
films as well. Includes a number of
unusual photos of Lone Ranger memorabilia. Also includes a list of radio
shows and books written by Striker,

Striker's pilot script for *The Lone Ranger*, and a chronology of important events in the media history of the Ranger.

9.17   Tatum, Stephen. *Inventing Billy the Kid: Visions of the Outlaw in American, 1881-1981.* Albuquerque: University of New Mexico Press, 1982.

In this important study, Tatum argues that history is more than a gathering of specific facts. Rather, history is the truth each generation makes of those facts. Thus, interpretation becomes its own historical artifact. The various legends, stories and histories of Billy the Kid over the course of a century becomes the central image Tatum uses to demonstrate his thesis. Tatum uses biographies, music, fiction, ballet and especially movies to show that the pre-occupations of each historical era have fashioned the story of the Kid to fit its own cultural needs. Billy fits the archetype of the outlaw-hero, but the way this archetype is detailed is in a state of constant flux, suggesting parallel changes in the cultural mindset. The discussion of the most important of the 40 movies about Billy the Kid are detailed and generally successfully located within their cultural contexts, although the box-office success or failure of the films is left out of the discussion. One significant flaw in the analyses, and in the use of the other materials as well, is a failure to detail the differing audiences for these arti-facts. Tatum tends to perceive American culture as a whole instead of a group of different audiences. Tatum's argument that no objective history of the Kid is possible may be compared with the book about Billy by Jon Tuska (6.27), which argues against works which run contrary to historical facts.

Articles

9.18   Aleiss, Angela. "Hollywood Adresses
            Indian Reform: *The Vanishing
            American.*" *Studies in Visual Commu-
            nication*, 10:4 (Fall 1984), 53-60.

            This short essay is packed with
            information about one of Hollywood's
            first efforts to address the problems
            caused by the federal government's Indian
            policies. Placing Zane Grey's novel in
            an historical and social context, the
            article also deals with the film's pro-
            duction, audience responses and the
            consequences of its success.

9.19   Axeen, David. "Eastern Western." *Film
            Quarterly*, 32 (Summer 1979), 17-18.

            Axeen looks at Michael Cimino's *The
            Deer Hunter* (1979) as a film which
            accepts the Western's chivalric values
            (such as male bonding, honor and martial
            skill) and its emphasis on the defense of
            the imperial being forced on "savage"
            cultures. The author's analysis includes
            a comparison of the film's central
            character with James Fenimore Cooper's
            Natty Bumppo.

9.20   Barson, Michael. "The TV Western." *TV
            Genres: A Handbook and Reference
            Guide*, ed. Brian G. Rose. Westport,
            Conn.: Greenwood Press, 1985, pp.
            57-71.

            An overview of the major developments
            in the television genre from the late
            1940s to its demise during the 1970s.
            Emphasis is on descriptive details rather
            than on analysis. Barson points out that
            the TV Western was a direct descendent of
            the movie genre. Includes a brief
            bibliography essay.

9.21   Bezanson, Mark. "Berger and Penn's West:
            Visions and Revisions." *The Modern*

American Novel and the Movies, ed.
Gerald Peary and Roger Shatzkin. New
York: Frederick Ungar Publishing Co.,
1978, pp. 272-281.

A comparison between Arthur Penn's
1970 Western *Little Big Man* and Thomas
Berger's novel of the same name.
Bezanson argues that Berger's novel
presents a cynical view of the old West
where both whites and Native Americans
are equally despicable. Penn's film, on
the other hand, clearly sides with the
Cheyenne, thereby allowing Penn to make
a Western which condemns American
involvement in Vietnam. The contrast
between novel and film is perceptive, but
the conclusions about the film had
already been articulated by 1978.

9.22   Boyd, David. "Prisoner of the Night."
        Film Heritage, 12 (Winter 1976-77),
        24-30.

        Boyd's comparative study of *The
        Searchers* (1956) and *Taxi Driver* (1976)
        argues that, though seemingly depicting
        antithetical worlds, the two films are
        virtually identical. The films' central
        characters, Ethan Edwards and Travis
        Bickle, are loners without a real home.
        Both regard themselves as defenders of
        their societies' values against the
        threat of alien intruders. See 3.25.

9.23   Brode, Douglas. "They Went Thataway."
        Television Quarterly, 19:2 (Summer
        1982), 33-41.

        An informal overview of the history
        of series television Westerns from their
        beginnings in the late 1940s through the
        early 1980s. Brode also argues for four
        types of television Westerns: historical
        hero Westerns (*Wyatt Earp*), wandering
        heroes (*Have Gun, Will Travel*), hero
        within a community Westerns (*Gunsmoke*),
        and family hero Westerns (*Bonanza*). In

addition, there are some interesting
comments about innovations that Walt
Disney brought to television Westerns.

9.24   Crain, Mary Beth. *"The Ox-Bow Incident*
         Revisited." *Literature/Film*
         Quarterly, 4:3 (Summer 1976),
         240-248.

         A comparison between Walter Van
Tilberg Clark's novel and the 1943 film
directed by William Wellman. Crain
argues that *"The Ox-Bow Incident* is an
existentialist novel, while the movie is
limited to an indictment of mob 'law' and
ultimately a reaffirmation of the basic
principles of democracy. The book leaves
the reader in despair for mankind; the
film, while exposing man in his sordid
reality, still leaves hope for justice
and those who carry it out." Crain
speculates that these differences between
film and novel perhaps were the result of
the Production Code and the Hollywood
penchant for uplifting drama, especially
during the war years.

9.25   Desser, David. "Kurosawa's Eastern
         'Western': *Sanjuro* and the Influence
         of *Shane*." *Film Criticism*, 8 (Fall
         1983), 54-65.

         Desser claims that English-language
critics' desire to establish the
"Japaneseness" of Japanese cinema has
forced them to neglect Akira Kurosawa's
Sanjuro (1962) and to underrate the
influence of the Western on Japanese
filmmaking. Arguing that *Sanjuro* can be
seen as a classic Western which is in
part a remake of George Stevens' *Shane*
(1953), the author uses the criteria for
Westerns drawn up by Will Wright in
Sixguns and Society (7.17) to point out
similarities and differences between the
two works.

9.26   Everson, William K. "Rediscovery."

Films in Review, 28 (February 1977),
100-103.

Author identifies a number of
"Fordesque" elements, including music,
camera manipulation and characters, in
Christian Jacques' *Boule de Suif* (1945).
Everson suggests the postwar French film
is a "textbook" example of John Ford's
influence outside the United States, and
draws a number of parallels between this
film and *Stagecoach* (1939).

9.27   Fultz, James R. "High Jinks at Yellow
        Sky: James Agee and Stephen Crane."
        Literature/Film Quarterly, 11:1
        (1983), 46-55.

A comparison between Stephen Crane's
1898 short story, "The Bride Comes to
Yellow Sky," and James Agee's 1952 film
adaptation (part of a two-part anthology
released as *Face to Face*). Fultz
emphasizes the comic elements in Agee's
script even though "all of Agee's
scripts, even this his most comic one,
are colored by his deep compassion, his
essentially tragic view of life."

9.28   Kendall, Martha. "Forget the Masked Man.
        Who Was His Indian Companion?"
        Smithsonian, 8:6 (September 1977),
        113-120.

Kendall, a linguistic anthropologist,
playfully describes her search for the
tribal origin of the Lone Ranger's best
friend, Tonto, by trying to locate the
language source for Tonto's term for the
masked man, *kemo sabe*. Various possibilities are discovered, but a definite
answer is never found. For a discussion
of wny the creator of *The Lone Ranger*,
Fran Striker, used this expression, see
the biography of Striker written by his
son, Fran Striker Jr., *His Typewriter
Grew Spurs* (9.16).

9.29   Marill, Alvin H. "The Television Scene:
            Westerns." *Films in Review*, 30:7
            (August/September 1979), 422-434.

            An interesting account of the state
            of television Westerns is provided in
            this review of those offered during the
            1978-79 prime-time season. *Little House
            on the Prairie* is the only regularly
            scheduled "Western" during this period
            (Marill does not comment on the irony of
            this perception). A number of "tele-
            features" and two miniseries, *The
            Chisholms* and *Centennial*, are also given
            cursory mention.

9.30   Marsden, Michael T. *"Shane*: From
            Magazine Serial to American Classic."
            South Dakota Review, 15:4 (Winter
            1977-78), 59-67. Reprinted as "The
            Making of *Shane*: A Story for All
            Media," in *Shane: The Critical
            Edition*, ed. James C. Work. Lincoln,
            Neb.: University of Nebraska Press,
            1984, pp. 238-253 (see 3.12).

            A reverential tracing of Jack
            Schaefer's story through its magazine,
            book, radio, movie and television series
            versions. The best section of the essay
            is a comparison between the magazine and
            novel versions, partly because Marsden
            uses detailed information supplied by
            Schaefer himself and partly because of
            limited information available on the
            radio and television versions.

9.31   Mayne, Richard. "Adventure Playgrounds:
            On Spaghetti Westerns." *Encounter*,
            58 (January 1982), 72-74.

            A set of speculations based on
            Christopher Frayling's book on
            "spaghetti Westerns" (9.3). Mayne
            concludes that Italian Westerns are
            "advertisements for violence." He
            further concludes that Westerns are
            "adventure playgrounds" for violent

fantasies, and that seeing them as
genuine political statements is to
"mistake an adventure playground for the
real world." In refusing to accept
Western films as possible metaphors for
contemporary politics or ideology, Mayne
sets himself against Frayling and most
other recent scholars of the Western.

9.32   McFee, Michael. "Via Ponderosa: Notes
        Toward a Theology of *Bonanza*."
        *Journal of Popular Film and
        Television*, 7:4 (1980), 426-432.

A tongue-in-cheek exercise in what
the author calls "nominal theology."
McFee finds that most of *Bonanza*'s
metaphors were Christian, Old Testament
and medieval. He argues that the theo-
logical character gave the series a
transcendent status within the genre.
Among the more provocative elements of
the essay is a Biblical interpretation
of the Cartwright boys' names, and the
equation of "their famous ten-gallon
toss" with archeological finds near
Corinth, Lindisfarne and Reno. A more
serious treatment of theology and
Westerns may be found in Marsden (7.31).

9.33   Newcomb, Horace. "Texas/TV." *Southwest
        Media Review*, 3 (Spring 1985),
        46-51.

Newcomb's basic argument is that, as
a mythic setting, Texas continues to
exert a powerful hold on our imagina-
tions, a hold which transcends the
vagaries of Nielsen ratings. This essay
appears in a special issue of *Southwest
Media Review* on "Texas Myth in Film."

9.34   Nichols, David. "Once Upon a Time in
        Italy." *Sight and Sound*, 50:1
        (Winter 1980-81), 46-49.

A highly appreciative discussion of
all of the Westerns directed by Sergio

Leone, especially *Once Upon a Time in the
West* (1970). Nichols describes how
Leone's Westerns are made up of American
mythology, Italian cynicism and an
operatic style. Through this combination
of theme and style, "legends are debunked
but somehow remain legends." A much more
detailed presentation of Leone's work
along similar lines was published about
the same time by Christopher Frayling
(9.3), but Nichols' brief essay is an
intelligent and informative overview.

9.35   Nolley, Kenneth S. "The Western as
          Jidai-Geki." *Western American
          Literature*, 11:3 (1976), 231-238.

A comparison of *Seven Samurai* (1954)
and the American adaptation, *The Magnificent Seven* (1960), based on how each film
is representative of its nation's
cultural values. Nolley concludes that
Seven Samurai is a more significant work
of art because the internal values within
the film are consistent. *The Magnificent
Seven*, on the other hand, contradicts
itself. While dialogue posits the values
of a passive agrarian life, the action of
the film glorifies aggressive violence.
Nolley's conclusions about *The Magnificent Seven*'s internal inconsistencies are
insightful, but his conclusion is
weakened by a failure to establish such
inconsistencies as a basis of making
aesthetic judgments. For analyses of
similarities and differences between the
formulas of Westerns and *jidai-geki*, see
earlier articles by Stuart Kaminsky (I,
9.24) and J.L. Anderson (I, 9.3).

9.36   Ramonet, Ignacio. "Italian Westerns as
          Political Parables." *Cineaste*, 15:1
          (1986), 30-35.

Ramonet argues that the "spaghetti
Western" uses the surface appearances of
the American Western to build, in effect,
"nothing less than the frontiers of a new

film genre"--a genre which allows for the
handling of a number of strongly
political subjects, particularly the
denunciation of aggressive United States
imperialism in Latin America, the support
of the progressive ideals of the Mexican
Revolution, antimilitarism and anti-
fascism. Ramonet's analysis of the
Italian Western includes an extensive
look at the form's "theatricality-
derived" conventions, as well as some
detailed examinations of several films,
refreshingly many of which were not made
by Sergio Leone. A challenging article
for anyone looking at post-1950s
strategies in the Western genre.

9.37   Reeder, Roberta. "*Red River*: The
        Literary Version and the Film."
        Cine-Tracts, 3 (Spring 1980), 56-57.

        The author compares the 1948 Howard
Hawks film with Borden Chase's story,
"The Chisholm Trail," which was the basis
of the film and which appeared in serial
form in *The Saturday Evening Post* in
December 1946 and January 1947. Though
Reeder points out the distinction
between "trail" (a route of travel) and
"river" (a crossing point), she supplies
little subsequent analysis. The article
is part of a special section of *Cine-
Tracts* on *Red River*, the result of a 1978
seminar on semiotics and film.

9.38   Roth, Lane. "*Vraisemblance* and the
        Western Setting in Contemporary
        Science Fiction Film."
        Literature/Film Quarterly, 13:3
        (1985), 180-186.

        Vraisemblance, according to Jonathan
Culler in his book *Structural Poetics*, is
the relationship between one cultural
artifact and another which is already
accepted and understood by the culture.
Roth uses this idea to argue that a
number of visual motifs of the Western

genre were utilized in six science
fiction films released between 1977 and
1980, including *Star Wars* (1977) and *The
Empire Strikes Back* (1980). These motifs
include the saloon, the devastated home-
stead, the campfire, the horse and the
wilderness. The article concludes with
speculations that science fiction movies
are probably more appealing to contemporary adolescents than Westerns. These
arguments are reasonable enough, but they
are also rather obvious to anyone
familiar with the films discussed.

9.39   Smith, James R. "Native American Images
         and the Broadcast Media." *American
         Indian Culture and Research Journal*,
         5:1 (1981), 81-92.

         An overview of images of Native
         Americans in popular radio and television
         series. Smith finds that images of
         Indians in these media were initially
         carryovers from film images but then
         evolved in their own ways for reasons of
         economics and demographics. In general,
         Smith finds images of Native Americans
         on the radio less offensive than images
         that developed on television in the late
         1950s, largely the result of a
         saturation of Westerns on TV. No series
         in either medium receives detailed
         attention, and it appears that Smith
         derived most of his material from
         secondary resources rather than from
         extensive listening or viewing.

9.40   Turner, John W. "*Little Big Man*, The
         Novel and the Film: A Study of
         Narrative Structure."
         Literature/Film Quarterly, 5:2
         (Spring 1977), 154-162. Reprinted in
         The Pretend Indians, ed. Gretchen M.
         Bataille and Charles L.P. Silet.
         Ames: Iowa State University Press,
         1980, pp. 156-162.

         A comparison between Thomas Berger's

novel and Arthur Penn's 1970 film reveals
that Penn's film lacks the narrative
consistency of the novel. The novel sets
up a binary opposition between savagery
and civilization. The movie cannot do
this because it is impossible to visually
show the spiritual essence of Indian
life. The second half of the film fails
because Penn continues in a comic mode
after the tragedy of the Washita massacre
demands a darker tone. Turner organizes
his arguments around earlier comments by
Leo Braudy and Pauline Kael, who also
found fault with the film but--says
Turner--for the wrong reasons. The
overall essay is meant to illustrate a
method for making useful comparisons
between movies and their literary
sources.

9.41   Wlaschin, Ken. "Birth of the 'Curry'
         Western: Bombay, '76." *Films and
         Filming*, 22 (April 1976), 20-23.

         A brief description of the Bombay
Film Festival in 1976. The article
focuses on *Sholay* (1976), a lavishly
produced Indian Western modeled partly
on *Butch Cassidy and the Sundance Kid*
(1969) and partly on *Duel in the Sun*
(1946).

Books

10.1   DeNitto, Dennis. *Film: Form and Feeling*.
        New York: Harper and Row, 1985.

        Chapter seven of this college intro-
        duction to film text (pp. 383-436)
        presents the film Western as "the United
        States' only indigenous major motion
        picture genre." DeNitto characterizes
        Westerns as myths, stories that reflect
        fundamental conflicts in human nature and
        in societies. Around this central
        concept, he presents a brief history of
        the Western and offers three detailed
        studies of famous individual films:
        Stagecoach (1939), the "classic Western
        in transition"; myth and realism in *Shane*
        (1953); and *The Wild Bunch* (1969) as an
        antihero Western. Discussion is aided by
        a number of excellent frame enlargements,
        but is hampered by frequent minor factual
        errors. As usual with single chapters
        covering the entire history and meaning
        of the Western, information is often
        covered too quickly, but this chapter is
        less guilty of that problem than chapters
        in most other texts.

10.2   Earley, Steven C. *An Introduction to
        American Movies*. New York: New
        American Library, 1978.

        A textbook introduction to American
        film divided into a general history and

an introduction to selected genres.
Chapter 19 (pp. 234-245) superficially
surveys the Western by attempting to
cover generic characteristics and a
history of the genre in only ten pages.
There are a number of factual errors.
The book also includes a glossary of film
terms, a bibliography and an index.

10.3   McDougal, Stuart Y. *Made Into Movies:*
            From Literature to Film. New York:
            Holt, Rinehart and Winston, 1985.

This textbook for undergraduate
courses in literature and film includes
the use of two Westerns as "case
studies." *Stagecoach* (1939) is discussed
as an example of allegory and *High Noon*
(1952) is used as an illustration of how
a film director can successfully manipulate time. The book also includes the
short story "The Tin Star" by John M.
Cunningham, the original source for *High
Noon.*

10.4   Schatz, Thomas. *Hollywood Genres:*
            Formulas, Filmmaking and the Studio
            System. New York: Random House,
            1981.

This college textbook describes and
analyzes six popular film genres, one of
which is Westerns. Schatz links
Westerns, detective films and gangster
movies as "rites of order," films
primarily about individuals in conflict
over "contested space" which is usually
resolved by violence. In a chapter
devoted to the Western genre, Schatz
very briefly sketches a history of the
Western, showing its changing themes and
preoccupations and then illustrating
these ideas by describing this evolution
in the Western films of John Ford. Many
of these ideas are presented by Schatz in
his book, *Old Hollywood, New Hollywood*
(7.12).

10.5   Sobchack, Thomas and Vivian C. Sobchack.
            An Introduction to Film. Boston:
            Little Brown and Co., 1980.

            Chapter four of this introductory
            film text (pp. 189-248) is devoted to
            defining the parameters and purposes of
            genre film. Westerns are among other
            genres used as examples of the narrative
            patterns, stereotypical characters and
            familiar images the authors see as the
            primary conventions in popular movie
            genres. The Western itself is described
            as one of a number of "genre melodramas."
            Some Westerns are also used as examples
            in sections of the chapter describing
            genres as myth, genre films and society
            and genre parody and anti-genre. No
            attempt is made to provide historical
            background, but the description of
            popular conventions is concise and clear.

Articles

10.6   Combs, Richard. "Westerns." *Anatomy of
            the Movies,* ed. David Pirie. New
            York: Macmillan Publishing Co., Inc.,
            1981, pp. 206-219.

            The central emphasis of Pirie's
            textbook anthology is to show how movies
            function as economic and commercial
            products. Combs' often disjointed
            chapter on the history of the Western
            genre include constant references to the
            box-office appeal of the films he
            discusses. The chapter also includes a
            handy listing of the most commercially
            successful Westerns after an inflation
            factor is built into the calculations.
            The most interesting element of the
            chapter, however, is a discussion of how
            Duel in the Sun (1946) influenced a
            decade or more of Westerns that followed
            it.

10.7   Frayne, John F. *"Stagecoach." Journal*

of Aesthetic Education, 9 (April
1975), 18-31.

A study guide to the famous John Ford
film meant for teachers preparing to
discuss the movie in the classroom.
Included is a brief overview of Ford's
career, the credits and an outline of the
sequences in *Stagecoach* (1939), and an
excellent series of study questions which
includes questions about the characters,
about implications of certain scenes and
about the significance of specific shots.
The article concludes with a very brief,
annotated bibliography. Although the
biographical sketch fails to carefully
place *Stagecoach* within Ford's career and
does not attempt to show any development
or changes in Ford's ideas or films, the
overall guide is a useful one for anyone
preparing to teach *Stagecoach* for the
first time.

10.8   Maynard, Richard A. "John Ford and the
        American Image." *Scholastic Teacher*
        (January 1974), 28-30.

        Argues that high school students
        should study Ford's films for two
        reasons: as an example of the work of a
        genuine *auteur* and "as a tapestry of
        American attitudes and values." A
        suggested classroom Ford film festival
        includes five Westerns.

10.9   Nachbar, Jack and Michael T. Marsden.
        "A Course File: Images of Native
        Americans in Popular Film." *The
        Native American Image on Film,* ed.
        Annette Traversie Bagley.
        Washington: The American Film
        Institute, 1980, pp. 39-58.
        Reprinted in part in *University Film
        and Video Association Monograph No.
        5: College Course Files,* ed. Patricia
        Erens with Marian Henley. University
        Film and Video Association, 1986, pp.
        136-139.

An outline for a six-unit course
syllabus (five units in the abridged
version), the main purpose of which is to
illustrate and discuss the implications
of Hollywood's images of Native Americans
from the late nineteenth century through
the 1970s. Each section includes an
annotated list of suggested films, and an
annotated list of suggested readings.
Also includes a brief, annotated list of
background readings. The complete
version also includes a list of film
distributors. Most of the suggested
films are Westerns.

APPENDIX A:
ADDITIONAL MATERIAL

A number of interesting and ambitious publications
related to Western films appeared between the time
the bulk of this work was organized and its
completion. The entries that follow include those
works dealing with Western films which were
available at the time of publication, and are noted
in the subject and author indexes.

Books

A.1   McDonald, Archie P., ed. *Shooting Stars:*
           Heroes and Heroines of Western Film.
           Bloomington: Indiana University
           Press, 1987.

           A collection of 12 biographical
           essays about a handful of major Western
           stars. Though not really fanzine
           material, most of the essays treat their
           subjects with a reverence usually
           reserved for fan magazines. Each chapter
           is a competent introduction to the work
           of an actor who made some or all of his
           reputation in Westerns; the majority of
           the chapters, however, present their
           subject as the embodiment of a single
           trait (William S. Hart as the serious,
           authentic cowboy, or Randolph Scott as
           the gentleman of honor) of the archetypal
           Hero of the West. Major Western stars
           profiled include Hart, Scott, Gary
           Cooper, Gene Autry, John Wayne, Ronald
           Reagan, Audie Murphy, Ken Maynard, Burt
           Lancaster and Clint Eastwood. Also

includes unfocused essays on women in
Westerns and TV cowboys. Chapters on
Murphy and Maynard, both rarely
discussed in scholarly work in the genre,
give the book some added value.

A.2   Nash, Robert Jay and Stanley Ralph Ross.
           The Motion Picture Guide. 12
           volumes. Chicago: Cinebooks, Inc.,
           1985-1987.

The most comprehensive filmography
of English language films in print.
Volumes one through nine are an alphabetical filmography of sound films from
1927 through 1983. Volume 10, by Robert
C. Connelly, covers silent features from
1910 through 1936. Volumes 11 and 12
are comprehensive name indexes. Each
entry includes title, year of release,
original running time, production and
releasing companies, color or black and
white designation, production and cast
credits, MPAA and *Motion Picture Guide*
ratings, genre classification, videocassette availability, and a one-
paragraph description of the film which
summarizes the plot and analyzes the
film's qualities, if any. Commentaries
tend to be highly opinioniated. Annual
updates are promised.

A.3   Pitts, Michael R. *Western Movies: A TV
           and Video Guide to 4200 Genre Films.*
           Jefferson, N.C.: McFarland and
           Company, Inc., 1986.

A filmography of 4,189 feature-length
Westerns from the silent era to the
present that are still available for
viewing. Each entry includes film title,
release company, year of release, running
time and whether the film is in color or
black and white, a cast listing, a very
brief plot synopsis and a one-sentence
critical review. A number of entries
also include video sources. Also has a
list of movie cowboy horses, a list of

pseudonyms, a list of names and addresses
of video sources, a brief bibliography
and a name index. Overall, a quite
useful resource.

A.4   Smith, Harold. *Saturdays Forever.*
                Knoxville, Tenn.: National Paperback
                Books, Inc., 1985.

Brief commentaries about 21 notable B
Western stars of the 1930s and 1940s,
with additional short chapters on related
topics such as B Western sidekicks.
Numerous photos accompany each chapter.
Smith admits to being an opinionated fan
of B Westerns, and most of his comments
reflect that perspective. The book makes
for pleasant browsing, but it is of
little or no use for research. It has no
indexes.

A.5   Swann, Thomas Burnette. *The Heroine or*
                the Horse. New York: A.S. Barnes and
                Co., 1977.

A brief history of the leading women
performers at Republic studios, including
those featured in Westerns. Emphasis is
on photos.

A.6   Weston, Jack. *The Real American Cowboy.*
                New York: Schocken Books, 1985.

A pro-cowboy, anti-capitalist
description of the working conditions of
"real" cowboys. Chapter seven, "The
Cowboy Myth" (pp. 209-252), describes how
the cowboy of popular Western novels and
movies is not an accurate representation
of genuine cowboys. Weston argues that
the deviations from reality in popular
Westerns generally favor the image of the
working cowboy over the more powerful
ranch owners, and that the popularity of
Westerns in the twentieth century
reflects a longing on the part of the
audience for a lost rural community.
While these arguments are provocative,

they are weakened somewhat by several
factual errors. Has no index.

Articles

A.7   Anderson, Christopher. "Jesse James, the
               Bourgeois Bandit: The Transformation
               of a Popular Hero." *Cinema Journal*,
               26:1 (Fall 1986), 43-64.

               Anderson analyzes *The True Story of
               Jesse James* (1957) within the context of
               the history of movie storytelling of the
               James legend, arguing that the Nicholas
               Ray film "is not primarily concerned with
               the material events in the life of Jesse
               James. Instead, it is more a film about
               the process of telling James stories and
               about the transformation of James into a
               cultural figure." A convincing argument
               for studying the depiction of popular
               heroes through their different incar-
               nations in popular culture, the essay
               asserts that figures like Jesse James
               transcend the notion of text, and instead
               Anderson effectively illustrates how the
               film positions itself in opposition to
               most early movie versions of the James
               legend, functioning as "both a parody of
               previous James films and a revisionist
               critique of them." A meticulous,
               balanced analysis of a neglected 1950s
               Western.

A.8   Gallagher, Tag. "Shoot-Out at the Genre
               Corral: Problems in the 'Evolution'
               of the Western." *Film Genre Reader*,
               ed. Barry Keith Grant. Austin:
               University of Texas Press, 1986,
               pp. 202-216.

               Argues against the consensus view, or
               recent studies of post-1950s Westerns
               that finds them to be more cynical and
               ambiguous than earlier "classic"
               Westerns. Using John Ford's Westerns as
               his main examples, Gallagher says that
               pre-1950 Westerns often contain many of

the characteristics of post-1950 works if
we look at them intensely. This thesis
leads Gallagher to conclude that too much
genre analysis errs in looking for
general patterns instead of the nuances
of specific films. The article tends to
oversimplify the studies it critiques,
and depends too much on somewhat
eccentric readings of the Westerns it
describes. Still, Gallagher's call for a
close examination of specific films is
well articulated.

A.9   Miller, Mary Jane. *"Cariboo Country*: A
       Canadian Response to American
       Television Westerns." *American
       Review of Canadian Studies*, 14:3
       (Fall 1984), 322-332.

       A discussion of how the CBC
television series about the modern
Canadian West, *Cariboo Country* (1960-67),
differed in important ways from popular
American TV Westerns of the same period.
Miller concludes that some of the main
differences were that *Cariboo Country*
used less formulaic plots, featured more
individualistic characters and relied
less on violence for its conclusions than
did American television Westerns. Brief
attempts to find cultural explanations
for these differences are explored, but
the emphasis in the article is on the
nature of the differences rather than on
the reasons for them.

A.10   Wood, Robin. *"Heaven's Gate* Reopened."
       Movie, nos. 31/32 (Winter 1986),
       72-83.

       Similar to Wood's analysis of
Heaven's Gate (1980) in his collection,
Hollywood from Vietnam to Reagan (see
5.53). This essay is more of an
apologia, celebrating the complexity of
Michael Cimino's film by defending some
of its more contested aspects. In
particular, Wood presents a nine-point

defense of the Harvard prologue and
analyzes Cimino's use of dance scenes and
battle sequences in both the Harvard
section and Wyoming segment of the movie,
showing how the director's non-linear
approach to *Heaven's Gate* reinforces its
central theme of personal--and
national--loss.

PERIODICALS ON WESTERN FILMS

This appendix lists names and addresses of periodicals intended primarily for fans and collectors that include news and information about Western films and performers. This list was compiled by Grady Franklin.

The Big Reel. Route 3, Box 83; Madison, N.C. Don Key, publisher.
Monthly newspaper. Mainly intended for collectors.

The Big Trail. 540 Stanton Ave.; Akron, Ohio 44301. Tim Lilley, editor.
Quarterly newspaper devoted to John Wayne.

Blazing West and Serial Classics. P.O. Box 64345; Los Angeles, Calif. 90064. Jeff Walton, publisher.
Bi-monthly newsletter. Information and features on Westerns and serials.

Classic Images. P.O. Box 809; Muscatine, Iowa 52761. Samuel K. Rubin, editor-publisher.
Monthly newsletter. Includes filmographies, profiles, reviews and information on all types of films, including Westerns.

Favorite Westerns and Serial World. P.O. Box 3325; Mankato, Minn. 56001. Norm Kietzer, publisher.
Quarterly magazine featuring information on Westerns and all types of serials.

Movie Collector's World. P.O. Box 309-C;

Fraser, Mich. 48026.   Brian Bukantis, editor.
Bi-weekly newsletter for collectors.

Norm's Serial News.   1726 Maux Dr.; Houston,
Texas 77043.   Norm Lynch, editor.
Bi-monthly newsletter primarily about serials,
but also includes information about Westerns.

*Roy Rogers-Dale Evans Collectors Association
Newsletter.*   P.O. Box 1166; Portsmouth, Ohio 45662.
Judy Wilson, editor.
Bi-monthly newsletter.

Under Western Skies.   Route 3, Box 263-H;
Waynesville, N.C. 28786.   Ron Downey, publisher.
Quarterly magazine.   Features numerous photos.

The Westerner.   610 57th St.; Vienna, W.V.
26105.   Roger Crowley, editor.
Quarterly magazine.   Information about Western
history and Western films.

The Western Film.   1943 Jasmine Dr.;
Indianapolis, Ind. 46219.   Grady Franklin, editor.
Quarterly newsletter.   Includes brief items
about Western films, Western stars and Western film
festivals.

Wrangler's Roost.   23 Sabrina Way, Stoke
Bishop; Bristol 9, England.   Colin Momber, editor.
Quarterly magazine.   Devoted entirely to
Westerns.

AUTHOR INDEX

Abbott, L.B. 3.14
Adams, Les 1.1
Adamson, Joe 5.17
Albert, Steven 3.15
Aleiss, Angela 9.18
Alloway, Lawrence 2.23
Alvarez, Max Joseph
  1.2
Amelio, Ralph J. 7.18
Anderson, Christopher
  A.7
Anderson, Lindsay
  3.16; 5.1; 5.56
Anderson, Robert 4.48;
  6.31
Appelbaum, Ralph 3.17;
  5.57
Apra, Adrian 2.24
Armes, Roy 2.25; 7.1
Armitage, Shelley 6.32
Arnett, Robert 8.1
Aros, Andrew 1.5; 1.6
Austen, David 2.26
Autry, Gene 4.1
Axeen, David 9.19

Bach, Steven 3.1; 3.18
Baer, Richard D. 1.8
Barkun, Michael 2.27
Barson, Michael 9.20
Basinger, Jeanne 4.49;
  5.2
Bataille, Gretchen M.
  1.9; 1.58; 1.59;
  1.60; 6.1; 6.33; 6.71

Bawden, Liz-Anne 1.10
Baxter, John 5.3
Bazin, Andre 3.19; 3.20
Beaver, Jim 4.50; 4.51
Behlmer, Rudy 2.1; 3.2
Belafonte, Dennis 4.2
Bell, Geoffrey 6.2
Belton, John 3.21; 4.3;
  5.4
Benequist, Lawrence 3.22
Bentley, Robert 8.2
Bergan, Ronald 6.34; 6.35
Berkofer, Robert F. 6.3
Bernstein, Gene M. 3.23
Bezanson, Mark 9.21
Billman, Carol W. 3.24
Biskind, Peter 6.4
Black, Louis 8.3
Bliss, Michael 5.5
Blumenberg, Richard M.
  6.36
Bobrow, Andrew C. 5.58
Bodeen, De Witt 4.52;
  4.53; 5.59
Bogdanovich, Peter 2.2;
  2.28; 2.29; 5.60
Bondanella, Peter 9.1
Boyd, David 3.25; 9.22
Boys, Barry 2.24
Bradshow, Bob 2.30
Braudy, Leo 7.2
Brode, Douglas 9.23
Broeski, Pat 5.61
Brooks, Tim 1.11
Brown, Gene 1.12

SUBJECT INDEX